Contents

Acknowledgements   vii
Foreword   ix

The Poet: *Julius Caesar* and the Democracy to Come   1
Not Now   21
Or Again, Meddling   38
Derrida's Event   59
Woo't   68
Jacques Derrida's Language (Bin Laden on the Telephone)   89
Impossible Uncanniness: Deconstruction and Queer Theory   113
Forgetting Well   135
Last   186

Index of Works by Derrida   188
Index of Names   190

Acknowledgements

I would like to record my warm gratitude to colleagues and friends who have, whether knowingly or not, helped with this book: Graham Allen, Emily Apter, Mikkel Astrup, Branka Arsic, Derek Attridge, Andrew Bennett, Geoffrey Bennington, Anne Berger, Jacob Bøggild, Rachel Bowlby, Peter Boxall, Hélène Cixous, Timothy Clark, Josh Cohen, Ellie Cook, Jennifer Cooke, Abi Curtis, Paul Davies, Marguerite Derrida, Christoforos Diakoulakis, Sarah Dillon, Jonathan Dollimore, Nikolai Duffy, Thomas Dutoit, Justin Edwards, Maud Ellmann, Michael Gasson, Sean Gaston, Noreen Giffney, Simon Glendinning, Hans Hauge, Marian Hobson, Joanna Hodge, Jenny Huynh, Stefan Iversen, Amber Jacobs, Campbell Jones, Peggy Kamuf, Susie Lingham, Charles Lock, Martin McQuillan, Marie-Louise Mallet, Laura Marcus, Elissa Marder, Alicia Meseguer, Ginette Michaud, J. Hillis Miller, Forbes Morlock, Michael Naas, Philip Newman, Henrik Skov Nielsen, Michael O'Rourke, Julian Patrick, Rob Penhallurick, Eftichis Pirovolakis, Eric Prenowitz, John David Rhodes, Dan Ringgaard, Mark Robson, Avital Ronell, Caroline Rooney, Kas Saghafi, Marta Segarra, Roy Sellars, Chris Stokes, Céline Surprenant, Keston Sutherland, Michael Syrotinski, James Theodosius, Sophie Thomas, Alex Thomson, Stephen Thomson, Jonty Tiplady, William Watkin, Elisabeth Weber, Sam Weber, David Wills, Richard Wilson, Julian Wolfreys, Sarah Wood, Simon Wortham and Robert Young.

Three of the pieces published here have earlier appeared in French translation: 'Le poète', trans. Geoffrey Bennington, in *La démocratie à venir: Autour de Jacques Derrida*, ed. Marie-Louise Mallet (Paris: Galilée, 2004), pp. 567–82; 'Pas maintenant', trans. Catherine Mazodier, in collaboration with Thomas Dutoit, in *Jacques Derrida*, eds Marie-Louise Mallet and Ginette Michaud (Paris: L'Herne, 2004), pp. 405–15; and 'Ou encore, interférence', trans. Pierre Vitoux, in *Derrida pour les temps à venir*, ed. René Major (Paris: Stock, 2007), pp. 250–80. Four pieces have appeared in journals or other essay-collections in English: 'The Poet: *Julius Caesar* and the Democracy to Come', in *Angles on Derrida: Jacques Derrida and Anglophone Literature*, eds Thomas Dutoit and Philippe Romanski, special issue of the *Oxford Literary Review*, vol. 25 (2003), 39–61; 'Not Now', in *Epochē: A Journal for the History of Philosophy*, 10:2 (Spring 2006), 379–93; 'Derrida's Event', in *Derrida's Legacies: Literature and Philosophy*, ed. Simon Glendinning and Robert Eaglestone (New York and Abingdon, UK: Routledge, 2008), pp. 36–44; and 'Jacques Derrida's Language (bin Laden on the Telephone)', in *Mosaic: A Journal for the Interdisciplinary Study of Literature*, vol. 39, no. 3 (September 2006), 173–95. I would like to express here (however belatedly) my profound thanks to the translators of these essays, as well as my gratitude to the editors and publishers for permission to reprint. Derrida's response to 'Meddling' at the 'Seminar with Jacques Derrida on the Occasion of his Honorary Doctorate from Queen Mary' (6 July 2004) is part of a larger body of material (DVD recordings and a transcript of the event) available for consultation in the library of Queen Mary, University of London: my particular thanks to Libby Saxton and Marian Hobson for permission to reproduce Derrida's response here. For the photographs reproduced in this volume, I would like to record my special thanks to Marie-Louise Mallet. Grateful acknowledgement is also made here to Andersen Press, for permission to reproduce material from David McKee's *Not Now, Bernard*.

I am grateful also to all those at EUP whose expert professionalism, patience, encouragement and good humour have guided this work into book-form, especially Padmini Ray Murray, Peter Williams, James Dale and, above all, my editor, Jackie Jones.

Finally, I would like to thank Sebastian, Alexander and Elena. They have been a ceaseless strength in the writing of these pages. Jinan, queen of the counter-hoax, continues to teach me how to live, what to do. She knows how I never find the wished-for words: 'Let everything become a post card again . . .'

Foreword

Jacques Derrida (1930–2004) was the most original and inspiring writer and philosopher of our time. He made – and his writing still makes and will continue to make – earthquakes in thinking. I believe that in many ways, indeed, the reading of his work is still ahead of us, scarcely begun. His work is about worldwide seismism. From the opening sentence of *Of Grammatology* (in 1967), his concern was with the trembling foundations of ethnocentrism and transformations of the world that we now so hastily name 'globalisation' and that he preferred to refer to as 'becoming worldwide' or 'worldwide-isation' (*mondialisation*).[1] His thinking on politics, ethics and responsibility, democracy, law and justice, will stimulate, encourage and empower for years to come. This thinking is at the same time inseparable from other, apparently less worldly or more intimate concerns, such as poetry, fiction and literature, memory and autobiography, friendship and mourning itself. Worldwide-isation, it might be said, is not only about the reaches of capitalist, hegemonic, colonial or imperialist violence or (in more benign mode) about the extensions of international law and democracy, but also about the ruses and aporias of narcissism and new ways of construing consciousness, interiority, writing and love.

Derrida's work has consistently provoked anxiety, anger and frustration, as well as pleasure, exhilaration and awe. One way or another he seems to get under people's skin. He questions everything. He refuses to simplify what is not simple. He works at unsettling all dogma. He meddles but always in a singular way, and he leaves it up to you how to meddle in turn. He is a great writer but can be difficult: the same goes, as his work shows, for other great writers (Plato, Mallarmé, Joyce, Blanchot, Cixous). He can also be wonderfully straightforward, poetic, funny and moving (and in these respects he is, perhaps, more like Nietzsche or Beckett). He is fascinated by religious topics and always sensitive, solicitous and respectful when writing about religion and the beliefs of others, but his own kind of thinking (deconstruction, the democracy to come, a new enlightenment, the demand for justice) is about what he calls a 'messianism without religion'.[2] He doesn't believe in any religious after-life: he is interested in surviving or 'living on', he says in an interview, 'precisely insofar as I do not believe that one lives on post mortem'.[3] His work is politically left-wing but he does not align himself with any particular party: many Marxists dislike him, even though he is arguably one of the sharpest and most sympathetic elaborators of 'Marxist thinking'.[4] He is a great admirer of Freud and subscribes to what he calls the 'ineluctable necessity of the psychoanalytic revolution'.[5] His conception of language is evidently troubling to some people. One is never entirely in control or ownership of what one is saying. There is, he contends, nothing essentially human about language. He argues that we need to rethink notions of the human, animals and animality: 'man is not the only political animal'.[6] He is very interested in Eros, sexuality and love, but he isn't ultimately taken with either 'the opposite sex' or 'the same sex': he suggests that everybody is queer and he dreams of polysexuality. Most of all, perhaps, his texts *do* very strange things, prompting comparisons with juggling or trapeze, a bizarre helter-skelter lighthouse ride with nobody at the bottom to pick you up, or again, an earthquake. And all of this because he is interested in the *experience of the impossible* – not everyone's cup of tea, perhaps.

♦

'Never will we believe either in death or in immortality': this proposition, which appears in the midst of Derrida's reflections on the death of his friend Paul de Man, constitutes a kind of silent refrain in the following pages.[7] In his *Mémoires: for Paul de Man* (1986), Derrida speaks of the 'terrifying lucidity' in which 'we know our friend to be gone forever' and yet, at the same time, we 'remain in *disbelief*' (p. 21). He has been meditating on the phrase 'in memory of'.[8] He notes that, since his friend's death, he can 'only speak in *memory of him*'. He then pauses, as if in incredulity, and begins a new paragraph: '*In memory of him*: these words cloud sight and thought. What is said, what is done, what is desired through these words: *in memory of. . .?*' (p. 19). It is a strange phrase, strangely familiar perhaps, haunting everybody and everything. As he goes on to suggest: 'any name, any nominal function, is "in memory of" – from the first "present" of its appearance, and finally, is "in virtually-bereaved memory of" even during the life of its bearer' (p. 54).

In Memory of Jacques Derrida: I thought cloudily and for a long time about what title might be least inappropriate for the pieces collected here. I would the reader might, in the end, imagine that this book has no title or else a ghostly but irreducible proliferation of titles. Derrida himself wrote on numerous occasions about the troubling and even insuperable difficulties of what title to attribute to a speech or piece of writing in response to death. How could I write 'in memory of' Jacques Derrida? Or even write in a way that might begin to do justice merely to what he has said about this seemingly simple but in truth unfathomable phrase 'in memory of'? It would require at least a book about his book about memory and Paul de Man, about Derrida and de Man, and another about memory and James Joyce, about Derrida and Joyce, about deconstruction and the gift, and so on. For besides his interminably ramifying meditations in *Mémoires: for Paul de Man*, Derrida also provides an inexhaustible and ineluctable modality of reflection on the phrase in an earlier essay, 'Two Words for Joyce' (1982).[9]

In that essay he talks about what constitutes 'greatness' in a writer and proposes to 'simplify outrageously' and categorise it in two ways. First, he says, there is the greatness of he or she who 'writes in order to give, in giving, and therefore in order to give to forget the gift and the given, what is given and the act of giving, which is the only way of giving, the only possible – and impossible – way' (p. 146). At issue here is a thinking of the gift as (like 'justice' or 'deconstruction') the 'dream of [a] possibility' (p. 147), linked to a certain 'experience of the impossible'.[10] The second way of considering a writer's greatness has to do with being *in memory of* him or her. He is speaking here about being 'in memory of Joyce', but it is difficult not to think, also, about being 'in memory of Derrida' in turn:

> Here the event is of such plot and scope that henceforth you have only one way out: *being in memory of him*. You're not only overcome by him, whether you know it or not, but obliged by him, and constrained to measure yourself against this overcoming. Being *in memory of him*: not necessarily to remember him, no, but to be in his memory, to inhabit his memory, which is henceforth greater than all your finite memory can, in a single instant or a single vocable, gather up of cultures, languages, mythologies, religions, philosophies, sciences, history of mind and of literatures. (p. 147)

We are all in memory of Jacques Derrida, whether we know it or not. And this, to follow the logic of his account here, can be a basis for 'gratitude without ambivalence' or for 'love', but also for 'resentment and jealousy' (p. 147). Derrida's work has already generated a great deal of both – 'resentment and jealousy' above all, perhaps, among those who have not read him, who misread or refuse to read him, in other words those who are especially susceptible to the effects of being in memory of him without knowing or being able to acknowledge it. But then this 'in memory of' is not just something peculiar to Joyce (or to de Man), or to Derrida. It is, as Derrida goes on to suggest, 'what happens already, from all time, with each event of writing' (p. 147). (It would then only remain to elucidate what is going on with that notion of *event of writing*: what is Derrida's 'event', how would writing be event, what is writing after Derrida, in memory of him, and so on? This book might thus just as well or just as ineptly be entitled *Derrida's Event*, or *Torn to Pieces*, or *Woo't*, or *Forgetting Well*, or *The Counter-Hoax*, or again *Or Again, Jacques Derrida . . .*)

Things are additionally complicated here. Derrida did not know Joyce personally, as the saying goes. They neither corresponded nor met 'in person': he was only ten years old when Joyce died. He notes that being in memory of Joyce is 'not necessarily to remember him, no, but to be in his memory, to inhabit his memory', whereas I can hardly begin to think about being *in memory of Derrida* without remembering him. He was a friend, over a good number of years, who showed me (among so many other things) what friendship is. Since his death, on 9 October 2004, I have felt at a loss for words while also knowing that I could not simply fall silent about it. On the one hand, faced with the death of a friend or loved one, we feel that all words of eulogy or elegy are inadequate and even a kind of violence – for how can we keep narcissistic impulses of appropriation out of the picture? How do we efface ourselves enough to be true or faithful to the other, and to the memory of the other? On the other hand, we also have to reckon with the fact that not saying anything can become another sort of injustice, indignity or violence, a different way of responding inadequately to his or her death. An analysis of this double-bind is one of the many profound contributions that Derrida has made to our thinking about the great riddle (as Freud described it) of mourning.[11]

♦

In what tense should one write of Jacques Derrida? He was a kind of magician of the future anterior. His thinking alters irrevocably the terms by which we might have understood the nature of a book, its time, the book to come. And life too, of course: *life will have been so short*, as he often remarked and as his writing constantly evinces. It is a question of 'a modality of the future anterior', he once wrote to me in a letter (15 September 1990), 'that does not modalise, as is often thought, the tense of the present'.[12] In the pages that follow I suggest that his work calls for new *ghost tenses*. 'Our time', I was saying at the beginning, a bit oddly perhaps, in the past tense. The pieces assembled here attempt to explore what Jacques Derrida has to say about time, about 'our time', the era of psychoanalysis, the era of deconstruction and worldwide-isation; about the now, anachronicity, untimeliness, deferred effect and the 'to come'; about the time of ghosts and mourning, reading and dreaming, the promise and the gift. To engage critically with such topics would not have been possible, at least for me, without Shakespeare. As I try to make clear, the relations between Shakespeare and Derrida are fascinating. Especially as regards memory, mourning and time out of joint, *Hamlet* is an indispensable focus here. What I hope might also emerge from all of these explorations is a sense of the sheer magnitude, richness and strangeness of Derrida's *œuvre*. We will have ended up with another way of beginning: Jacques Derrida was, perhaps, the Shakespeare of our time.

◆

Written over a period of six years, the pieces that follow are linked by numerous motifs: justice, 'globalisation' and democracy, love and friendship, fiction and poetry, terror and religion, psychoanalysis and dreams, queerness and ghosts, memory and forgetting. The order in which they appear will be construed (rightly and wrongly) as chronological: I would prefer to think of them as a sort of distracted chronicle of anachronicity. The first three pieces were written while Jacques Derrida was alive, the others after his death. 'The Poet' was originally delivered at the Cerisy-la-Salle conference on 'La démocratie à venir (autour Jacques Derrida)', in July 2002. It is about the 'to' in *Julius Caesar* (today, to come, to murder, to be torn to pieces, and so on). In the discussion afterwards Derrida made jokey reference to its being too much: *'"To" too much!'* No doubt he was right. Exorbitance, excess and exaggeration are, after all, integral to many of his own concerns, as well as to a reading of Shakespeare. I try to show this in relation to the promise, the gift and poetry or the poematic, as well as the 'democracy to come'. By the time I was writing 'Not Now', in the following year, I knew that he was ill. A section of 'Or Again, Meddling' was presented at a seminar with him on the occasion of his receiving an honorary doctorate from Queen Mary, University of London, on 6 July 2004. Part of his improvised response to this presentation has been included here.

'Derrida's Event' was the title of one of the series of talks organised by the Forum for European Philosophy, at the Tate Modern in London, under the heading 'For Derrida' in the spring of 2005. These brief remarks constitute my first attempt to respond formally in public to the painful and still singularly strange *event* of Derrida's death. An early version of 'Woo't' was presented at La Bretesche, in Missillac, Brittany, in June that year. 'Jacques Derrida's Language (Bin Laden on the Telephone)' was initially delivered as a Richard Hoggart Lecture, at Goldsmiths College, University of London, in February 2006. 'Impossible Uncanniness' was written for a conference on 'Deconstruction and Queer Theory', at University College, Dublin, in July 2007. 'Forgetting Well' was presented in various forms in the same year (at seminars in Bangor, Leicester and Århus), but continued to alter and expand over the months that followed. 'Last' dates from a night in March 2008. In concluding the book on an oneirophilic note, with dream, with a kind of uncanny giving or given, a dream-memory or *dream in memory of Jacques Derrida*, I recall what he says in 'Fichus':

> dreaming is the element most receptive to mourning, to haunting, to the spectrality of all spirits and the return of ghosts . . . The dream is also a place that is hospitable to the demand for justice and to the most invincible of messianic hopes.[13]

Seaford, East Sussex
August 2008

Notes

1. In the opening sentence of *Of Grammatology*, trans. Gayatri Chakravorty Spivak (Baltimore, MD: Johns Hopkins University Press, 1976), Derrida refers to 'the *ethnocentrism*' that, until now, has necessarily 'controlled the concept of writing' (p. 3). On 'becoming worldwide' and 'worldwide-isation', see, for example, 'Autoimmunity: Real and Symbolic Suicides. A Dialogue with Jacques Derrida', trans. Pascale-Anne Brault and Michael Naas, in Giovanna Borradori, *Philosophy in a Time of Terror: Dialogues with Jürgen Habermas and Jacques Derrida* (Chicago and London: Chicago University Press, 2003), pp. 85–136; and *Rogues: Two Essays on Reason*, trans. Pascale-Anne Brault and Michael Naas (Stanford, CA: Stanford University Press, 2005).
2. Jacques Derrida, *Spectres of Marx: The State of the Debt, the Work of Mourning, and the New International*, trans. Peggy Kamuf (London: Routledge, 1994), p. 59.
3. 'I Have a Taste for the Secret', Jacques Derrida in conversation with Maurizio Ferraris and Giorgio Vattimo, in Derrida and Ferraris, *A Taste for the Secret*, trans. Giacomo Donis (Cambridge: Polity, 2001), p. 88.

4. See, for example, *Ghostly Demarcations: A Symposium on Jacques Derrida's 'Spectres of Marx'*, ed. Michael Sprinker (London: Verso, 1999).

5. Jacques Derrida and Elisabeth Roudinesco, *For What Tomorrow . . . A Dialogue*, trans. Jeff Fort (Stanford, CA: Stanford University Press, 2004), p. 179.

6. See Jacques Derrida, 'Afterword: Toward an Ethic of Discussion', trans. Samuel Weber, in *Limited Inc* (Evanston, IL: Northwestern University Press, 1988), p. 136.

7. Jacques Derrida, *Mémoires: for Paul de Man*, trans. Cecile Lindsay, Jonathan Culler and Eduardo Cadava (New York: Columbia University Press, 1986), p. 21. Further page references are given parenthetically in the main body of the text.

8. The original French phrase is '*en mémoire de*': see *Mémoires pour Paul de Man* (Paris: Galilée, 1988), p. 42.

9. 'Two words for Joyce', trans. Geoff Bennington, in *Post-Structuralist Joyce: Essays from the French*, eds Derek Attridge and Daniel Ferrer (Cambridge: Cambridge University Press, 1984), pp. 145–59. Further page references to this essay are given parenthetically in the main body of the text.

10. Derrida writes explicitly on numerous occasions about deconstruction and the 'experience of the impossible': for some particularly helpful general remarks, see 'Deconstructions: The Im-possible', trans. Michael Taormina, in *French Theory in America*, eds Sylvère Lotringer and Sande Cohen (New York: Routledge, 2001), pp. 13–31.

11. See Sigmund Freud, 'On Transience', trans. James Strachey, in *Art and Literature*, Pelican Freud Library, vol. 14, ed. Albert Dickson (Harmondsworth: Penguin, 1985), 288–9.

12. Jacques Derrida, 'Afterw.rds: or, at least, less than a letter about a letter less', trans. Geoffrey Bennington, in *Afterwords*, ed. Nicholas Royle (Tampere, Finland: Outside Books, 1992), tr. sl. mod., p. 200; 'Afterw.rds: ou, du moins, moins qu'une letter sur une letter en moins', in *Afterwords*, p. 210.

13. Jacques Derrida, 'Fichus', in *Paper Machine*, trans. Rachel Bowlby (Stanford, CA: Stanford University Press, 2005), tr. sl. mod., pp. 173–4; *Fichus* (Paris: Galilée, 2002), p. 36.

The Poet: *Julius Caesar* and the Democracy to Come

> In sweet music is such art,
> Killing care and grief of heart
> Fall asleep, or hearing die.[1]

> You have to let yourself be 'charged', as they say in English.[2]

How are we to murder the poet today? Tear him to pieces?

'Today': what a word, already in pieces. 'To': to day. 'Today', that is to say this, now, these 'present times', this 'today' that is a double word, prepositionally a bit mad, touched by 'to' as towards, in the direction of, as far as, until, at, for, of, before, before the hour of, this 'today' is perhaps not yet. What is the place, if there is one, of this 'to'? What is this 'to' that marks time, in English, from Shakespeare to this day? How to hear 'to' in the democracy to come? In question is 'something that remains to be thought', Jacques Derrida declares, 'not something that is certain to happen tomorrow, not the democracy (national or international, state or trans-state) of the *future*, but a democracy that must have the structure of a promise – *and thus the memory of that which carries the future, the to-come, here and now*'.[3] It is a matter of the experience of a promise, the appeal of and to 'a new tone', as he describes it, at the end of *The Other Heading*, 'beyond the "revolutionary day"'. At the end of the day, it is today in pieces. Derrida writes:

> Already the days are numbered: *at another speed*, the day is announced, the day is coming, when the *day* reaches its end. The day is announced when the day (the visibility of the image and the publicity of the public, but also the unity of daily rhythm, but also the phenomenality of the political, but also perhaps, and at the same time, its very essence) will no longer be the *ratio essendi*, the reason or the ration of the telemetatheoretical effects that we have just been speaking about.
>
> Has the day ever been the measure of all things, as one pretends to believe?[4]

♦

'Tear him to pieces', take him out, take him inside you.[5] You're talking in my mind, through my lips, it's only you.

♦

'What is't o'clock?' (II, ii, 114; II, iv, 23). As Hélène Cixous remarks in her extraordinary essay 'What is it o'clock?', that is the question at the heart of *Julius Caesar.*[6] 'What, Lucius, ho! / I cannot by the progress of the stars / Give guess how near to day' (II, i, 1–3). Brutus's words, their curiously unfinished syntax, mark the uncertain beginning of the great 'orchard scene'. How near 'to day' is this now? Is this today? A little later, the conspirators Decius, Casca and Cinna reiterate the uncertainty:

> DECIUS   Here lies the east, doth not the day break here?
> CASCA   No.
> CINNA   O, pardon, sir, it doth, and yon grey lines
>   That fret the clouds are messengers of day.
> CASCA   You shall confess that you are both deceived.
>   Here, as I point my sword, the sun arises.
>
> (II, i, 101–6)

'Today' is the time of murder, of what is planned, feared, waited for. Calpurnia, Caesar's wife, tells him: 'You shall not stir out of your house today' (II, ii, 9). 'What say the augurers?' asks Caesar. To which his servant replies: 'They would not have you to stir forth today' (II, ii, 37–8). 'Do not go forth today' (II, ii, 50), Calpurnia insists: 'We'll send Mark Antony to the Senate House / And he shall say you are not well today' (II, ii, 52–3). Caesar appears to have decided: 'tell [the senators] I will not come today . . . / . . . / I will not come today. Tell them so, Decius' (II, ii, 62, 64).

At the end of Act II, scene ii, Caesar says:

> I am to blame to be thus waited for.
> Now, Cinna, now, Metellus. What, Trebonius,
> I have an hour's talk in store for you.
> Remember that you call on me today.
>
> (II, ii, 119–22)

As Marvin Spevack observes, 'blame' here is perhaps an adjective: the First Folio (1623) has 'too blame'. How much to blame is Caesar to be thus waited for? 'Remember . . . today': the 'to' of 'today' signals motion towards, at the same time as excess, hyperbole, exorbitance. Of the movement from 'to' to 'too', E. A. Abbott concludes: 'The transition from the meaning of progressive motion to that of "increasingly" or "excessively", and from "excessively" to the modern "to excess", is

too natural to require more than mention' (§73). 'To' is 'too natural'.
'Too': untranslatable hyperbole, supplement or addition invisible in
Shakespearean English. 'Too', as Abbott notes, 'is only an emphatic
form of "to" . . . [It] is often spelt "to" by Elizabethan writers (Sonnets
38, 86); and conversely, "too" is found for "to" (Sonnets 56, 135)'.[7]
Thus, in Sonnet 56, 'today' is 'too daie': 'although too daie thou fill /
Thy hungrie eies . . .'.[8]

There is a 'to'-effect to *Julius Caesar*. 'To': how to translate? I dedicate
this essay today, naturally, to Geoff Bennington.[9]

◆

'The time is out of joint.' Derrida suggests that, in saying this, Hamlet
'thereby opened one of those breaches, often they are poetic and thinking peepholes [*meurtrières*], through which Shakespeare will have kept
watch over the English language and at the same time signed its body,
with the same unprecedented stroke of some arrow'.[10] Shakespeare is
already in the château. Peggy Kamuf translates '*meurtrières*' as 'peepholes': one might also think of 'loopholes', a term that would refer to the
slits in the walls of the castle as well as to forms of ambiguity or double-
meaning (the loophole as the way out of a contract, for example). This
second sense of 'loophole' is what, up 'to' Derrida, might have been
called an anachronism. The *OED* dates the first figurative use of 'loophole' to 1663. But anachronism, in Shakespeare as in Derrida, proves a
loophole.[11] '*Meurtrières*' also means 'murderesses' and 'murder-holes'.
'To' would, perhaps, be a murder-hole. '*Meurtrière*' appears already to
generate a sense of strangeness, not only to do with the oblique evocation of the uncanniness of the female genitals and ghostly feminisation
of Shakespeare's act of keeping watch over the English language, but
also to do with an act (the act of murdering) that is prescribed but has
perhaps not (yet) taken place.[12] *Julius Caesar* gives us to think the time,
the time of today as the time of murder: when does Caesar die? When
does 'the poet' die? As Derrida says of *Hamlet*: 'One must indeed know
at what moment death took place, really took place, and this is always
the moment of a murder'.[13]

Shakespeare's *Hamlet* has a decisive role in Derrida's thinking in the
exposition of the democracy to come. Hamlet's 'The time is out of joint'
is the epigraph that watches over *Spectres of Marx*, though it appears
in numerous other texts as well.[14] The 'New International' is, in part,
elaborated out of Shakespeare: the 'New International' is, we are told,
'"out of joint", without coordination, without party, without country,
without national community (International before, across, and beyond

any national determination), without co-citizenship, without common belonging to a class' (SM, p. 85). Derrida's preoccupation with *Hamlet* has directed attention to a new sense of the political in the reading of Shakespeare.[15] In its staging of questions of friendship, tyranny and the destruction of the Roman republic, the mob, the epitaph or funeral speech, the power of spirits and spectrality, and what he has termed 'the homo-fraternal and phallogocentric schema' (PF, p. 306), however, *Julius Caesar* might appear to offer a more obvious focus for the exploration of Derrida's concerns. Before anything else, however, *Julius Caesar* is a sort of sister-play to *Hamlet* in its out of jointedness by the clock. 'Indeed, it is a strange-disposèd time' (I, iii, 33), observes Cicero, letting this 'disposèd' sound in at least doubly antithetical fashion. 'Disposèd' means both 'inclined' (time anthropomorphised, as if in a strange affair of internal time consciousness) and 'settled' or 'ordered' (time as what we might call external, spatialised, objective). It is possible to be 'well disposed' (that is to say, 'well employed', as in *All Is True,* I, ii, 117) or 'ill-disposed' (that is to say 'unwell', 'bad-tempered', as in *Troilus and Cressida*, II, iii, 70). But to be strangely disposèd or disposèd to what is strange, strangely disposèd to strangeness? 'Strange-disposèd': this striking double-word or two-fold appears nowhere else in Shakespeare's writings. 'Disposèd' to (or 'unto')? 'To' haunts the sense, along with the ghostliness of the gift, legacy or bequeathal ('to dispose' in the sense of 'to bestow': cf. *Julius Caesar*, III, i, 178).

Cicero's formulation suggests how 'disposèd' is already strange to itself: the posing is at once a disposing, placing a dis-placing, time apart from itself, time (in) pieces. As in, for example, *Macbeth* (where it comes and comes back insistently), 'strange' would perhaps be Shakespeare's word for 'uncanny', *unheimlich*. Cicero is responding to Casca's expressing belief in omens, in 'prodigies' (I, iii, 28) and 'portentous things':

CASCA	For I believe they are portentous things
	Unto the climate that they point upon.
CICERO	Indeed, it is a strange-disposèd time.
	But men may construe things after their fashion
	Clean from the purpose of the things themselves.
	Comes Caesar to the Capitol tomorrow?
CASCA	He doth, for he did bid Antonio
	Send word to you he would be there tomorrow.

(I, iii, 31–8)

The strangeness of this 'strange-disposèd time' is traced through the tenses of the lines that follow, leading to 'tomorrow'. The 'to' of 'tomorrow' conveys that sense of movement towards which eerily transfers, iterates and reiterates itself in the 'to' of 'today' and 'tonight'.

As if to equate these 'to's, Cicero and Casca both deploy the present tense ('Comes Caesar to the Capitol tomorrow?', 'He doth'). The 'to' of 'tomorrow' is not to come: it 'comes' already. As if to cover over this strange disposition of tense and time, Casca concludes by returning 'tomorrow' to the future: 'he did bid Antonio / Send word to you he *would be* there tomorrow'. But the momentary concord ('Comes Caesar . . . tomorrow?', 'He doth') seems to dispose of the future, opening in turn perhaps towards a thinking of what Derrida has referred to as a '"now" without present'.[16] The 'to' of 'tomorrow' here will have prefigured the 'to' that characterises the appearance of 'tonight' at two crucial, linked moments which we will come to later.

♦

The insane anachronism of the clock in *Julius Caesar*. This medieval invention that strikes in Act II, scene i is one of Shakespeare's most dramatic, metadramatic anachronisms.[17] It takes us to the heart perhaps of what Derrida has called the stroke [*le coup*], the 'unprecedented stroke of some arrow' (SM, p. 18), the 'stroke of genius', 'the signature of the Thing "Shakespeare"' (SM, p. 22). What is this Shakespearean stroke, this coup of the signature of the poet? What is the time of this *coup de théâtre*? What is't o'clock?

             Clock strikes
BRUTUS   Peace, count the clock.
CASSIUS   The clock hath stricken three.
TREBONIUS 'Tis time to part.
CASSIUS   But it is doubtful yet
           Whether Caesar will come forth today or no.
(II, i, 192–4)

The anachronism of the Elizabethan clock in ancient Rome strikes the note of artifice, of that 'contretemps of ironic consciousness' that Derrida detects elsewhere in Shakespeare.[18] We might link this to Thomas M. Greene's contention that 'A text that somehow acknowledges its historicity self-consciously would seem better fitted to survive its potential estrangement than a text that represses history.'[19] Shakespeare's coup concerns a peculiarly ironic spectralisation of time. Shakespearean anachronism inscribes its own ghostly 'to come', submitting to the incalculable and 'unknown'. As Cassius remarks of the assassination: 'How many ages hence / Shall this our lofty scene be acted over / In states unborn and accents yet unknown!' (III, i, 111–13). Phyllis Rackin comments that at this moment 'Shakespeare's English audience was reminded of their situation in the playhouse and the actors' status as actors representing an event that had taken place so long ago that even the English language the actors were in fact speaking was yet unknown.' She suggests that an anachronistic moment such as this 'invades the time-frame of the audience . . . its effect is no less striking than that of a character stepping off the stage to invade the audience's physical space or addressing them directly to invade their psychological space'.[20]

O my democratic friends. (PF, p. 306)

Rackin foregrounds the disruptive and dislocating effects of anachronisms: they 'can dissolve the distance between past events and present audience in the eternal present of dramatic performance'.[21] To whom does she think she is addressing these words? In what present? Having assassinated Caesar the conspirators cry out 'Liberty! Freedom! Tyranny is dead!' (III, i, 78), but the cry is already doubled, theatrical, an iteration, crying out to be cried out. Cinna: 'Run hence, proclaim, cry it about the streets' (III, i, 78–9); Cassius: 'Some to the common pulpits, and cry out, "liberty, freedom, and enfranchisement!"' (III, i, 80–1); Brutus: 'Let's all cry, "Peace, freedom, and liberty!"' (III, i, 110). For Rackin, Shakespeare's 'plebeian characters' in particular 'belong to the ephemeral present moment of theatrical performance, the modern, and socially degraded, world of the Renaissance public theatre'.[22] The aporetic disjunction between what she at one point calls 'the eternal present of dramatic performance' and at another this 'ephemeral present moment of theatrical performance' is perhaps illustrative of a more general presentism characteristic of Shakespearean criticism and historiography. The plebeians or 'tag-rag people', as Casca calls them, are always already 'in the theatre' (I, ii, 252–4). Shakespeare's poetry cries out for another thinking of what we are here trying to explore under the rubric of the 'strange-disposèd time' of his 'poetic or thinking peepholes'.

◆

'Tear him to pieces.'

◆

Jacques Derrida does not name any poets in 'Che cos'è la poesia'.[23] If he tears up the poet, he does so indirectly, tearing himself up too. There is a certain anthropomorphism at work in this brief, elliptical essay, a haunting transubstantiation: the poem says 'destroy me'. It says: 'Eat, drink, swallow my letter, carry it, transport it in you' (p. 293). Not only are no poets named, but the word 'poetry' itself becomes radically displaced, first by the term 'poetic', then by the neologism of the 'poematic' (p. 297). The poematic is characterised by what 'can reflect language or speak poetry, but . . . never relates back to itself'. It entails the logic and experience of what Derrida calls the 'demon of the heart'. He writes: 'This "demon of the heart" never gathers itself together, rather it loses itself and goes astray (delirium or mania), it exposes itself to chance, it would rather let itself be torn to pieces by what bears down upon it' (p. 299). There is a cryptic tension, it seems, between this figure of demonisation and what Derrida tells us in his great essay on Valéry, 'Qual Quelle':

> At a certain point in history, for reasons to be analysed, the poet ceased being considered the prey of a foreign voice, in mania, delirium, enthusiasm, or inspiration. Poetic 'hallucination' is then accommodated under the rubric of the 'regime': a simple elaboration of hearing-oneself-speak, a regulated, normed exchange of the same and the other, within the limits tolerated by a kind of general organisation, that is, an individual, social, historical system, etc.[24]

If Derrida stresses a certain domestication of the figure of the poet and a certain normativisation of 'poetic "hallucination"', he nevertheless affirms a demonic poematic or poematic demonisation, the madness of the poem, which is also to say the madness of the gift and the madness of the poem as gift. He opens up the possibilities of other ways of thinking 'hallucination' and 'the "regime"'. How might we try to think the 'gift of the poem' (p. 297) in the context of *Julius Caesar*? 'Che cos'è la poesia' is written in the second person ('tu'). It addresses itself to you, regarding the time of a signature and its dispersion, a certain 'now' which would be the experience of a 'to come': in French '*désormais*' (a word Derrida elsewhere describes as 'one of the most beautiful, and one of the most untranslatable, words . . . in the French language'[25]), in English, 'henceforth', 'henceforward', 'from now on'. Derrida writes: 'You will call poem *from now on* [emphasis added: N.R.] a certain passion of the singular mark, the signature that repeats its dispersion, each time beyond the *logos*, ahuman, barely domestic, not reappropriable into the family of the subject' (p. 297).

No *Julius Caesar*, no Shakespeare, no drama without 'learning by heart'. From now on.

◆

It is a question of a '"political" translation' (a translation into and of the political) that would twist the 'history of friendship', a 'scansion', as

Derrida names it, 'which would have introduced dissymmetry, separation and infinite distance in a Greek *philía* [friendship] which did not tolerate them *but nevertheless called for them*' (PF, p. 232). The democracy to come is '*a matter of thinking an alterity without hierarchical difference at the root of democracy*': 'this democracy would free a certain interpretation of *equality* by removing it from the phallogocentric schema of *fraternity*' (PF, p. 232). The question of poetry, the poetic or poematic offers, perhaps, a way of scanning this 'political' translation. Speaking of rhyme, of 'the insane linking [*appariement*, "matching", "mating", "coupling"] of a couple', he notes that 'a friendship should always be poetic. Before being philosophical, friendship concerns the gift of the poem' (PF, p. 166). Before engaging with what *Julius Caesar* might be explicitly analysing with regard to questions of monarchy, democracy, republicanism and a well-established view of Rome as 'the best historical model of the mixed regime', it would be a matter of trying to construe the logic of multiple voices that is the condition of any such engagement.[26] Before encountering the apparent division of social space into public and private, a division on which (as Richard Halpern stresses) all classical political theory has relied,[27] there is the question of what Derrida calls 'writing in the voice', its 'differential vibration'.[28] *Julius Caesar* will thus perhaps open to that 'call to come' which, as Derrida evokes it in the polyphonic drama of quotation marks at the end of 'Psyche: Inventions of the Other', 'happens only in multiple voices'.[29]

◆

Water wells up there, at the origin, imaginary. Like a mirage or buried spring: uncanny.[30] As Samuel Weber shows in an admirable recent essay on 'uncanny thinking', the uncanny and the theatrical belong together. He writes: 'A theatrical scenario . . . never takes place "once and for all" but rather "one scene at a time". It is singular and yet repetitive, ongoing and yet never complete. It is both nearby and distant, familiar and strange.'[31] But can we even speak of '"one scene at a time"', a phrase that Weber is careful to put in quotation marks? Where will *Julius Caesar* have begun? We have perhaps not yet begun to take the measure of the strange dispositions of language in Shakespeare's work. We require another vocabulary, new 'concepts' to elaborate what is going on where, for example, criticism has for so many years, even centuries, talked about 'mirror scenes in Shakespeare', larger scenes 'in miniature' or 'vignette', one speech or phrase or character or episode 'echoing' another.[32] Here is Act III, scene iii, what is often referred to as the Cinna episode. The location is a street in Rome:

Enter CINNA THE POET, *and after him the* PLEBEIANS

CINNA THE POET	I dreamt tonight that I did feast with Caesar, And things unluckily charge my fantasy. I have no will to wander forth of doors, Yet something leads me forth.
1 PLEBEIAN	What is your name?
2 PLEBEIAN	Whither are you going?
3 PLEBEIAN	Where do you dwell?
4 PLEBEIAN	Are you a married man or a bachelor?
2 PLEBEIAN	Answer every man directly.
1 PLEBEIAN	Ay, and briefly.
4 PLEBEIAN	Ay, and wisely.
3 PLEBEIAN	Ay, and truly, you were best.
CINNA THE POET	What is my name? Whither am I going? Where do I dwell? Am I a married man or a bachelor? Then to answer every man directly and briefly, wisely and truly. Wisely I say I am a bachelor.
2 PLEBEIAN	That's as much as to say they are fools that marry. You'll bear me a bang for that, I fear. Proceed directly.
CINNA THE POET	Directly I am going to Caesar's funeral.
1 PLEBEIAN	As a friend or an enemy?
CINNA THE POET	As a friend.
2 PLEBEIAN	That matter is answered directly.
4 PLEBEIAN	For your dwelling – briefly.
CINNA THE POET	Briefly, I dwell by the Capitol.
3 PLEBEIAN	Your name, sir, truly.
CINNA THE POET	Truly, my name is Cinna.
1 PLEBEIAN	Tear him to pieces, he's a conspirator.
CINNA THE POET	I am Cinna the poet, I am Cinna the poet.
4 PLEBEIAN	Tear him for his bad verses, tear him for his bad verses.
CINNA THE POET	I am not Cinna the conspirator.
4 PLEBEIAN	It is no matter, his name's Cinna. Pluck but his name out of his heart and turn him going.
3 PLEBEIAN	Tear him, tear him! Come, brands ho, fire brands! To Brutus', to Cassius', burn all! Some to Decius' house, and some to Casca's, some to Ligarius'! Away, go!

Exeunt all the Plebeians [forcing out Cinna]

In *Romeo and Juliet*, Romeo remarks of his name: 'Had I it written, I would tear the word' (II, i, 99). But the name can only be plucked out of your heart. In the name of the name (not only 'Cinna' but also 'the poet'), Cinna is to be torn to pieces. In North's translation of Plutarch (from which Shakespeare is borrowing here) we read:

But there was a poet called Cinna, who had been no partaker of the conspiracy but was alway one of Caesar's chiefest friends. He dreamed, the night before, that Caesar bade him to supper with him and that, he refusing to go, Caesar was very importunate with him and compelled him, so that at length he led him by the hand into a great dark place, where, being marvellously afraid, he was driven to follow him in spite of his heart. This dream put him all night into a fever. And yet, notwithstanding, the next morning when he heard that they carried Caesar's body to burial, being ashamed not to accompany his funerals, he went out of his house, and thrust himself into the press of the common people that were in a great uproar. And because some one called him by his name, Cinna, the people thinking he had been that Cinna who in an oration he made had spoken very evil of Caesar, they falling upon him in their rage slew him outright in the market-place.[33]

North's Plutarch goes on to state that the 'fickle and unconstant multitude' had 'torn poor Cinna the poet in pieces'.[34] 'In pieces' or 'to pieces'? Shakespeare prefers 'to' – 'Tear him *to* pieces, he's a conspirator.' But Shakespeare also keeps to a certain now, deepens and divides, encrypts it we might say. From now on. The poet is *to be* torn to pieces, perhaps. We never hear anything more of the poet.[35] But we also will never have heard about anything else. Such would be the 'strange-disposèd time' in which the poet is to be torn to pieces. In a slight and doubtless improper deformation of an archaic (Spenserian) usage, we might say that the poet is *to-torn*. ('To-tear': this is to tear in pieces, the prefix 'to' as 'asunder'. To sunder, to tear asunder. From Orpheus to Cinna and beyond, the poet is to be torn to pieces, to-torn.)

Norman N. Holland remarks that 'Cinna's death serves as an echo to Caesar's' and argues that '[t]he Cinna episode, as a miniature of Caesar's death, identifies Brutus' motives with those of the mob and establishes the attitude of the play toward the assassination'.[36] We categorise it by Act and Scene number (III, iii: is it by chance, I wonder, that the Christological 33 imprints itself here, just as Shakespeare's Caesar, unlike Suetonius' or Plutarch's, is said to have 'three and thirty wounds' (V, i, 53)?). We term it 'episode', 'miniature' or even (in the phrasing of Frank Kermode) 'a little insertion'.[37] Holland speaks of Cinna's death 'echoing' Caesar's and 'establish[ing] the attitude of the play toward [this] assassination'. But things are perhaps stranger, more complex and cryptic than such descriptions might suggest. The 'to-torn' of Cinna directs us to what Samuel Weber, in a related context, has called 'the theatrical derangement of the "work"'.[38] 'Then to answer': What is the name? What is your destination? Where do you come from? What are the politics of *Julius Caesar*? What are the politics of deconstruction? Answer directly, answer all of these questions at once, briefly, wisely and truly.

♦

How 'to answer'? As William Archer put it in a theatre review in 1898, *Julius Caesar* has 'no comic relief'.[39] At once because and in spite of appearing so close to comical, this is the stuff of terror.[40] The poet's life is suspended, paralysed in the time of this 'to', picking up from the spectral 'to' that lingers tacitly at the end of the initial barrage of the plebeians' questions: 'you were best [to]'. Cinna knows: 'to answer every man directly and briefly, wisely and truly': it is impossible. The scene, if it is one, the 'to-torn' of the poet (which is also the time of the today of the murder of Caesar, the 'strange-disposèd time' of the play) might be read as a theatrical prefiguring of a remark Derrida makes in *Politics of Friendship*: 'it is impossible to address only one person, only one man, only one woman. To put it bluntly and without pathos, such an address would have to be *each time one single time*, and all iterability would have to be excluded from the structure of the trace' (PF, p. 215). Derrida goes on to refer to this as precisely a 'drama' (p. 215). *Julius Caesar* seems to inscribe a thinking of 'theatrical derangement' in terms of what might be called the iteraphonic.[41] There is a spectrality of address already under way. The words of one character eerily repeat, singularly, without that character's knowledge or control. This would be the language of peepholes, an uncanny thinking of contagion prior to the socius or mass, or to any distinction between public and private.

To consider just a few instances, by way of moving towards a conclusion: to 'answer directly' (III, iii, 9, 14–15, 21) is a demand made already in the opening words of the play, when one of the tribunes, Murellus, informed by a cobbler that the cobbler is, 'as you would say, a cobbler', demands: 'But what trade art thou? Answer me directly' (I, i, 10–12). The 'Cinna episode' is a strange replaying of the so-called opening scene. The opening scene is itself spooked: it is mutely revisited in the very next scene, when we learn that Murellus and his fellow tribune Flavius are already 'put to silence' (I, ii, 275).[42] But the iteraphonic also interrupts, overturns and disposes quite differently the sequentiality of acts and scenes: the time of the poem, of the work as writing, disposes you to the sense of the opening scene as already haunted by the so-called Cinna episode. Act III, scene iii opens onto other times, above all to the time of reading as to come. The time of the words of 'the poet' (to be torn to pieces) engulfs the play of which it is ostensibly a part. It is no longer a question of saying that one scene or one speech 'echoes' an earlier one, in the 'strange-disposèd time' of the iteraphonic.

'I dreamt tonight that I did feast with Caesar', begins Cinna the poet, in that astonishing four-line soliloquy the fourth line of which leads him, finds him led forth, into the madness of the day. In North's Plutarch you read that Cinna 'dreamed, the night before, that Caesar bade him to supper'. Shakespeare interrupts, or we might say *iterrupts* the time. 'Tonight', at this strange moment in *Julius Caesar*, is strangely *before* today. The 'to' comes to belong to a past that never existed. As Abbott observes apropos this rare usage of 'to': '*To* was [on occasion] used [by Shakespeare] without any notion of "motion toward the future" in *to-night* (last night)' (§190).[43] But the singular, dreaming 'tonight' in Act III, scene iii is already iteraphonic, a striking repetition of the account of Calpurnia's dream, earlier in the play, before the assassination, but at the same time, the same 'tonight'. As Caesar says: 'She dreamt tonight she saw my statue, / Which like a fountain with an hundred spouts / Did run pure blood' (II, ii, 76–8). Who says 'I dreamt tonight'? At least three speakers, we might suppose. Caesar may appear to speak *for* Calpurnia, in place of her ('She dreamt tonight'), but this in fact only underscores the dream's peculiarity and power.[44] The almost incredible effacement of the presence of woman in *Julius Caesar* is integral to the cold, lucid exposition of its homo-fraternal, phallogocentric schema. Prior to any determination of Portia as a 'female terrorist',[45] or blood as a 'trope of gender',[46] or Brutus as (in Antony's final declaration) 'a man!' (V, v, 75),[47] however, the logic of the iteraphonic would entail turning our ears to what Derrida has described as 'sexual differences in the plural'. He writes:

> Why don't we turn our ears toward a call which addresses and provokes *above all else*, above and beyond whatever says 'me', my 'body', as a 'man' or a 'woman', or my sex? To turn one's ears to the other when it speaks to 'whom', to 'what', to 'this' 'who' which has not yet been assigned an identity or, for example, since we have to speak of it, to either one sex or the other?[48]

'What is't o'clock?' Iteraphonically this question recurs, or occurs twice, in separate scenes involving two characters who never hear each other speak: 'What is't o'clock?' (II, ii, 114), asks Caesar; 'What is't o'clock?', asks Portia (II, iv, 23).

🖑

I dreamt tonight of the democracy to come. You are talking in my mind, through my lips, it's only you.

🖑

I have been trying to evoke a few, perhaps especially explicit instances of the iteraphonic in *Julius Caesar*. If the signature of the poet is to be felt here, we should also have to reckon with a thinking of the iteraphonic as 'unbounded generalisation':[49] in Cinna's four-line soliloquy at the start of Act III, scene iii we might also pick up on the strange appearance or reappearance of 'will' (a celebrated signature-word that occurs twenty-seven times in thirty-six lines in the preceding scene: see III, ii, 126–61)[50] or the phrase 'forth of doors' that weirdly iterates Antony's description of the blood leaving Caesar's body as 'rushing out of doors' (III, ii, 170). It would be possible to elaborate notions of the iteraphonic or, perhaps, iteraesthesia (for it is a matter of a spectralisation of sense and feeling) across the entirety of Shakespeare's text, thus engaging with micrological analyses of apparently single words such as 'blood', 'noble', 'honourable', 'man', 'friend' or, perhaps, 'to'.

Julius Caesar is an inexhaustibly rich text for any attempt to think about the nature and politics of friendship. In this play, perhaps more deliberately and succinctly than in any other of Shakespeare's works, we are brought up against the strangeness of a friend and friends. In *Julius Caesar* Trebonius, Brutus and Caesar can be 'like friends' (II, ii, 127), uncertainly 'as' friends, similar to but not the same as 'friends'; it is apparently possible to 'befriend [one]self' (II, iv, 29); 'friend' can mean 'lover' or vice versa (II, iii, 6); yet at other moments the distinction between 'lovers' ('Romans, countrymen, and lovers' (III, ii, 13), as Brutus addresses the people) and 'friends' ('Friends, Romans, countrymen' (III, ii, 65), as Antony addresses them) can appear decisive; and above all, perhaps, friends can do you a good turn by turning against you, indeed by disposing of you altogether (as Brutus puts it, in what is perhaps the most shocking formulation of friendship in the play: 'So are we Caesar's friends, that have abridged / His time of fearing death' (III, i, 103–4)). 'Friendship would be *unheimlich*', suggests Derrida. He asks: 'How would *unheimlich, uncanny*, translate into Greek? Why not translate it by *atópos*: outside all place or placeless, without family or familiarity, outside of self, expatriate, extraordinary, extravagant, absurd or mad, weird, unsuitable, strange but also "a stranger to"?' (PF, p. 178).

A stranger to friend. Kirby Farrell has suggested that there is a 'deep taboo in [Shakespeare's] plays against attempts to seize the future by force'.[51] *Julius Caesar* dramatises the 'strange-disposèd time' of the 'being-promise of a promise' (SM, p. 105). It is a play about attempts to predict and seize the future, and in particular about faith in friendship. In the aftermath of Caesar's murder Brutus claims to know the future, as regards the friendship of Antony. He tells Cassius: 'I know that we shall have him well to friend' (III, i, 143). Abbott notes of the 'to' in 'to friend' here: '*To*, from meaning "like", came into the meaning of "representation", "equivalence", "apposition"' (§189). Has the meaning of 'to' come, or is it still to come? What is this 'to friend'? It is as if Brutus says to Cassius: O my friend, there are friends: I know the future, we will certainly have Antony as friend. Ironised by the knowledge that there can be no such knowledge, no grounds for such knowledge, the 'to' is the mark of interruption, the very disjunction with the future.

Is there (in Derrida's terms) a 'suitable' reading of Shakespeare's play? *Julius Caesar* is a stranger to friend. *Atópos* of the iteraphonic. The play can always be torn to pieces. As is obvious from its stage history, it is susceptible to innumerable different 'political' readings and renditions, including those of ostensibly 'politically opposing' kinds.[52] Eighteenth-century productions presenting Brutus as hero, and thus promoting what Francis Gentleman (writing in 1770) called 'one of the noblest principles that actuates the human mind, the love of national liberty', generally entailed tearing the play to pieces by omitting, in particular, the so-called Cinna episode.[53] The time of Shakespeare's play is haunted by this, just as strangely as it is by the ghost of Caesar, by the ghost of Caesar in the play but also by the ghost of Caesar as Shakespeare, the play as the ghost of Caesar. Double is the ghost, the ghost is always (at least) double. Great play of the two: a play of two parts, two 'central characters', two poets, two Caesars.[54] As Brutus discovers, reading can always call up a ghost:

> Let me see, let me see, is not the leaf turned down
> Where I left reading? Here it is, I think.
>   *Enter the* GHOST OF CAESAR
> How ill this taper burns! Ha, who comes here?
>
> (IV, iii, 273–5)

How to answer?

Julius Caesar keeps 'to', keeps to itself. '*Et tu, Brute?*' (III, i, 76). This familiar but strange, strangely familiar, anachronistic foreign language at the heart of *Julius Caesar* is the only Latin in all of Shakespeare's so-called Roman plays.[55] How would one hear this '*tu*'? How would it have sounded, how should it sound, in what language or languages? In 'accents yet unknown', a new international? Rhyming with, haunted by 'you'? You, too? Suetonius records that Caesar at this moment spoke Greek: Καὶ σὺ τέκνον? In English: 'You too, my child?'[56] (The use of the word τέκνον, it may be recalled, is linked to the not uncommon belief that Brutus was Caesar's illegitimate son.) The Latin phrase in *Julius Caesar* seems to circle around and back on itself, a sort of palindrome in the ear (et tu . . . rb . . . ut te), petering out, interrupted. 'Tu' falls, brutish in reverse. I conclude with a supplement, centuries later, in translation. You might have felt it coming from the start:

Before all else I am seeking to produce effects (*sur toi, on you*. What do they do here in order to avoid the plural? Their grammar is very bizarre. I would not have been able to love you in English, you are untranslatable. Or I would have had recourse, more than ever, to anachronistic procedures, even more retro, I would have made you theatrical, divine. Do you think it would have changed something, you, *toi*, this singular in disuse?).[57]

Notes

1. William Shakespeare, *All Is True*, III, i, 12–14, in *The Norton Shakespeare: Based on the Oxford Edition*, eds Stephen Greenblatt, Walter Cohen, Jean E. Howard and Katherine Eisaman Maus (New York and London: W. W. Norton, 1997).
2. Jacques Derrida, 'Circumfession', in *Jacques Derrida*, trans. Geoffrey Bennington (Chicago: Chicago University Press, 1993), p. 301.
3. Jacques Derrida, *The Other Heading: Reflections on Today's Europe*, trans. Pascale-Anne Brault and Michael B. Naas (Bloomington, IN: Indiana University Press, 1992), p. 78.
4. Ibid., pp. 108–9.
5. William Shakespeare, *Julius Caesar*, ed. Marvin Spevack (Cambridge: Cambridge University Press, 1988), III, ii, 26. Unless otherwise stated, further references to *Julius Caesar* are to this edition and given parenthetically in the text. Unless otherwise indicated, all references to other works by Shakespeare are to *The Norton Shakespeare*.
6. Hélène Cixous, 'What is it o'clock? or The door (we never enter)', trans. Catherine A. F. MacGillivray, in *Stigmata: Escaping Texts* (London: Routledge, 1998), pp. 57–83.
7. E. A. Abbott, *A Shakespearian Grammar*, 3rd edn (London: Macmillan, 1870), §73. Further section references are to this edition and given parenthetically in the text.
8. See *Shakespeare's Sonnets*, ed. Stephen Booth (New Haven, CT: Yale University Press, 1977), p. 50. In the earliest (1623 First Folio) version of *Julius Caesar*, 'today' is consistently printed as 'to day'.
9. As noted in the Foreword, this text was originally presented at the château at Cerisy-la-Salle, on the occasion of the ten-day conference on 'La démocratie à venir (autour Jacques Derrida)', in July 2002. The text was delivered in English with a French translation (by Geoffrey Bennington) accompanying on an overhead projector.
10. Jacques Derrida, *Spectres of Marx: The State of the Debt, the Work of Mourning, and the New International*, trans. Peggy Kamuf (London: Routledge, 1994), p. 18. Further references will appear in the main body of the text, abbreviated 'SM'.
11. The term 'anachronism' itself, in the sense of 'an error which implies the misplacing of persons or events in time', has been traced back to 1629: see Herman L. Ebeling, 'The Word "Anachronism"', *Modern Language Notes*, 52 (1937), 121. Cited by Phyllis Rackin, who provides a valuable account of anachronism in Shakespeare in her *Stages of History: Shakespeare's*

English Chronicles (London: Routledge, 1991): see, in particular, Chapter 3, 'Anachronism and Nostalgia', pp. 86–145.

12. The *meurtrière* is also of course a question of writing: to whom is Shakespeare's work addressed? In the 'Envois' Derrida writes: 'for me this is the only *meurtrière*: one kills someone by addressing a letter to him that is not destined to him, and thereby declaring one's love or even one's hatred. And I kill you at every moment, but I love you'. See *The Post Card*, trans. Alan Bass (Chicago: Chicago University Press, 1987), p. 112.

13. Jacques Derrida, 'The Time is Out of Joint', trans. Peggy Kamuf, in *Deconstruction is/in America: A New Sense of the Political*, ed. Anselm Haverkamp (New York: New York University Press, 1995), p. 20.

14. See, for example, 'The Time is Out of Joint'; *Politics of Friendship*, trans. George Collins (London: Verso, 1997) (hereafter abbreviated 'PF' in the main body of the text), p. 103; 'I Have a Taste for the Secret', trans. Giacomo Donis, in Jacques Derrida and Maurizio Ferraris, *A Taste for the Secret* (Cambridge: Polity, 2001), pp. 6–7, 56–7. For Gilles Deleuze also, Hamlet's 'The time is out of joint' marks a crucial moment in the history of philosophy and conceptions of temporality: 'Time *out of joint*, the door off its hinges, signifies the first great Kantian reversal: movement is now subordinated to time. Time is no longer related to the movement it measures, but rather movement to the time that conditions it . . . It is Hamlet . . . who completes the emancipation of time . . .. Hamlet is the first hero who truly needed time in order to act, whereas earlier heroes were subject to time as the consequence of an original movement (Aeschylus) or an aberrant action (Sophocles) . . . Time is no longer the cosmic time of an original celestial movement, nor is it the rural time of derived meteorological movements. It has become the time of the city and nothing other, the pure order of time.' See Gilles Deleuze, *Essays Critical and Clinical*, trans. Daniel W. Smith and Michael A. Greco (London: Verso, 1998), pp. 27–8.

15. I have attempted to explore this in more detail elsewhere: see, in particular, 'Night writing: deconstruction reading politics', in *The Uncanny* (Manchester: Manchester University Press, 2003), pp. 112–32.

16. 'I Have a Taste for the Secret', p. 13.

17. Cf. Matthew H. Wikander, 'The Clock in Brutus' Orchard Strikes Again: Anachronism and Achronism in Historical Drama', in *The Delegated Intellect: Emersonian Essays on Literature, Science, and Art in Honor of Don Gifford*, ed. Donald E. Morse (New York: Peter Lang, 1995), p. 149.

18. Jacques Derrida, 'Aphorism Countertime', trans. Nicholas Royle, in *Acts of Literature*, ed. Derek Attridge (London and New York: Routledge, 1992), p. 431. Further examples of anachronism in *Julius Caesar* would include the hats that are worn by the conspirators (II, i, 73); the kerchief worn by the sick Ligarius (II, i, 322); the 'watch' or night watchmen who have seen 'most horrid sights' (II, ii, 16) during the night before the murder; and, most insidiously and profoundly perhaps, the Christification of Caesar, above all in the context of Calpurnia's dream and the Christian typology of Caesar's blood. As Decius tells him, the dream 'Signifies that from you great Rome shall suck / Reviving blood and that great men shall press / For tinctures, stains, relics, and cognizance' (II, ii, 87–9).

The Norton editors gloss the final line: 'Heraldic colours and emblems ("tinctures", "stains", and "cognizance"); venerated properties of saints ("tinctures", "stains", and "relics"): see Norton p. 1555. As David Kaula has argued, the account of Calpurnia's dream is strongly suggestive of 'the medieval cult of the Holy Blood, which featured not only the proliferation of phials of Christ's blood but also stories about bleeding statues and paintings of Christ'. See David Kaula, '"Let Us Be Sacrificers": Religious Motifs in *Julius Caesar*', *Shakespeare Studies*, 14 (1981), 204. Cf. also Gail Kern Paster who observes: 'Caesar, as Decius Brutus anticipates, responds positively to this sacerdotal image of himself (perhaps even becoming a victim of witty anachronism on Shakespeare's part in Caesar's ignorance of basic Christian typology about the self-sacrificial nature of the Christ he is made to resemble here).' See Paster's essay, '"In the spirit of men there is no blood": Blood as Trope of Gender in *Julius Caesar*', *Shakespeare Quarterly*, 40: 3 (1989), 294. Anachronism here is not simply a matter of being 'witty', however: the Christification of Caesar is in keeping with the play's more general dramatisation and questioning of what Derrida has referred to as 'the Christianisation of fraternisation, or fraternisation as the essential structure of Christianisation' (PF, p. 96).

19. See his essay 'History and Anachronism', in *The Vulnerable Text: Essays on Renaissance Literature* (New York: Columbia University Press, 1986), p. 224. Shakespeare's exploration of 'strange-disposèd time' is, however, perhaps more radical than is suggested by Greene's conception of 'potential estrangement', which would seem to imply some logic of originary non-estrangement.

20. Phyllis Rackin, *Stages of History: Shakespeare's English Chronicles*, p. 94.

21. Ibid., p. 94.

22. Ibid., p. 103.

23. Jacques Derrida, 'Che cos'è la poesia?', trans. Peggy Kamuf, in *Points . . . Interviews, 1974–1994*, ed. Elisabeth Weber (London: Routledge, 1995), pp. 288–99. Further references are given parenthetically in the main body of the text.

24. Jacques Derrida, 'Qual Quelle: Valéry's Sources', in *Margins – of Philosophy*, trans. Alan Bass (Chicago: Chicago University Press, 1982), p. 298.

25. Jacques Derrida, *Demeure: Fiction and Testimony* (with Maurice Blanchot's *The Instant of My Death*), trans. Elizabeth Rottenberg (Stanford, CA: Stanford University Press, 2000), p. 102.

26. For a discussion of republicanism and the 'mixed regime' in particular, see John R. Kayser and Ronald J. Lettieri, '"The Last of All the Romans": Shakespeare's Commentary on Classical Republicanism', *Clio*, 9: 2 (1980), 197–227. They argue that '[t]he essence of Roman republicanism consisted of its mixed constitution or regime' (p. 198). They thus follow Kurt von Fritz whose study *The Theory of the Mixed Constitution in Antiquity: A Critical Analysis of Polybius' Political Ideas* (New York: Columbia University Press, 1954) provides an especially detailed account of the notion of the mixed constitution or regime as comprising the three elements of monarchy, oligarchy and democracy. Kayser and Lettieri seek to

situate Shakespeare's work in an Elizabethan context: 'Fully conscious of the depraved conditions of monarchy gone awry (tyranny) and the bestial proclivity of democracy (anarchy), many late sixteenth-century Englishmen advanced the notion that some semblance of a mixed regime was necessary to establish an effective and stable polity' (p. 200).

27. Richard Halpern, 'That Shakespeherian Mob: Mass Culture and the Literary Public Sphere', *Shakespeare Among the Moderns* (Ithaca, NY: Cornell University Press, 1997), p. 78.
28. Jacques Derrida, 'Dialanguages', trans. Peggy Kamuf, in *Points*, p. 140.
29. Jacques Derrida, 'Psyche: Inventions of the Other', trans. Catherine Porter, in *Psyche: Inventions of the Other*, vol. 1, eds Peggy Kamuf and Elizabeth Rottenberg (Stanford, CA: Stanford University Press, 2007), p. 47.
30. I refer here, in the subterranean space of a footnote, to Derrida's discussion of the *unheimlich* or uncanny in relation to the argument that 'The timbre of my voice, the style of my writing are that which for (a) me never will have been present. I neither hear nor recognise the timbre of my voice. If my style marks itself, it is only on a surface which remains invisible and illegible for me'. See 'Qual Quelle: Valéry's Sources', pp. 296–7, n. 25.
31. Samuel Weber, 'Uncanny Thinking', in *The Legend of Freud*, Expanded Edition (Stanford, CA: Stanford University Press, 2000), p. 7. He goes on to say that the theatrical scenario is 'present and passing. It is marked not by acts or even by actors but rather by acting. Its tense and temporality is that of the *present participle*. [It is] "presenting rather than "present"' (p. 7). I would associate this thinking of the present participle with the 'to' (the 'coming' as never completely come, as still keeping, indeed as structured by, the 'to come').
32. The phrase 'mirror scenes in Shakespeare' is Hereward T. Price's. See 'Mirror Scenes in Shakespeare', *Joseph Quincy Adams Memorial Studies*, ed. James G. McManaway (Washington, DC: Folger Shakespeare Library, 1948).
33. Plutarch, 'The Life of Marcus Brutus', trans. Sir Thomas North, in *Julius Caesar*, ed. Spevack, pp. 170–1.
34. Ibid., p. 171.
35. Rather, in Act IV, scene iii, we are presented with the figure of another poet, a 'cynic', a 'jigging fool' who is dismissed by Brutus for not knowing his time: 'Get you hence, sirrah; saucy fellow, hence! / . . . / I'll know his humour when he knows his time' (IV, iii, 134–6). 'Time' here of course carries a double sense, both 'proper occasion' and sense of rhythm or 'poetic metre' (see Spevack, p. 126 n.). The question remains: what is the time of the poet?
36. Norman N. Holland, 'The "Cinna" and "Cynicke" Episodes in *Julius Caesar*', *Shakespeare Quarterly*, 11: 1 (1960), 441, 443.
37. He suggests that the 'little insertion' of this scene (III, iii) 'was meant as an ironic denial that poets, except by unhappy chance, have anything to do with politics', before adding: 'yet this is an intensely political play, a fact that has a controlling influence over its language'. See Frank Kermode, *Shakespeare's Language* (London: Penguin, 2000), p. 86.
38. Samuel Weber, 'Uncanny Thinking', p. 30.

39. William Archer, review of a performance of *Julius Caesar*, produced by Herbert Beerbohm Tree, at Her Majesty's Theatre, London; reprinted in *Shakespeare in the Theatre: An Anthology of Criticism*, ed. Stanley Wells (Oxford: Oxford University Press, 1997), p. 152.

40. On the question 'Where are you from?' as a 'terroristic' question, see David Punter, *Postcolonial Imaginings: Fictions of a New World Order* (Edinburgh: Edinburgh University Press, 2000), p. vii and *passim*.

41. Elsewhere I have tried to explore this in relation to a (correspondingly anachronistic) notion of theatrical or dramaturgic telepathy. See, for example, *The Uncanny*, Chapters 8 and 18. I elaborate further on the itera-phonic in the pages that follow (see, in particular, 'Not Now', 'Woo't' and 'Forgetting Well'), as well as in 'Fear of Freud (On the Universal Tendency to Debasement in the Sphere of Literature)', *Oxford Literary Review*, 30: 1 (2008), 85–121.

42. This 'to'-effect ('to silence' = 'to death') is, again, peculiarly Shakespearean: as Spevack notes, in Plutarch we are told only that Murellus and Flavius are 'deprived . . . of their Tribuneships' (p. 157).

43. Elsewhere, 'tonight' indeed carries this sense of 'motion toward the future' – hence, for example, Cassius' asking Casca 'Will you sup with me tonight?' (I, ii, 277) or Brutus' telling Lucilius and Titinius: 'bid the commanders / Prepare to lodge their companies tonight' (IV, iii, 139–40). Cassius' death is described specifically in terms of a movement 'to night' (retained as two words in Spevack's edition). Titinius declares: 'But Cassius is no more. O setting sun, / As in thy red rays thou dost sink to night, / So in his red blood Cassius' day is set' (V, iii, 60–2).

44. Cynthia Marshall picks up on a similar sense of paradox in this context, though she reads the scene and the 'place' of Calpurnia rather differently: 'That [Calpurnia] is denied even the articulation of her dream, which is narrated by the appropriating Caesar, demonstrates an effacement of her linguistic presence; Calpurnia is largely without the power of words in the play. But her relative muteness also confers on Calpurnia the paradoxi-cal freedom of one unconfined by limiting verbal structures.' See Cynthia Marshall, 'Portia's Wound, Calpurnia's Dream: Reading Character in *Julius Caesar*', *English Literary Renaissance*, 24: 2 (1994), 471–88: here, pp. 483–4.

45. Ibid., p. 477.

46. I refer here in particular to Gail Kern Paster's thought-provoking essay, '"In the spirit of men there is no blood": Blood as Trope of Gender in *Julius Caesar*'. (See note 18 above.)

47. On 'man' and 'manliness' in particular, see Jan H. Blits, 'Manliness and Friendship in Shakespeare's *Julius Caesar*', *Interpretation: A Journal of Political Philosophy*, 9: 2–3 (1981), 155–67.

48. Jacques Derrida, 'Voice II', trans. Verena Andermatt Conley, in *Points*, p. 163.

49. See Jacques Derrida, 'The Time of a Thesis: Punctuations', trans. Kathleen McLaughlin, in *Philosophy in France Today*, ed. Alan Montefiore (Cambridge: Cambridge University Press, 1983), p. 40.

50. See Richard Wilson, '"Is This a Holiday?": Shakespeare's Roman Carnival', *English Literary History*, 54 (1987), 39. Cf. Gail Kern Paster, '"In the spirit

of men there is no blood": Blood as Trope of Gender in *Julius Caesar*', p. 297. Wilson reads 'will' as a 'phallic pun' in Act III, scene ii. As Eric Partridge has made clear, however, 'will' can also signify the female genitals, as well as the name of the poet himself (Will Shakespeare). See Eric Partridge, *Shakespeare's Bawdy* (3rd edn 1968; London: Routledge, 2001), pp. 284–6.

51. Kirby Farrell, 'Prophetic Behaviour in Shakespeare's Histories', *Shakespeare Studies*, 19 (1987), 21.

52. For two accounts of this history, see Michael Dobson, 'Accents Yet Unknown: Canonisation and the Claiming of *Julius Caesar*', in *The Appropriation of Shakespeare: Post-Renaissance Reconstructions of the Works and the Myth*, ed. Jean I. Marsden (New York: Harvester Wheatsheaf, 1991), pp. 11–28; and Alan Sinfield, *Faultlines: Cultural Materialism and the Politics of Dissident Reading* (Berkeley: University of California Press, 1992), pp. 10–28.

53. See Alan Sinfield, *Faultlines*, p. 11.

54. My thanks here to Avital Ronell who, in the discussion at Cerisy, finely stressed the importance of the 'two' in the context of *Julius Caesar*.

55. See Kayser and Lettieri, who also remark on the 'obviously anachronistic' nature of this Latin phrase (p. 219).

56. Suetonius, *History of Twelve Caesars*, trans. Philemon Holland (1606), with an introduction by Charles Whibley (New York: AMS Press, 1967), vol. 1, p. 76.

57. Jacques Derrida, 'Envois', *The Post Card*, p. 113.

Not Now

'Not Now': to whom will these words have been addressed, in what tone are they to be heard?[1]

Everything is to be or not to be knotted and unknotted in this strange couple. Not now – 'neither a statement nor a sentence' as Derrida says of a corresponding phrase 'out of joint', in the essay that will figure as a sort of ghost text for my remarks here, 'The Time is Out of Joint'.[2] Already at issue, then, is that 'traditional gesture of deconstruction' which consists, as Derrida says, in 'interrogating, so as to put them back into play, titles in general: the title of the title, the justification and authority of the title. And to do so by marking a multi-referentiality, which is to say . . . a *differeferentiality* [différéférentialitée] of the title that is thus suspended. The reference of the title, that to which it refers, the thing in play becomes at once multiple, different, and deferred' (p. 24). The title ('The Time is Out of Joint'), as Derrida goes on to remark, thus announces both the subject and form of the text it entitles, the question of 'a certain difference within time, a temporal and temporalising differance' (p. 24). The title-phrase 'Not now' (which is of course not mine) would likewise perhaps say something about titles in general, about the dislocations, anachronies, contretemps, dismaintenances and other nots of time in deconstruction.

There is a question of love here, as always with Derrida. Concerning the sentence 'The time is out of joint', he notes at the start of his essay that it is not his. He has neither 'signed [nor] countersigned it' (p. 25). It is a quotation. But he has loved it, and that is a definition of love: 'one can never love anything other than that: what one cannot sign, he or she in the place of whom one neither can nor wants to sign'. Love renders this title-phrase 'desirably ineffaceable within [him]' (p. 25). Derrida's reported feeling about this reported sentence, 'The time is out of joint', recalls his extraordinary account of the poematic (in 'Che cos'è la poesia?'), the reporting and transporting of a word or phrase, the cryptic ellipticality of a poem, not to be signed, one never signs it, keeping it within oneself, a foreign body, desirably ineffaceable.[3] 'Not now': as just noted, this title is not mine, it is a quotation – from at least three places, three places in my heart, three cryptic instances I love.

♦

The first is David McKee's *Not Now, Bernard* (1980),[4] an example of that impossible genre called 'children's literature', a genre not (not at present, or not yet) especially often associated with the work of Derrida, despite the fact that 'the problem of the child' is a consistent focus of attention in that work, and despite the sense that he is, in Hélène Cixous's striking phrase, 'the forever-child'.[5] As Derrida comments in a footnote in 'Passions: "An Oblique Offering"': 'The child is the problem. As always. And the problem is always childhood.'[6] Or as he declares in one of the 'Envois' in *The Post Card*: 'the child remain[s], alive or dead, the most beautiful and most living of fantasies, as extravagant as absolute knowledge. As long as you don't know what a child is, you won't know what a fantasy is, nor of course, by the same token, what knowledge is.'[7] On its back cover *Not Now, Bernard* is described as 'the all-time classic story of Bernard whose parents are too busy to understand'. The curious hyperbole of the 'all-time' ('all-time classic') is perhaps already strangely at odds with the ironic 'not now' that marks and remarks this very short text:

> 'Hello, Dad,' said Bernard. 'Not now, Bernard,' said his father. 'Hello, Mum,' said Bernard. 'Not now, Bernard,' said his mother. 'There's a monster in the garden and it's going to eat me,' said Bernard. 'Not now, Bernard,' said his mother. [Bernard then goes out into the garden and meets a monster.] 'Hello, monster,' he said to the monster. The monster ate Bernard up, every bit. [The monster then goes into the house; tries in vain to get the attention of Bernard's parents, being met only with another 'Not now'; eats Bernard's dinner; watches TV; reads one of Bernard's comics; breaks one of his toys; then goes up to bed. Bernard's mother comes to turn out the light.] 'But I'm a monster,' said the monster. 'Not now, Bernard,' said Bernard's mother. [These are the final words as she turns out the light.]

I cannot pretend to do justice to the simplicity and profundity, the gentleness and violence of this tiny text, this 'mini treasure' as it is called in its latest reprinting. There is a picture above each of the brief lines of text, so that we are immediately drawn in, so to speak, to the question of the decapitational time of reading, the junctions and disjunctions between the picture and the caption.

On the first page there is a picture of a man in pinky-white blank-faced concentration, sleeves rolled up, holding a nail to the wall with his left hand and raising a hammer with his right. He is, perhaps, in the process of trying to put up a picture in the picture. On his left wrist he is wearing a watch. Behind him, smiling and open-mouthed, is a little boy with his hands behind his back. The caption beneath offers: '"Hello, Dad," said Bernard.' The correspondence between this opening image and the Matthew Paris picture of Socrates and Plato on which Derrida wrote his 'Envois' is no doubt coincidental, as is the fact that both works (McKee's and Derrida's) appeared in the same year (1980). But what is coincidence in the context of reading Derrida? No encounter without chance, chance encounter and the incalculable. We should no doubt always be careful about philosophising with a hammer. On the next page the father has smashed his finger: the finger is red with blood and his face is entirely green. His eyes apparently are now shut and his mouth open, groaning or crying out in pictorial agony. The nail, fallen from his left hand, is still in mid-air. The child has already turned around and, looking wide-eyed and innocent, is apparently leaving the picture. The caption is at once accompanying and dislocating, pertinent and foreign: '"Not now, Bernard," said his father.' Again, the only visibly useless prosthesis in the picture is the father's watch: we cannot tell its time or significance, we cannot but speculate on whether it is Bernard's greeting ('Hello, Dad') or perhaps the father's watching his watch, momentarily distracted by this single, apparently non-instrumental prosthetic supplement (supplement to the father and, if one can say so, to the pictorial narrative), or something else that has him injure himself. Cause and effect are interrupted, colliding, smashed. The time is out of joint: the father's 'Not now, Bernard' is out of joint with the picture (and of course is also strangely out of joint with itself, since it is a quotation, the first – but at the same time the second – appearance in the text of the title of the text); but the picture (especially in the imaged simultaneity of the nail still in mid-air and the child already making his way out of the picture) is also out of joint with itself.

McKee's book is both funny and appalling. Like any 'not now' it can always seem to be appropriated, domesticated in the name of the child, children or children's literature; but at the same time, without perhaps wanting to push the homology too far, it might be said that – just as 'deconstruction is/in America' (that being the other beloved sentence on which Derrida meditates in 'The Time is Out of Joint' (p. 25)) – deconstruction is/in children's literature. Everything comes back to the name, the name of the name and the unnamable. The appeal of McKee's 'all-time', 'not now' classic would doubtless lie in the name of Bernard, its singularity, but also in its substitutability, its replaceability. As Derrida writes in *Demeure*: 'The example is not substitutable; but at the same

"Hello, Dad," said Bernard.

time . . . this irreplaceability must be exemplary, that is, replaceable. The irreplaceable must allow itself to be replaced on the spot', in the 'pointed instant' of 'a here-now' [*un ici-maintenant*].[8] Bernard is indeed 'replaced on the spot': McKee's story is that of precisely such replaceability.

If *Not Now, Bernard* has to do with the monstrous, it is perhaps less in the figure of the so-called monster itself (the monster that eats Bernard) than in the unspoken monstrosities that haunt this little text: the terrible somnambulism of the parents as if Bernard were dead already or, conversely, as if he were an orphan, in a deaf world of orphaned speech; or, in the event of the apparently unremarked disappearance of the child into the monster's mouth ('every bit' swallowed up, leaving the monster, tongue sticking out, holding up the remains, a single trainer:[9] think of all Derrida has said, in *The Truth in Painting*, and in particular about 'letting a picture drop like an old shoe'[10]), that insidious movement by which Bernard himself becomes 'not now', that 'most monstrous thing',

"Not now, Bernard," said his father.

as Derrida has described it, of a child dying before its parents;[11] or in the eerily reverse but simultaneous movement by which the child becomes the monster, a monstrosity begot upon itself. One can always turn out the other: substitutability will have been the law. *Not Now, Bernard* can always also be read, in its title and in each singular repetition of its title-phrase, as a 'not now' addressed not only to Bernard but to the name of Bernard, in the name of Bernard and in the name of the name, a 'not now' addressed to and on the subject of anyone. Already with this name of 'Bernard', we are perhaps not far from Barnardo and the opening words of Shakespeare's *Hamlet*: 'Who's there?'[12]

◆

Second instance. 'Not now' is a quotation from part of the title of a lecture Derrida gave at Cornell University in April 1984, 'No Apocalypse,

Not Now (full speed ahead, seven missiles, seven missives)'.[13] Inverting the title of Francis Ford Coppola's 1979 war film about Vietnam, *Apocalypse Now*, Derrida's 'not now' is at once playful and perfectly serious. It is an encounter, perhaps before anything else, unsettling tone and tonality. The question 'what is seriousness?' (p. 391) is indeed an explicit focus of attention in this text. In all seriousness, then, Derrida affirms and elaborates on the singular competence of those studying philosophy and literature to speak, write and make public interventions on the topic of nuclear war, the arms race, nuclear deterrence and so on. 'Not Now' is not only an ironic allusion to a film, but also a sort of summary of Derrida's work, in particular on the subject of apocalypse, tone, revelation, and truth.

'Not now' communicates with the 'come' evoked by Derrida in the essay that shadows and guides the 'seven missives' of the 1984 text, namely the great essay on 'the ends of man', 'Of an Apocalyptic Tone Newly Adopted in Philosophy' (1980). As he writes in the final pages of that text: 'Now here, precisely, is announced – as promise or threat – an apocalypse without apocalypse, an apocalypse without vision, without truth, without revelation . . . Our *apocalypse now* . . . there is not, there has never been, there will not be apocalypse.'[14] At issue here is Derrida's consistent concern with what he describes in *Monolingualism of the Other* as not 'an ultimate unveiling, but . . . what will have remained alien, for all time, to the veiled figure, to the very figure of the veil'.[15] His desire to 'demystify' or 'deconstruct apocalyptic discourse itself' (AT, p. 51) is doubtless in various respects apocalyptic. It is linked to the notion of affirmation itself, or what he elsewhere calls the yes, the 'irrecuperable' yes, the yes that 'does not wait'.[16] Derrida's 'not now' is not negative, it is 'full speed ahead' (*à toute vitesse*). As Sean Gaston has glossed this, in a fine account of the notion of speed in Derrida: 'To go ahead – to anticipate, to go in advance, to go before – is to go beyond one's own head or heading, beyond any calculation or programme'.[17]

'*In the beginning there will have been speed*' (p. 387), Derrida asserts at the beginning of 'No Apocalypse, Not Now': this strange future anterior affirmation of speed tallies with a thinking of the trace, writing and the disseminal divisibility of the now. We are led back here to the extraordinary work of 1968, '*Ousia* and *Grammē*: Note on a Note from *Being and Time*'.[18] In this essay Derrida analyses and disturbs the meaning and presuppositions of the 'now' as it is inscribed in philosophical writings from Aristotle onwards, through Hegel to Heidegger. For Aristotle, Derrida comments,

> time is . . . time has as its essence, the *nun*, which is most often translated as *instant*, but which functions in Greek like our word 'now' (*maintenant*).

The *nun* is the form from which time cannot ever depart, the form in which it cannot not be given; and yet the *nun*, in a certain sense, is not. If one thinks time on the basis of the now, one must conclude that it is not. The now is given simultaneously as that which is *no longer* and as that which is *not yet*. It is what it is not, and is not what it is. (p. 39)

Derrida shows that this 'aporia' (as Aristotle calls it) itself entails a certain presupposition of simultaneity, the element of 'a certain same'. Of the Aristotelian view that '[a] now cannot coexist, as a current and present now, with another now as such', Derrida declares: 'This is *meaning*, sense itself, in what unites meaning to presence' (pp. 54–5). And yet, Derrida goes on to argue:

This impossibility implies in its essence, in order to be what it is, that the other now, with which a now cannot coexist, is also in a certain way the same, is also a now as such, and that it coexists with that which cannot coexist with it. The impossibility of coexistence can be posited as such only on the basis of a certain coexistence, of a certain *simultaneity* of the non-simultaneous, in which the alterity and identity of the now are maintained [or 'nowed', as the French verb '*maintenir*' might suggest] together in the differentiated element of a certain same. (p. 55)

In this way Derrida broaches the question of the operation and effects of 'the trace of difference' (O&G, pp. 63ff.), differance and originary delay.

In an excellent exposition of '*Ousia* and *Grammē*', in an essay entitled 'Time after Time: Temporality, Temporalisation', Timothy Clark summarises Derrida's argument as follows:

What is called 'time' has the structure of an originary delay. However, both 'originary' and 'delay' must at once be qualified. 'Delay' is inaccurate to the extent that it suggests something 'present' that is held back rather than a 'delay' that, in constituting the present, only appears in so far as it is over. Nor is there anything 'originary' in this retro-action. It is *always already* over and thus both succeeds and precedes itself.[19]

This recalls Derrida's qualifications in the reading of Husserl in *Speech and Phenomena*. 'No now can be isolated as a pure instant, a pure punctuality': Husserl recognises this but his account is 'nonetheless thought and described', says Derrida, 'on the basis of the self-identity of the now as point, as a "source-point"'.[20] '*Ousia* and *Grammē*' concludes, in a sort of 'no apocalypse, not now', with an account of differance as what 'give[s] us to think a writing without presence and without absence, without history, without cause, without *archia*, without *telos*, a writing that absolutely upsets all dialectics, all theology, all teleology, all ontology' (O&G, p. 67).

As Derrida specifies in *Of Grammatology*: 'It is not a matter of complicating the structure of time while conserving its homogeneity and its fundamental successivity.' His concern is with trying to reckon with the effects of 'arche-writing as dead time within the living present'.[21] Derrida's 'not now' is neither not nor now, unknowable knot as we might say in English, picking up on the French 'pas', the step or not.[22] We might think here of Werner Hamacher's characterisation of the performative or (as Derrida himself names it in the 'Envois') *perverformative*:[23] 'The performative does not perform – unless it still "performs" the possibility of the "not" of its performing and is in-formed by this "not"; it is, in French once again, a *pas-formative*.'[24] Derrida's *pas-formative* or perverformative 'not now' will have gone full speed ahead, starting out from what he calls 'the deferral within the now of writing [*la différance dans le maintenant de l'écriture*]', in the very instant, at the very moment of inscription.[25] The 'not now' of the 'dead time' or 'dead hour' is at work in any act of writing in the so-called narrow sense, whether this is a work of philosophy or fiction, a signature or a shopping list. '*At the very moment* "I" make a shopping list', Derrida comments in 'Limited Inc', 'I know . . . that it will only be a list if it implies my absence, if it already detaches itself from me in order to function beyond my "present" act and it is utilisable at another time, in the absence of my-being-present-now'.[26] At issue here is the unarrestable logic of 'necessary possibility', the '*possibility of an absence* [which is] necessarily inscribed in the functioning of the mark' (p. 48).

This strange attention to what Derrida calls 'the absence of the now of writing' (LI, p. 49) transforms our understanding of a signature, a date, an oeuvre and a reading. In 'Signature Event Context' he notes:

> By definition, a written signature implies the actual or empirical nonpresence of the signer. But, it will be claimed, the signature also marks and retains his having-been-present in a past *now* or present [*maintenant*] which will remain a future *now* or present [*maintenant*], thus in a general *maintenant*, in the transcendental form of presentness [*maintenance*].[27]

The condition of possibility of a signature, however, is 'simultaneously', at the same time, in a certain 'not now' or now-without-presence, its condition of impossibility. Writing is thus figured, at the end of 'Signature Event Context', as something that is not, that perhaps 'does not exist', 'a disseminating operation *removed* from the presence (of being) according to all its modifications' (p. 21).

Finally, I would like to note, in this all-too-telegrammatic sketch, that we could hardly hope to approach the 'not now' in the context of Derrida's work without trying to acknowledge the importance of the notion of the gift. As he remarks in *Given Time*: 'One would never have the time of a gift. In any case, time, the "present" of the gift, is no longer thinkable as a now, that is, as a present bound up in the temporal synthesis.'[28] Correspondingly, there is the inscription of a sort of instant, radical forgetfulness without which no gift would be possible: 'For there to be gift, not only must the donor or donee not perceive or receive the gift as such, have no consciousness of it, no memory, no recognition; he or she must also forget it right away [*à l'instant*: instantly] and moreover this forgetting must be so radical that it exceeds even the psychoanalytic categoriality of forgetting' (GT, p. 16). 'For there to be forgetting . . . there must be gift. The gift would . . . be the *condition* of forgetting.' The gift, if there is any, must involve something that comes about 'in an instant, in an instant that no doubt does not belong to the economy of time, in a time without time' (GT, p. 17).

♦

Third cryptic instance: Shakespeare's *Hamlet*. (In passing we might note that if this play is a work of literature, our reading here is guided by Derrida's proposition, in *Demeure*, that 'literature is not' [*la littérature n'est pas*]: 'There is no essence or substance of literature: literature is not. It does not exist.'[29]) Derrida's 'The Time is Out of Joint' proposes that Shakespeare's play is about the 'At once (*sur l'heure*). As if there were a dead time in the hour itself' (TOJ, p. 19). It is as if Derrida were quoting himself from *Of Grammatology*, on the 'dead time'. He goes on:

> Everything in fact begins, in *Hamlet*, with the dead time of this 'dead hour', at the moment when, in an already repetitive fashion, the spectre arrives by returning . . . (Act I, scene I, *Marcellus*: 'Thus twice before, and jump at this dead hour, / With martial stalk hath he gone by our watch'). The vigilance of the watching guard, the very watch of consciousness, is also a maddened watch or timepiece that, turning on itself, does not know how to guard or regard the hour of this 'dead hour'. It is delivered over to another time for which the timeclock and the calendar no longer are the law. They no longer are the law or they are not yet the law. (TOJ, p. 19).

Not now, not yet the law: such would be the 'other time' of the play. (And we might hear here also the '*pas maintenant*', the 'not yet' of differance as Derrida explores this, for example, in relation to Kafka's 'Before the Law'.[30])

'Jump at this dead hour' says Derrida's edition of *Hamlet*: this is the wording in the First and Second Quartos; the First Folio has 'just at this dead hour'. The jump and the just: the question of the present, exactly at this instant, is already haunted by an undecidable knotting concerning the exact text. 'Jump' is beautiful, not least because of its connotations (elsewhere in Shakespeare) of danger, hazard, death and the incalculable, as in Macbeth's speculation 'We'd jump the life to come' (*Macbeth* I, vii, 7). Not now. Just jump.

Derrida describes his essay as taking up a phrase ('The time is out of joint') which had already, in *Spectres of Marx*, been 'cited, recited, analysed, and also loved there like an obsession', but which he had not 'until today' thought to read in terms of contretemps and 'the time of mourning' (TOJ, p. 18). Of *Hamlet* he now says, in the lecture delivered in New York in the autumn of 1993 at a conference concerning 'the present state of deconstruction':[31] 'No one can agree about the time of mourning, which is finally the true subject of the play. It is just now, upon rereading the play recently, that I have noticed this, so late, too late, as if by contretemps' (p. 18). No encounter with Derrida or with Shakespeare without contretemps. It has to do, Derrida says, with 'a contretemps within the contretemps because it is a question of a contretemps on the subject of an utterance that says the contretemps' (p. 18). The contretemps would be of the now and the utterance that says it. As he remarks in a conversation with Maurizio Ferraris earlier in the same year (16 July 1993): 'There is a "now" of the untimely; there is a singularity which is that of this disjunction of the present . . . There is "now" without present; there is singularity of the here and now, even though presence, and self-presence is dislocated. There are instances of dislocation that are singular, irreplaceable.'[32]

'The Time is Out of Joint' explores this in particular through the question of the time, the date and instant of death. Derrida writes:

> One must indeed know *when*: *at what instant* mourning began. One must indeed know *at what moment* death took place, really took place, and this is always the moment of a murder. But Hamlet, and everyone in *Hamlet*, seems to be wandering around in confusion on this subject. Now, *when* and *if* one does not know *when* an event took place, one has to wonder *if* indeed it took place. (pp. 20–1)

Derrida's 'now' here ('Now, *when* and *if* one does not know *when* an event took place . . .') conforms to that teasingly, testingly ironic sense defined in *Chambers Dictionary* as: '**now**: . . . used meaninglessly or conversationally, or with the feeling of time lost or nearly lost, in remonstrance, admonition, warning, or taking up a new point'.[33] 'Now, *when and if* one does not know *when* an event took place': we must indeed wonder about the time of this singular, perverformative 'now'.

Derrida goes on to offer a definition of deconstruction specifically in terms of this singularity, this 'now' of the untimely, contretemps of the now. 'Deconstruction', he suggests, has to do with 'putting "out of joint" the authority of the "is"' or 'rather . . . of measuring itself against the *historical* experience . . . of that which in the "is", in time or in the present time of the "is", remains precisely "out of joint"' (p. 25). A little later, he ties the knot between deconstruction and the delirious mad 'now' of Shakespeare's play in this figure of death and dying. For decades, he says, 'we have been told that deconstruction is dying' and 'it is true'. 'Deconstruction begins . . . by dying', he suggests, elucidating this as follows: 'one must stop believing that the dead are just the departed and that the departed do nothing. One must stop pretending to know what is meant by "to die" and especially by "dying". One has, then, to talk about spectrality' (p. 30).

I would like to conclude with a brief consideration of Derrida's haunting remarks in relation to a few words from Hamlet:

HORATIO	You will lose this wager, my lord.
HAMLET	I do not think so. Since he [Laertes] went into France, I have been in continual practice. I shall win at the odds. But thou wouldst not think how ill all's here about my heart. But it is no matter.
HORATIO	Nay, good my lord –
HAMLET	It is but foolery. But it is such a kind of gain-giving as would perhaps trouble a woman.
HORATIO	If your mind dislike anything, obey it. I will forestall their repair hither, and say you are not fit.
HAMLET	Not a whit. We defy augury. There's a special providence in the fall of a sparrow. If it be now, 'tis not to come. If it be not to come, it will be now. If it be not now, yet it will come. The readiness is all. Since no man knows aught of what he leaves, what is't to leave betimes? Let be.

(V, ii, 156–70)

Derrida's injunction that 'One must stop pretending to know what is meant by "to die" and especially by "dying"' (it is time to stop, not now, not anymore, from now on stop pretending to know) is perhaps already resonating for us in this passage. Here, so close to the end, 'not' and 'now' become, perhaps more than ever, knotted. But from the very opening of the play (in which Barnardo's seemingly straightforward response to Francisco's 'You come most carefully upon your hour' – "Tis now struck twelve' (I, i, 6–7) – in fact bespeaks a 'now' of uncertain time, the 'now' of the clock's striking is not now), 'now' is deranged. We could say that Shakespeare's play comprises a dislocated, eerie series – 'Now to my word' (I, v, 111), 'Now could I drink hot blood' (III, ii, 373), 'Now might I do it pat, now he is praying' (III, iii, 73), 'Where be your gibes now, your gambols, your songs, your flashes of merriment that were wont to set the table on a roar' (V, i, 180–2), so many 'nows' that are 'not nows' – so long as we mark a disjunction here with the presupposition, still monolithically prevalent in Shakespeare criticism, that *Hamlet* is about forms of deferral, delay or afterwardness to be thought *on the basis of the present*.

'If it be now, 'tis not to come. If it be not to come, it will be now. If it be not now, yet it will come': at once reasonable and not, it is the second of these 'If X, then Y' formulations that is perhaps most sharply out of joint. 'If it be not to come, it will be now': what will be (not now) is not to come. Do we believe Hamlet? Does he or anyone else know what he is saying? Is it himself? Everyone can perhaps pretend to know 'the readiness is all', but what is it, what are the 'readiness' and the 'all' of this 'is'? As measured against what? As witnessed by whom? We might recall here Derrida's words about the Shakespearean 'rendezvous with death' in 'Aphorism Countertime': '*Untimely. Never on time.*'[34] If everyone can pretend to be able to read 'The readiness is all', the sentence that succeeds it will have retroactively destroyed it. Harold Jenkins has a long and impressive note on the chaos: the Second Quarto has 'since no man of ought he leaues, knowes ‸ '; the Folio has 'since no man ha's ought of what he leaves'. Neither makes much sense: the text of *Hamlet* 'itself' is not now. A supplement is required. G. R. Hibbard (editor of the OUP text) proposes: 'Since no man knows aught of what he leaves, what is't to leave betimes?' Jenkins (editor of the Arden), perhaps more adventurously, has: 'Since no man, of aught he leaves, knows aught, what is't to leave betimes?'[35] Since no man knows anything about what he leaves, or rather perhaps about what he will have left, what does it matter if he leaves early? The repetition of the verb 'leave' is also a disjointing: what one leaves has in a sense of course no relation to one's leaving; moreover, 'leaves' (present) is not 'to leave' (betimes, not now, not yet). To leave, to depart, not now. How could one read Hamlet's words here without thinking of the ghost whose 'word' has led him all the way up to this very instant, this strangely fitting, out of joint moment in which he proclaims that he is 'fit', and that he (or 'we') 'defy', that is to say dare, flout, resist, reject 'augury', including any Biblical omens or omniscience of falling sparrows watched over by the heavenly father (Matthew 10:29)? 'One must stop believing that the dead are just the departed and that the departed do nothing': this affirmation of the logic of spectrality on Derrida's part is drawn from Hamlet himself, 'the heir of a spectre concerning which no one knows any longer *at what moment* and therefore *if* death has happened to him' (TOJ, p. 30).

If we are reading *Hamlet* as literature here, this would be on condition of trying to reckon with Derrida's contention that 'literature . . . always is, says, does something other, something other than itself, an itself which moreover is only that, something other than itself'.[36] Literature 'does not maintain itself', says Derrida, 'it does not maintain itself abidingly (*elle ne se maintient pas* à demeure)'.[37] Its now is not now, its not now to come. It will always have been leaving, itself and us. I would like to add here just one further remark concerning the cryptic, inexhaustible, inconsistent consistency or consistent inconsistency of this dialogue between Hamlet and Horatio from the final scene of Shakespeare's play. This has to do with the peculiar ways in which specific words in Shakespeare come to be traced, in a sort of 'now without present', by other appearances or apparitions of the 'same' words. I hesitate to describe these as 'earlier' or 'later' appearances because the logic in question here is precisely that of another time, a 'dead time' perhaps, or time without time. It is a matter of dramaturgic telepathy, the iteraphonic and iteraesthesia.[38] I am thinking here of the sort of strangeness, for example, whereby Hamlet's soliloquised determination to 'speak daggers to [his mother], but use none' (III, ii, 379) is repeated and made different in the closet scene when his mother cries: 'O speak to me no more. / These words like daggers enter in my ears' (III, iv, 86–7).[39] Such effects exceed any notion of authorial intention, even as they necessarily complicate and perhaps transform any notion of characterisation or plot.

In his remarks to Horatio, jump before the arrival of 'Claudius, Gertrude, Laertes, Osric, and all the State, and Attendants with foils and gauntlets' (stage direction, following V, ii, 170), Hamlet is and is not fit, after all.[40] As he says, there is this 'gain-giving' in the region of his heart, of 'such a kind' as 'would perhaps trouble a woman' (V, ii, 162–3). 'Gain-giving' would be a strange sort of counter-gift encounter, a giving against, a singular disturbance, at once somatic and linguistic, of what is given. It is the first instance of the word in English (according to the *OED*) and the first and last time it occurs in any of Shakespeare's writings. Apparently in cryptic correspondence with 'gainsaying' (denial, dispute, contradiction), 'gain-giving' is invariably translated by modern editors (without any evident misgivings) as 'misgiving'. What is the time of this 'gain-giving' and to whom or what should we refer it? Is Hamlet himself, woman or man? 'Since no man knows aught of what he leaves, what is't to leave betimes?' 'Betimes': what a word. Weird plural singular of 'time', 'betimes' can also be 'betime': at an early time, in good time. 'Now cracks a noble heart' (V, ii, 312), Horatio will declare: what and when is this 'now'? To leave or die 'betimes': Hamlet's use of the word doubtless suggests dying early, as well as soon (the *OED* additionally defines 'betimes' as 'In a short time, soon, speedily, anon, forthwith': sense 4), but there is also the sense of 'betimes' as 'while there is yet time, before it is too late' (*OED*, sense 3). What would be the right time and speed at which to read or think 'betimes'? The word, in its singular form, is used on only one other occasion in the play, in a scene of terrifying 'foolery' in which Hamlet himself is not present. It is Ophelia, another spectre haunting the 'not now', she who scarcely appears in any of the discussions in or around *Spectres of Marx* or 'The Time is Out of Joint' but who, in this iteraphonic nonpresent, affirms a nonknowledge of the future (of 'what we may be') that comes back in Hamlet's claim that 'no man knows aught of what he leaves': 'Lord, we know what we are, but know not what we may be', she says, 'Pray you let's have no words of this. But when they ask you what it means, say you this: [and here the work passes into song, into what – as Derrida says in one of the 'Envois' – like tears, cannot be sent[41]] [*She sings*] Tomorrow is Saint Valentine's day, / All in the morning betime . . .' (IV, v, 42–8). I leave you to read or listen to the rest.

Notes

1. By way of a first note that would be as much a pre-script as post-script, I must recall a detail here regarding what drove me to write this essay and what, for me at least, pervades it from start to finish. I received a phone call from Jacques Derrida in early May 2003. He was due to come to speak on the subject of 'the uncanny' at the University of Sussex the following month. He confided to me then that he was ill and explained that he would be unable to come: perhaps at a later date, he said, but 'not now'. 'Not now' thus echoed and resonated on the line, though otherwise unspoken in our conversation, to the terrible news of his illness. 'Forgive me', he said in his disarmingly humble way, 'for this uncanny situation.' The text that follows was originally given at the opening of a two-day conference entitled 'Encounters with Derrida', at the University of Sussex, in September 2003. I would like to thank the organisers, Persephone Lioliou, Vicky Margree and Eftichis Pirovolakis, for inviting me to speak.

2. Jacques Derrida, 'The Time Is Out of Joint', trans. Peggy Kamuf, in *Deconstruction is/in America: A New Sense of the Political*, ed. Anselm Haverkamp (New York: New York University Press, 1995), pp. 14–38: here, p. 28. Further page references to this essay appear parenthetically in the text, preceded by 'TOJ' where appropriate.

3. Jacques Derrida, 'Che cos'è la poesia?', trans. Peggy Kamuf, in *Points . . . Interviews, 1974–1994*, ed. Elisabeth Weber (London: Routledge, 1995), pp. 288–99.

4. David McKee, *Not Now, Bernard* [1980] (London: Red Fox, 1996).

5. Hélène Cixous, 'What is it o'clock? or The door (we never enter)', trans. Catherine A. F. MacGillivray, in *Stigmata: Escaping Texts* (London: Routledge, 1998), p. 64.

6. Jacques Derrida, 'Passions: "An Oblique Offering"', trans. David Wood, in *Derrida: A Critical Reader*, ed. David Wood (Oxford and Cambridge, MA: Basil Blackwell, 1992), pp. 5–35: here, p. 30. For a recent exception to this, see Stephen Thomson's fascinating essay, 'Derrida and the Child: Ethics, Pathos, Property, Risk', in *Angles on Derrida*, special issue of *Oxford*

Literary Review, 25 (2003), eds Thomas Dutoit and Philippe Romanski, 337–59.

7. Jacques Derrida, 'Envois', in *The Post Card: From Socrates to Freud and Beyond*, trans. Alan Bass (Chicago: Chicago University Press, 1987), p. 39.

8. Jacques Derrida, *Demeure: Fiction and Testimony* (with Maurice Blanchot's *The Instant of My Death*), trans. Elizabeth Rottenberg (Stanford, CA: Stanford University Press, 2000), p. 41.

9. I am grateful to Peter Boxall for alerting me to the force, the pictorial punctum of this shoe.

10. Jacques Derrida, *The Truth in Painting*, trans. Geoff Bennington and Ian McLeod (Chicago: University of Chicago Press, 1987), p. 328.

11. 'Envois', p. 199.

12. William Shakespeare, *Hamlet*, ed. G. R. Hibbard (Oxford: Oxford University Press, 1994), I, i, 1. Further references to *Hamlet* are based on this edition, unless otherwise indicated. References to other writings by Shakespeare are drawn from *The Norton Shakespeare: Based on the Oxford Edition*, eds Stephen Greenblatt, Walter Cohen, Jean E. Howard and Katherine Eisaman Maus (New York and London: W. W. Norton, 1997).

13. Jacques Derrida, 'No Apocalypse, Not Now (full Speed Ahead, Seven Missiles, Seven Missives)', trans. Philip Lewis and Catherine Porter, in *Psyche: Inventions of the Other*, vol. 1, eds Peggy Kamuf and Elizabeth Rottenberg (Stanford, CA: Stanford University Press, 2007), pp. 387–409. Further page references to this essay appear parenthetically in the text.

14. Jacques Derrida, 'Of an Apocalyptic Tone Newly Adopted in Philosophy', trans. John P. Leavey, Jr, in *Derrida and Negative Theology*, eds Harold Coward and Toby Foshay (Albany, NY: State University of New York Press, 1992), p. 66. Further page references to this essay appear parenthetically in the text, preceded by 'AT' where appropriate.

15. Jacques Derrida, *Monolingualism of the Other; or, The Prosthesis of Origin*, trans. Patrick Mensah (Stanford, CA: Stanford University Press, 1998), p. 73.

16. See, for example, 'Negotiations', in *Negotiations: Interventions and Interviews, 1971–2001*, ed. Elizabeth Rottenberg (Stanford, CA: Stanford University Press, 2002), pp. 27–9.

17. Sean Gaston, 'Une accélération affolante', in *Oxford Literary Review*, 25 (2003), 361–84: here, in particular, see p. 367.

18. Jacques Derrida, '*Ousia* and *Grammē*: Note on a Note from *Being and Time*', in *Margins of Philosophy*, trans. Alan Bass (Chicago: Chicago University Press, 1982), pp. 29–67. Further page references are given parenthetically in the main body of the text, abbreviated 'O&G' where appropriate.

19. Timothy Clark, 'Time after Time: Temporality, Temporalisation', *Oxford Literary Review*, 9 (1987), 134.

20. Jacques Derrida, *Speech and Phenomena and Other Essays on Husserl's Theory of Signs*, trans. David Allison (Evanston, IL: Northwestern University Press, 1973), p. 61.

21. Jacques Derrida, *Of Grammatology*, trans. Gayatri Chakravorty Spivak (Baltimore, MD: Johns Hopkins University Press, 1976), pp. 67–8.

22. Of the phrase 'not now' we might note, in a sort of playful negotiation between French and English, Derrida's comment in the 1987 interview 'Negotiations': 'A phrase is a knot.' See *Negotiations: Interventions and Interviews, 1971–2001*, p. 28.
23. See 'Envois', p. 136.
24. Werner Hamacher, 'Lingua Amissa: The Messianism of Commodity-Language and Derrida's *Spectres of Marx*', in *Futures of Jacques Derrida*, ed. Richard Rand (Stanford, CA: Stanford University Press, 2001), p. 164.
25. See Jacques Derrida, 'Ellipsis' in *Writing and Difference*, trans. Alan Bass (London: Routledge & Kegan Paul, 1978), p. 300; 'Ellipse', *L'écriture et la différence* (Paris: Éditions du Seuil, 1967), p. 436.
26. Jacques Derrida, 'Limited Inc a b c . . .', trans. Samuel Weber, in *Limited Inc* (Evanston, IL: Northwestern University Press, 1988), p. 49. Further page references appear parenthetically in the text, preceded by 'LI' where appropriate.
27. Jacques Derrida, 'Signature Event Context', trans. Samuel Weber and Jeffrey Mehlman, in *Limited Inc* (Evanston, IL: Northwestern University Press, 1988), p. 20. Further page references appear parenthetically in the text, preceded by 'SEC' where appropriate.
28. Jacques Derrida, *Given Time: I. Counterfeit Money*, trans. Peggy Kamuf (London: Chicago University Press, 1992), p. 9. Further page references appear parenthetically in the text, preceded by 'GT' where appropriate.
29. *Demeure: Fiction and Testimony*, p. 28 (*Demeure, Maurice Blanchot*, p. 29).
30. See Jacques Derrida, 'Préjugés: devant la loi', in Jean-François Lyotard et al., *La faculté de juger* (Paris: Minuit, 1985), pp. 87–139: esp. p. 120. The English translation ('Before the Law', trans. Avital Ronell and Christine Roulston, in *Acts of Literature*, ed. Derek Attridge (London: Routledge, 1992), pp. 181–220) renders Derrida's 'pas maintenant' as 'not yet': see 'Before the Law', p. 204. For a brilliant discussion of the deconstructive 'not yet', especially in relation to Marxism, see Geoffrey Bennington, *Legislations: The Politics of Deconstruction* (London: Verso, 1994), pp. 74–87.
31. *Deconstruction is/in America: A New Sense of the Political*, p. vii.
32. 'I Have a Taste for the Secret', Jacques Derrida in conversation with Maurizio Ferraris and Giorgio Vattimo, in Derrida and Ferraris, *A Taste for the Secret*, trans. Giacomo Donis (Cambridge: Polity, 2001), pp. 12–13.
33. This 'now' is what Peggy Kamuf's excellent English translation gives for the '*or*' of Derrida's original ('*Or* quand *et* si *on ne sait pas* . . .') ['The time is out of joint', unpub. ts.]: we shall return to the 'or' (in French *and/or* English) in 'Or Again, Meddling' and Derrida's remarks on this (below).
34. Jacques Derrida, 'Aphorism Countertime', trans. Nicholas Royle, in *Acts of Literature*, p. 432.
35. See *Hamlet*, ed. Harold Jenkins (London: Methuen, 1982), pp. 565–6.
36. 'Passions: "An Oblique Offering"', p. 33.
37. *Demeure: Fiction and Testimony*, p. 28 (*Demeure, Maurice Blanchot*, p. 29).

38. On dramaturgic telepathy, permit me to refer to *Telepathy and Literature: Essays on the Reading Mind* (Oxford: Blackwell, 1990), pp. 142–59, and *The Uncanny* (Manchester: Manchester University Press, 2003), pp. 126–7, 249–50. An elaboration of the iteraphonic and iteraesthesia, on the other hand, constitutes a sort of guiding thread of the so-called present work.
39. I return to this particular example in 'Forgetting Well' (below).
40. For more on the 'fit' and 'fitting' in the context of *Hamlet*, permit me to refer to *The Uncanny*, pp. 318–22.
41. See 'Envois', pp. 14–15.

Or Again, Meddling

When a text quotes and requotes, with or without quotation marks, when it is written on the brink, you start, or indeed have already started, to lose your footing. You lose sight of any line of demarcation between a text and what is outside it.[1]

Or again, meddling. I offer these three words as a way of thinking about the works of Jacques Derrida. 'Meddling' is a strange word that has no current counterpart in French but came into English from French, from the old French verb *medler*, a variant of *mêler*, deriving from the Latin *miscēre*, to mix. It is obsolete or spectral French. It meddles English and French. 'Meddling' is related to a mix or medley of other words, at least a couple of which (*mélange* and *mêlée*) are the same, as one too hastily says, in both languages. 'Meddling' in its accepted current usage is interfering or tampering with; in archaic or obsolete senses, it is mixing, concerning oneself with, contending, fighting or engaging in conflict (meddling would here be in the fray with *mêlée*), combining or blending (culinary or medical ingredients, as in a pharmakon perhaps), or (a sense still current in parts of the US) having sexual intercourse with. The erotic and sexual associations of the verb 'to meddle' are especially striking in Shakespeare: to meddle or mell is 'to mingle sexually with', as Eric Partridge puts it.[2] There is meddling with 'women's matters' in *Julius Caesar* (I, i, 21–2) and meddling with a 'mistress' in *Coriolanus* (IV, v, 45–6).[3] Shakespeare also plays on the sexual connotations of 'meddler' (one who meddles) and the fruit called 'medlar' (*Timon of Athens*, IV, iii, 304–9). Meddling is an organising trope in *Troilus and Cressida*, and yet it operates in a peculiarly negative, tacit or ironic mode: three times in the opening scene Pandarus says that he will 'not meddle' or will neither 'meddle nor make' (I, i, 14, 63, 78), but he never uses the word again. One of the notable aspects of the conventional and current meaning of 'meddling' has to do with a sort of pejorative moralism: it is figured as interfering or making trouble *unnecessarily*. 'Tampering' has a similar aspect: to tamper (usually *with* something) is to interfere unwarrantably, in a pejorative fashion. In what ways might the unnecessary be necessary? What if meddling were, before anything else, to be meddling with itself? What might be going on in the intimacies of 'meddling'? What might it mean to speak of meddling with 'meddling'? It would be a question here of trying to think about the reserves within a word, and about what Derrida has called 'the possibilities within the language to dissociate words, to graft, to integrate many languages in one, and to exploit the hidden possibilities in the language'.[4]

♦

Where will we have begun? 'Or again, meddling': this title might recall the traditional formula of subtitles or substitute titles that begin with the word 'or'. These days such titles are comparatively rare, though one can think of certain instances in the writings of Derrida: there is *Monolingualism of the Other; or, The Prosthesis of Origin*, for example, or the short text entitled 'Afterw.rds: or, at least, less than a letter about a letter less'.[5] 'Or again, meddling': what is going on here with syntax and grammar? What is the subject? Is it 'or' or is it 'meddling'? Or again, is it 'or again'? Apparently supplementary, what precedes and frames this title, if it is one? These are perhaps not insignificant questions, especially if we acknowledge, with Derrida, the force of the notion that deconstruction begins with an *and* [et], an *and* that is in 'dangerous liaisons' [liaisons dangereuses] *and* (or) '*déliaisons*' with 'or' [ou]. I am referring here to his remarkable essay on the 'and' in relation to deconstruction, 'Et Cetera . . . (and so on, und so weiter, and so forth, et ainsi de suite, und so überall, etc.)'.[6] Recalling Husserl's remarks on 'the forms of conjunctive liaison', namely 'that of the *and* and the *or* (*die des* Und *und* Oder)', Derrida notes that Husserl could just as well have said 'that of the *or* or the *and*' (p. 297). 'Or' again: having begun with the proposition that 'in the beginning, there is the *and*' (p. 282), Derrida develops the argument that 'the most constant task of any deconstruction' is to wonder about 'what *and* – and even a syncategoreme in general – means and does not mean, does and does not do' (p. 285). The 'and' might always be 'or', the 'and' *or* even a syncategoreme in general. Of the one and the other, the one or the other, he writes:

> Even 'the one *or* the other' (disjunction or alternative) presupposes some 'the one *and* the other'. Even the oblique bar of the opposition, and for example *and/or* between *and* and *or*, or between *and* or *or*, still presupposes an 'and'. Or *or* [Ou *ou*]. (pp. 289/25)

'Or *or*': this is, perhaps, one of the shortest, most undecidably grammatical, most immeasurably rich sentences in Derrida's work. And/or: impossible to decide, he suggests.

Or again, even when, at the start of 'Et Cetera', he is evoking the strange loneliness of deconstruction, the or of the other sticks its oar in. (The word 'or', we might recall, is an abbreviated form of the Middle English word 'other'.) 'Or' again, meddling. It's happening in an airport lounge, the very scene of writing introduced by an 'or': 'And if only you knew how independent deconstruction is, how alone, so alone, all alone! And as if it had been abandoned, right in the middle of a colloquium, on a train platform – *or* in an airport lounge which would look like this one, changing planes *or* leaving for I know not what destination . . .' (p. 282, my emphases; Derrida's ellipsis). The form and structure of 'Et Cetera' would appear to enact this undecidability of and/or. Like numerous other of his texts, it is a dialogue comprising one voice and/or another: Derridean dialogue disseminates through this irreducibly, undecidably polyphonic logic of the *and/or*. The statement just cited concerning the aloneness of deconstruction, for example, is immediately followed by another voice that declares: 'And well no, I believe on the contrary that nothing is less lonely and thinkable on its own' (p. 282).

'Or again': this phrase is of course a quotation. Derrida calls it 'sublime'. It crops up repeatedly in the works of J. L. Austin, in *How to Do Things with Words* (1962) and elsewhere. It might even be described as a sort of Austinian signature-effect: 'or-again-Austin'. Apparently averse to producing finalised written versions of his texts, giving different versions of the 'same' paper repeatedly, Austin's discourse is punctuated and dispersed through the force of the 'or again'.[7] There are intriguing affinities between the works of Austin and Derrida: we could list, among others, a certain sense of humour, irony, or again, meddling. This is perhaps legible in the interfering ambiguity of the English translation, in the word 'works' as I have just used it in the context of these writers. In a long and beautifully spooling essay entitled 'Typewriter Ribbon: Limited Ink (2)', Derrida analyses some of the ways in which Paul de Man 'reckon[s] with the works of Austin'.[8] He then pauses to qualify this use of the word 'works' ('*travaux*'): 'I say purposely, and vaguely, the "works" of Austin because one value of these works is to have not only resisted but marked the line of resistance to systematic work, to philosophy as formalising theorisation, absolute and closed, freed of its adherences to ordinary language and to so-called natural languages' (p. 123). Austin and Derrida put a spanner, or *spanner after spanner*, in the works. Austin seeks to play Old Harry, the devil or (as one also says) Old Nick, with what is called philosophical discourse.

He does so, like Derrida, in a way that brings into question – exposes what Austin calls 'unhappiness' in – the very nature of 'doing things with words'. In a teasingly naughty admission to having devilish inclinations, in a devilish advocacy that is by its very utterance tied up in performative knots, Austin notes that there are 'two fetishes which I admit to an inclination to play Old Harry with, viz. (1) the true/false fetish, (2) the value/fact fetish'.[9] How serious is this admission? How genuine or true? In his earlier essay on Austin, Searle and speech act theory, 'Limited Inc', Derrida declares himself set on meddling in similar fashion when he queries the notion of the genuine, attacking Searle for his use of the term 'genuinely graphematic' as a way of characterising 'the traditional concept of "written language".'[10] Derrida comments that he does not consider the 'graphematic instance' to be 'genuine'; and, as if in a more brazen version of Austin, he then peremptorily asserts: 'I do not seek to establish any kind of authenticity.'[11]

The example of 'or again' that Derrida picks out in 'Typewriter Ribbon' comes from Austin's paper 'Performative Utterances'.[12] It is the celebrated passage in which Austin presents a series of instances of performative utterance that he describes in a characteristically proleptic and ironic fashion, as 'not . . . odd at all' and indeed 'decidedly dull'. We are asked to prepare ourselves, then, for three or four 'decidedly dull' utterances in which 'we should say' a person 'is *doing* something rather than merely *saying* something'.[13] Here, in a sort of citational meddling or *mêlée*, is Derrida citing Austin: 'Suppose, for example, that in the course of a marriage ceremony I say, as people will, "I do" – (sc. take this woman to be my lawful wedded wife). Or again [this "Or again" is sublime], suppose that I tread on your toe and say "I apologise". Or again . . .'[14] He interrupts Austin at this point, letting the 'or again' stand alone, as if on its own two feet, or again leaving it to resonate all by itself, a singular aposiopesis, these two words trailing off with an ellipsis, as if (in the words of 'Et Cetera') 'leaving for I know not what destination . . .' As ever, Derrida makes us acutely aware that to quote is to interfere, touch and meddle with (*toucher, toucher à*). We might here recall the rhetorical question that haunts the double-text called 'Living On / Border Lines' (and I will come back to this strange work again shortly): 'How can one text, assuming its unity, give or present another to be read, without touching it, without saying anything about it, practically without referring to it?'[15]

'Or again . . .', Derrida quotes, then begins a new sentence: 'This linking by additive contiguity, without transition ("Or again") from the marriage ceremony to the excuse when I tread on another's toes makes me think irresistibly of an Algerian Jewish rite' (TR, p. 128). He then leads us into a marvellous little scene in which he recounts the 'more or less superstitious custom' in which 'the wedded couple is advised, at the precise moment when their marriage is consecrated in the synagogue, to hurry up and place a foot on the other's foot so as to guarantee for himself or herself power in their conjugal life . . . One has to hurry and take the other by surprise. One must create the event' (p. 128). We might spend a very long time with this brief but also perhaps lifelong moment in Derrida's text. It is difficult to read these few sentences, for example, without thinking of all that he says elsewhere about the hymen or again about the step (*marche*) of deconstruction. It is a remarkably concentrated and suggestive moment of power (*pouvoir*), violence (*coup de force*) and forgiveness. And it is also very funny. '"I do take you for husband (or wife), oh, excuse me, sorry"' (p. 128). Derrida nevertheless concludes quite seriously:

> At any rate, whatever the response might be to a marriage proposal, it would be necessary to excuse oneself and ask forgiveness. 'Marry me, I want to marry you.' Response: 'Yes, I beg your pardon' or 'No, I beg your pardon.' In either case, there is fault and thus forgiveness to be asked – and it is always as if one were treading on the other's toes. (p. 128)

This is, apparently, the end of the scene: a new section of 'Typewriter Ribbon' then begins, under the heading 'The "One Certain Monument": Of a Materiality Without Matter'. In fact, however, there is a grafting of one onto the other. For the next section begins with a sort of refrain, an impish transfer of a phrase that occurs twice in the preceding paragraph and once in the immediately preceding sentence: '*As if . . .*' (p. 128), begins the new section. This grafting of 'as if' ('it is always *as if* one were treading on the other's toes') seems to pick up the repetition of the 'or again', as if in these snatches of syntax a sort of ghostly medley were underway. Or again, *as if.* What Derrida does with Austin's words, through the seemingly 'irresistible' anecdote about the Algerian Jewish marriage rite, is to produce an undecidable *and/or* of the 'or again', meddling with the examples, showing how the second ('I apologise') is already in the first (the 'I do' of the marriage ceremony). In this way he traces something perhaps of the 'sublime' effect he detects in Austin's 'or again'. 'Or again' would figure as another term for thinking about Derrida's notion of the open chain of 'non-synonymous substitutions' that he talks about in the essay 'Différance' and, in effect, everywhere in his work, an open chain that would include deconstruction, reserve, supplement, hymen, *différance* and iterability, and *and*, et cetera.[16]

'Or again': a supplement – strange meddling with repetition and difference. Let us merely note its cryptically Austinian reappearance at the end of another essay by Derrida, written around the same time as 'Typewriter Ribbon', '"Le Parjure", *Perhaps*: Storytelling and Lying ("abrupt breaches of syntax")'. 'Or again [*Ou encore*]', he writes, at the end of '"Le Parjure", *Perhaps*', in the context of the madness of marriage and, again, the question of forgiveness and repentance:

> Conclusion: one ought *never* to get married, *whether or not one is Christian.* Marriage is a madness in Christian lands, but it has no absolute sacramental sense outside of Christianity. Or again [*Ou encore*], which comes down to the same thing, one ought never to marry more than once, like Hölderlin in America. One does not marry twice, and if one can marry twice, that's because marriage is impossible or destined to perjury, to the impossibility of repenting together. Whether it takes place once or twice, marriage would be that madness. Impossible to decide if it is more mad to lose one's senses in a Christian land or a non-Christian land. But it is perhaps even more impossible today to decide where the frontiers of Christian lands are drawn.[17]

'Or again': this passage offers a remarkable example, I think, of Derrida's contention, in 'Living On', that 'each text is a machine with multiple reading heads for other texts'.[18] The concluding passage of '"Le Parjure", *Perhaps*' is ostensibly a reading of J. Hillis Miller, Paul de Man, Henri Thomas' *Le Parjure*, Kafka's *Letter to the Father* and Kierkegaard – which would seem like quite enough reading heads or writing heads to be contending or meddling with already – but it is perhaps also difficult not to pick up a cue to Austin.

'Or again' directs us back to the earlier scene of the 'or again' and the question of marriage in Austin's work. We might then appreciate more clearly the madness about which Eve Kosofsky Sedgwick memorably writes:

> The marriage ceremony is, indeed, so central to the origins of 'performativity' (given the strange, disavowed but unattenuated persistence of *the exemplary* in this work) that a more accurate name for *How to Do Things with Words* might have been *How to say (or write) 'I do' hundreds of times without winding up any more married than you started out.*[19]

As if. And we might also in this way come to sense how deeply Austin's account of how to do things with words is a Christian work, starting with the 'I do' of the Christian marriage ceremony. Like *How to Do Things with Words*, the essay on 'Performative Utterances' is pervaded, for example, by the language of christening, a christening that is also a christianising of 'performative utterances'. Here is the complete version of the sentence from Austin's text that Derrida cuts off after the opening two words: 'Or again, suppose that I have a bottle of champagne in my hand and say "I name this ship the *Queen Elizabeth*".' A few lines later Austin specifies: 'When I say "I name this ship the *Queen Elizabeth*" I do not describe the christening, I actually perform the christening.'[20]

Mad medley of the 'or again' and 'as if'. Permit me to conclude this discussion of Derrida and Austin with a brief anecdote. It has to do with one of the photographs that I have on my desk in front of me here as I write. It shows the two of us in the bright sunshine outside the château at Cerisy in July 2002. It was during the ten-day conference on 'the democracy to come'. There was a 'photo-opportunity' and Marie-Louise Mallet, the organiser of the event, asked if she could take a picture of us (as I remember she had done in the same place, five years earlier). Jacques and I posed for the photograph. As we did so, I remember I was thinking about something he says in an interview ('"There is No *One* Narcissism" (Autobiophotographies)'), concerning what he calls the '*effect of the idiom for the other*': 'whatever pose you adopt, whatever precautions you take so that the photograph will look like this or like that, there comes a moment when the photograph surprises you and it is the other's gaze that, finally, wins out and decides'.[21] Marie-Louise took a couple of shots and at some point in the proceedings Jacques and I became aware of precisely the same thing. We had positioned ourselves for these pictures arm in arm, posing in such a way that we both came to be surprised by the same thought more or less simultaneously. It was he who articulated it, as we separated with a flash of strange embarrassment. He said, in English, in the language of the other, both of us virtually already laughing: 'It is as if we were married!'

♦

What are the limits or borders of meddling? In 'Living On' (originally published in English in 1979), Derrida writes:

> The question of the text, as it has been elaborated and transformed in the last dozen or so years, has not merely 'touched shore' [*touché au bord*] (scandalously tampering, as in Mallarmé's declaration, '*On a touché au vers*'), tampering with all those boundaries that form the running border of what used to be called a text, of what we once thought this word could identify, i.e., the presumed end and beginning of a work, the unity of a corpus, the title, the margins, the signatures, the referential realm outside the frame, etc. What has happened, if it has happened, would be a sort of overrun [*débordement*] spoiling [*mettant à mal*] all these boundaries and divisions, and forcing us to extend the accredited concept, the dominant notion of 'text', of what I still call 'text', for reasons partially strategic – a 'text' that would henceforth no longer be a finished corpus of writing, some content enclosed in a book or its margins, but a differential network, a fabric of traces referring endlessly to something other than itself, to other differential traces. Thus the text overruns all the limits assigned to it so far, not submerging or drowning them in an undifferentiated homogeneity, but on the contrary making them more complex, dividing and multiplying strokes and lines – all the limits,

everything that was to be set up in opposition to writing (speech, life, the world, the real, history, and what not, every field of reference – to body or mind, conscious or unconscious, politics, economics, etc.).[22]

Derrida recalls Mallarmé's formulation: '*On a touché au vers.*' Verse has been touched, affected, interfered with. *Toucher à*: to meddle with, especially in the context of laws, regulations or traditions. Poetry, writing on poetry, becomes meddling. Elsewhere the *poematic* (that which the 'I' can never sign, that which affirms that we must 'set fire to the library of poetics') transpires as one of Derrida's terms for such meddling.[23] But it is never simply a question of an aesthetic tampering, a playing about with poetic or literary language. 'Meddling' is never purely meddling with language, not least perhaps because this word, if it is a word, is never pure, it announces the logic of the impure, con-taminated, parasitical. It would be meddling with institutions, with our understanding of law, regulation and tradition. Meddling overruns.

A dozen or so years after the publication of *Of Grammatology* (1967), Derrida declares (in what is a quite unusually specific historical declara-tion, a peculiar performative utterance of its own) that '[t]he question of the text, as it has been elaborated and transformed in the last dozen or so years', has meddled with 'all [the] boundaries . . . of what we once thought this word could identify'. As so often with Derrida, there is something remarkable going on in the syntax, in the shifts and mixings and touches of his sentences. Meddling is the experience of a question ('the question of the text') that has not yet reached its question mark or perhaps even begun. It is the elaboration and transformation of a *question* that has meddled with 'the presumed end and beginning of a work, the unity of a corpus, the title, the margins, the signatures, the referential realm outside the frame, etc.'. The immediately following sentence might on first sight appear to be a retraction, a withdrawing as of a wave: 'What has happened, if it has happened, would be a sort of overrun [*débordement*, overflowing] spoiling all these boundaries and divisions . . .' Has this meddling happened or hasn't it? The second sen-tence is not so much a turning away, however, as a further specification of meddling as meddling *with* happening or event. Meddling here is not tampering in the sense merely of tinkering or fiddling, but more strongly of *spoiling, mettant à mal*, corrupting, damaging, messing up, playing Old Harry or Old Nick with. Meddling with the question of *le bord* (the edge, border, side, brink) is first of all to be meddling with the borders of what happens, with the framing of an event. As Derrida affirms in 'Border Lines', the text that accompanies, mixing and meddling with 'Living On': 'The question of the borderline [*bord*] precedes, as it were, the determination of all the dividing lines . . . between a fantasy and a "reality", an event and a non-event, a fiction and a reality, one corpus and another, and so on.'[24]

'Living On / Border Lines' sets out the stakes of that meddling which some call or used to call 'deconstruction'. ('Deconstruction' was always dying, it 'begins . . . by dying',[25] as he remarks elsewhere: deconstruction will always have been meddling with what we think we understand as archaic or obsolete sense, from 'arche-writing' and 'paleonymy' to everything that might be dubbed neologism or invention in language; what is out of use, obsolete or obsolescent can always come back, show up as, in certain contexts, more effective, more useful, less obsolete than any so-called 'current sense'.) In 'Border Lines', Derrida goes on to write:

> A politico-institutional problem of the University: it, like all teaching in its traditional form, and perhaps all teaching whatever, has as its ideal, with exhaustive translatability, the effacement of language [*la langue*]. Deconstruction of a pedagogical institution and all that it implies. What this institution cannot bear, is for anyone to meddle with [*toucher à*] language, meaning *both* the national language *and*, paradoxically, an ideal of translatability that neutralises this national language. Indissociable nationalism and universalism. What this institution cannot bear is a transformation that leaves intact neither of these two complementary poles. It can bear more readily the most apparently revolutionary ideological sorts of 'contents', if only these contents do not meddle with the borders of language [*la langue*] and of all the juridico-political contracts that it guarantees.[26]

Meddling with French or English, for example, but also with 'an ideal of translatability that neutralises this national language', involves a sense of the 'intolerable': it 'brings out the limits of the concept of translation on which the university is built'.[27] As Derrida goes on to argue, 'we must pause to consider [*on devra s'arrêter*] translation. It brings the *arrêt* of everything, decides, suspends, and sets in motion'.[28] Meddling sentences. (How will a French translator deal with this rather improbable two-word sentence?)[29] It is a question of drawing all the consequences of the fact that, as Derrida puts it: 'One never writes either in one's own language or in a foreign language.'[30] It is a matter of what he calls 'the hymen or the alliance *in the language of the other*, this strange vow by which we are committed in a language that is not our mother tongue', a matter of what he elsewhere terms an 'inalienable alienation'.[31]

◆

What are Derrida's texts like? Genres are not to be meddled with. I will not meddle with genres. I am translating and no doubt deforming the opening words of his essay 'La loi du genre': *Ne pas mêler les genres. Je ne mêlerai pas les genres.*[32] I dream of a meddling with French and

English, French and English meddling (with) the other. Every Derrida text meddles differently, even if it might appear to be up to the same thing. It would be as if to say, every time: *or again, Jacques Derrida.* Meddling is always related to a context, it is always singular, but also a meddling *with* something in a double sense. What is meddled with proves also to be what is effectively doing the meddling. There is something here perhaps of meddling as making love (as he has said: 'the texts I want to read from the deconstructive point of view are texts I love, with that impulse of identification which is indispensable for reading'[33]), but also of meddling as a certain violence, meddling in the sense of the *mêlée* or fighting, the logic of a 'strategy without finality' linked to the need for what he has called 'a new discourse on war'.[34] As Derrida proclaims in one of the early interviews in *Positions*: 'Deconstruction, I have insisted, is not *neutral.* It *intervenes.*'[35] Deconstruction meddles. And while the point of this intervention, this meddling or interfering, is always in a specific context, it is always also a question of the deformation or transformation of that context, meddling *in* and *with* context. This is why every text by Derrida is in a sense written in a new genre or rather a new mixing or meddling with genres.

♦

I would like to conclude this perhaps rather haphazard-seeming miscellany with a gothic footnote, a step to the side, as if on a spiral staircase, in other words with a few words about Horace Walpole. One of the things I love about Derrida's work has to do with the way it says: be free, come, go, read, think, see what you can do as concerns the possibilities of inventing, intervening, or again meddling. It is never enough (though it can often seem like a lot) to try to read and elucidate how Derrida's texts are meddling. It is crucial to the logic of what I have been attempting to trace here that reading Derrida means meddling *with* Derrida in the double senses just outlined. His texts call to be read differently, anew, every time: they affirm the open-endedness of the *or again.* There is no knowing where or how we might find Derrida's texts being read: meddling with the notion of the calculable, decidable or programmable is one of the most consistent and implacable features of his work. But one of the perhaps more surprising areas of literary and cultural theory in which Derrida's work has been making an impact in recent years is 'the Gothic'. I am thinking here of work by numerous critics and theorists, including Ruth Parkin-Gounelas, Jodey Castricano and Julian Wolfreys.[36]

Derrida's essay 'Fors', on the psychoanalytic notions of the crypt and phantom, published as the foreword to Abraham and Torok's *The Wolf*

Man's Magic Word, together with his book *Spectres of Marx* (1993) in particular have provided critics with a new conceptual vocabulary and new imaginative possibilities for approaching Gothic literature. It is doubtless not by chance that the increased critical interest in the Gothic in recent years should have coincided with what is generally seen as an increased interest in ghosts and spectrality in Derrida's own writings. The links between his work and the Gothic have to date had to do largely with the ghostly, crypts and secrets. As Jodey Castricano suggests, Derrida's writings offer an indirect but powerful illumination of the sense that 'tropes and topoi of the Gothic [such as] haunting, mourning, and revenance' are not 'unique to the Gothic' but rather are 'integral components of subjectivity, language, and thought'.[37] I would like to cut things off here with a different or at least additional hypothesis, a hypothesis indeed concerning the additional or supplementary, viz.: Derrida's work throws new light, patterns and shadows on 'the Gothic' as meddling, 'the Gothic' as a figure of meddling and as a meddling figure. It encourages a new understanding of the fascination and importance of 'the Gothic', in terms of notions of mixing up, interposing, tampering and interfering, dangerously supplementing.

Horace Walpole's dazzling masterpiece *The Castle of Otranto* (1765) is generally reckoned as the first example of the Gothic novel in English.[38] Its subtitle, 'A Gothic Story', was added on the publication of the second edition. It is with the second edition also, coming only a few months after the first, that Walpole abandons the persona of a translator, one William Marshall, who had presented the story as the translation of a recently discovered ancient Italian manuscript. As E. J. Clery puts it: 'it was precisely the moment that *Otranto* was revealed to be a modern work that the adjective "gothic" was first applied to it. There is a dislocation: "Gothic" is no longer a historical description; it marks the initiation of a new genre.'[39] Strangely supplementary, 'Gothic' here appears to mark the making explicit (but therefore also the peculiar enfolding or complication) of a logic of anachrony. It is in this context of anachrony that we might also see a rapport between *Spectres of Marx* and the 'Gothic': 'Gothic' entails a meddling with what we think we understand by history, linearity, genealogy. To deploy a phrase from Shakespeare's *Measure for Measure* in a somewhat impish way, we might say that 'Gothic' is a 'temporary meddler' (V, i, 144). Shakespeare's phrase alludes to a 'ghostly father', 'a meddling friar' (V, i, 126–7) called Lodowick. A temporary meddler is a meddler in temporal matters, that is to say primarily in worldly as opposed to spiritual or sacred matters. But for present purposes, tampering a little with Shakespeare's language, I would like to describe 'Gothic' as meddling with time, a temporal meddler. (I will come back to the 'meddling friar' again in a moment.)

'For the reader of today, coming to *Otranto* after more than two centuries of Gothic writing, many of its elements will appear instantly, if not uncannily, familiar,' writes E. J. Clery.[40] These would include the figure of the castle itself, trap-doors and subterranean passageways, shrieks and screams, creaking and slamming doors, ghosts and skeletons, a virtuous young damsel or two in distress, murder, a disruptive questioning of the nature of marriage (its lawfulness, its strange taking or not taking place), madness, refused or impossible mourning, disturbances of legacy and inheritance, interferences in the 'family line', the return of the past and/or of the repressed. (In passing it may be noted that in at least the last half-dozen of these elements we might also begin to elaborate the deconstructive interest of 'the Gothic', in particular regarding a notion of deconstruction as 'uncanny politics'.[41]) The identification of *The Castle of Otranto* as 'A Gothic Story', its participation in the genre of 'Gothic novel', or even its somewhat fantastical status as the first in that genre, is doubtless a *'participation without belonging'*, as Derrida formulates the law of the law of genre: there is, he says, a taking part in without being part of. There is 'a law of impurity or a principle of contamination', of mixing or meddling that is 'lodged within the heart of the law itself'.[42] One of the ways in which we might explore this meddling with genre in *The Castle of Otranto* is in terms of drama and poetry, and especially the work of Shakespeare. In the Preface to the Second Edition (1765) Walpole proclaims that Shakespeare is his 'model' and goes on to suggest that what characterises Shakespeare's work is a sort of lawlessness, or meddling with law: 'Shall the critic', he asks rhetorically, 'give laws to Shakespeare?' (CO, pp. 10, 12). If, as Derrida suggest in *Spectres of Marx*, Shakespeare 'keeps watch over the English language', he does so in a formidably ghostly and meddlesome way.[43]

At issue here is a quite different conception of 'the Gothic novel', drawing on its links to poetry or (in Derrida's phrase) the poematic, as well as to the language of theatre and theatricality. In the astonishing compactness, skidding turns, interruptions and whirling velocities of Walpole's writing, there are many allusions to Shakespeare, especially to *Hamlet* and *Macbeth*. There is perhaps always in the play or ludic character of such allusion a sense and dissemination of meddling. The obvious Shakespearean references in *The Castle of Otranto* have to do with the ghostly, in particular with invocations or evocations of the Ghost of Hamlet's father and the Ghost of Banquo.[44] There are many others, too many indeed to enumerate here. Let us confine ourselves simply to the play of what is, apparently, a single word: 'meddling'. It occurs twice in the novel, on both occasions in reference to the 'holy father Jerome' who resides at 'the convent adjoining the church of saint Nicholas' (p. 44), who intervenes and schemes to protect first the peasant Theodore and later Matilda, daughter of Manfred Prince of Otranto. Jerome is described on one occasion as a 'meddling priest' (p. 48) and again, towards the end of the novel, as 'this meddling friar' (p. 97). On both occasions the phrase issues from Manfred himself. But in the linear unfolding of the story, 'meddling' will always have meant more, less or other than Manfred thinks it means. In fact this 'holy father' is more meddling, less holy, more holey, than might at first appear, either to Manfred or to the reader, on account of 'the secret [which] remain[s] locked in [his] breast' (p. 115) until the final page of the novel, namely the revelation that Theodore is 'the true prince of Otranto' (p. 113). 'Meddling', in other words, operates at the level of narrative as well as character: quite how 'meddling' this friar is is kept secret *by the text* as well as by the meddling character *in* the text.

The novel is meddling with the reader. But this is not to say that we will ever have known what 'meddling' *is*. Walpole's novel silently gestures, if you will, to and through the strangeness of this word. Is 'meddling' an adjective and/or a verb? What is the time of 'meddling'? Is the meddling happening now? Does it belong to the present, as a casual reading of the word, especially as a so-called present participle, might suggest? Or is the meddling already underway? Or already past? Or again, is 'meddling' not also just as much a hearkening towards, a promise or threat of something to come? Manfred's deictic 'this' ('this meddling friar') perhaps helps to make explicit a sense that 'meddling' is performative, a sort of micrological performative utterance, an act of naming that is not readily dissociated from questions of blasphemy and malediction. But at the same time it would be a sort of poematically meddling performative, a meddling *with* performative. As I have already indicated, the phrase 'meddling friar' is Shakespearean: Walpole's text appears to be echoing (and parenthetically we might begin to wonder how *Gothic* the notion of the echo is in this scenario, how much 'literary' or 'textual' echo is, from the beginning, caught up in supplementary distortion, interference, or again, meddling) the passage in *Measure for Measure* in which we witness the appearance of the 'meddling friar' Lodowick.

Now the word 'meddling' is comparatively rare in Shakespeare: it occurs in only four places. Without wanting to overload the significance of the modest appearances of this curious word, I think that together they suggest a certain consistency and intrigue, the consistency of a certain intrigue. There is the 'meddling friar' in *Measure for Measure*, a 'meddling priest' in *King John* (III, i, 89), the 'meddling fiend' in *2 Henry VI* (III, iii, 21) and a 'meddling monkey' in *A Midsummer Night's Dream* (II, i, 181). In each case 'meddling' seems to suggest itself as a peculiar supplement, superfluity or *débordement*. We might suppose, in other words, that every monkey is a meddling monkey, and that the same could be said of the friar, priest and fiend or devil (or again, Old Harry). Associations of the divine (and/or devilish) and the animal: 'meddling' seems to carry these, in cryptic fashion. In *How to Do Things with Words*, Austin concludes his discussion of the act of naming a ship by considering what is going on in a case where the performative fails (and, in this prosthetic extension to my gothic footnote, we might notice how the feet come in again here, walking and kicking, along with the Austinian signature-phrase 'or again'): 'I see a vessel on the stocks, walk up and smash the bottle hung at the stern, proclaim "I name this ship the *Mr Stalin*" and for good measure kick away the chocks: but the trouble is, I was not the person chosen to name it.' In this case, Austin declares, 'there is not even a pretence of capacity . . . there is no accepted conventional procedure; it is a mockery, like a marriage with a monkey. Or again one could say that part of the procedure is getting oneself appointed . . .'[45] The monkey and the 'I' in Austin's text are up to monkey-business. Or again, one could say: it is as if they were married.

There is something curiously canny about 'meddling', a sense of uncertain, secretive or cryptic knowledge, of uncertain knowingness. In the passage concerning the 'meddling friar' in the Oxford edition of *Measure for Measure*, the editor N. W. Bawcutt proposes that 'meddling' here means 'fond of intrigue'.[46] This gloss is doubtless reductive, but it nicely evokes the sense of a certain affection and loving, even to the point of folly, together with a sense of secrecy. The 'meddling' figure of the friar in *The Castle of Otranto* mixes up the genres of poetry, drama and novel. 'Meddling' overruns genre and text, even as it encrypts what we might call (after Derrida) a poematic love of Shakespeare, a loving madness of citation at the heart of the work. Walpole's text is meddling, is about meddling, at the level of plot, character and also (as I have tried to suggest) narration: the 'meddling friar' is simply a counterpart to the meddling Manfred, but more or less every character in the story is meddling in one way or another. 'Meddling' in the text is attributable to Manfred, but the word is also the narrator's and of course the author's. If there is something singularly meddling about 'the Gothic', however, in the context of Walpole's novel, it has to do not only with a fondness of intrigue at these levels but also, and in some sense *before* this, in terms of the sentence and syntax, as a matter of tone, or tones, of mixing or meddling voices, of interrupting and cutting off. Consider the passage in which Manfred first accuses Jerome of meddling:

> – But first, my lord, I must interrogate the princess, whether she is acquainted with the cause of the lady Isabella's retirement from your castle. – No, on my soul, said Hippolita; does Isabella charge me with being privy to it? – Father, interrupted Manfred, I pay due reference to your holy profession; but I am sovereign here, and will allow no meddling priest to interfere in the affairs of my domestic. (pp. 47–8)

Voices mingle and clash in this *mélange* and *mêlée*. The reader is called upon to keep constant watch over changes of speaker, the irruption of another voice or other voices. And of course also over the meddling of a voice within a voice, the voice perhaps of a narrator, or author, or again (perhaps) God. As the 'meddling priest' says in response to Manfred: 'I forgive your highness's uncharitable apostrophe: I know my duty, and am the minister of a mightier prince than Manfred. Hearken to him who speaks through my organs' (p. 48).

Walpole's text is an obsessive work of interruption, of incidents or events – such as a 'clap of thunder' (p. 74) or other 'sudden noise' (p. 76) – interrupting the action, and of voices interrupting one another. Interruption tells the story, punctuating, stopping short, diverting, meddling sentences. There is a consistent intrigue around 'inter-' and 'interring' words. Along with so many cases of 'interruption' (with all the numerous forms of the verb 'to interrupt'), for example, we find 'interred' (p. 39), 'interpose' (p. 91) and 'interposition' (p. 61), 'interest' (pp. 62, 84, 89), 'intercede' (pp. 95, 109) and 'intercession' (pp. 66, 107), 'interrogate' (p. 47), 'intercourse' (p. 66), 'interview' (p. 74), 'interfere' (pp. 48, 88), 'intervention' (p. 96) and 'intermarriage' (p. 104). But what is interred, interrupted, interfered with is, finally perhaps, something intervening in the grammar and syntax itself. Meddling, in *The Castle of Otranto*, concerns the singular speed, force and beauty of Walpole's scheming sentences. 'I detest grammatical mistakes', Derrida has said.[47] A similar love of precision, correctness and propriety characterises Walpole's writing. Meddling with sentences is always conducted in the most canny, meticulous and exacting fashion. Walpole omits all quotation marks and makes constant use of the strange, interruptive force of the dash and – in the marvellously compact and rigorous ordering of its polyphonic disorder – a privileged place (place without place) is given to the rhetorical figure of aposiopesis, the interrupted or unfinished sentence.

Permit me to step off into the dark with just two abrupt examples of such abruption. Isabella is speaking of the love she allegedly bore

Conrad, the son of Manfred, who has just died: 'How! my lord, said Isabella; sure you do not suspect me of not feeling the concern I ought? My duty and affection would have always – Think no more of him, interrupted Manfred; he was a sickly puny child, and heaven has perhaps taken him away that I might not trust the honours of my house on so frail a foundation' (p. 24). The dash following the words 'My duty and affection would have always' marks the aposiopesis. Or again: shrieking at, then speaking to, what she had at first believed to be 'the ghost of her betrothed Conrad', Isabella interrupts Theodore, who is in the midst of saying: 'I will die in your defence; but I am unacquainted with the castle and want – Oh! said Isabella, hastily interrupting him, help me but to find a trap-door that must be hereabout' (p. 29). Theodore's speech is literally dashed: 'but I am unacquainted with the castle and want . . .' If there is some rapport here between 'the Gothic', as it manifests itself in Walpole's novel, and the writings of Jacques Derrida, it would perhaps have to do also with this intrigue of ellipsis, interruption, death sentence and aposiopesis. Hauntological polyphony with uncertain beginning and end, beginning *or* end: 'or again, meddling'.

Meddling AfterwORd

[A shortened version of the foregoing text, in particular omitting the gothic footnote about *The Castle of Otranto*, was presented at a seminar with Derrida on the occasion of his receiving an honorary doctorate from Queen Mary, University of London, on 6 July 2004. His response, improvised in English, and concerned with 'the problem of meddling', is cited below.]

Jacques Derrida: [. . .] Meddling, of course, has to do with what we previously said about contamination and the unavoidable meddling or contamination, spoiling and so on and so forth. But, instead without really adding something or answering something, I would give an example of the way this meddling compels me to admit that two logics, two different axioms or logics are at the same time – and/or, and/or – at the same time, absolutely heterogeneous and absolutely indissociable. There is 'and/or', you cannot choose between the 'and' and the 'or'. Let me take the example of hospitality, an example that I treasure because I've been for a long time working on this problem of hospitality. Pure hospitality, what I call unconditional hospitality, would consist in, let's say, not only inviting the other, or letting the other come, and so on and so forth, but in exposing oneself to the coming of the other unconditionally, without asking any questions, without making any . . . [*sic*] asking for any conditions or for the other to respect my rules, my language, my house, my culture, and so on and so forth. The unconditional hospitality is just a way of exposing oneself in one's vulnerability to the coming of the other. That's a hospitality worthy of the name, pure hospitality, unconditional. No border, no visa, no passport, just the uninvited visitor comes in and is well received. But such an unconditional hospitality or unconditional gift, to become real, to become effective must become concrete and must give something. That is, must go through a number of conditions. If you want, for instance, to organise hospitality, and to make hospitality possible then you have to make rules, you have to condition hospitality. The logic of unconditional hospitality and the logic of conditional hospitality are absolutely heterogeneous; they have nothing to do with one another. What I call the 'hospitality of invitation', that is, when you invite someone and say 'well, please come for dinner or come in my house or in my country but don't destroy anything, don't disturb anything', and so on and so forth. That is, when I make some laws of hospitality, then I limit the hospitality, that's the hospitality of invitation, I invite someone according to my own rules: 'this is my house, you are welcome in my house', that's the hospitality of invitation. So when we invite we are not purely hospitable. We are purely hospitable when we do not invite, when the uninvited guest comes in as a visitor, as an unexpected visitor, that's the 'hospitality of visitation', if you want, as opposed to 'hospitality of invitation'. And these two hospitalities – the unconditional and the conditional – are absolutely heterogeneous, they have nothing to do with one another. And nevertheless, they are indissociable. If you want hospitality to become effective, then you have to organise the conditions and to give something to determine hospitality. So, in another example, you have this couple of concepts which are absolutely heterogeneous to one another and absolutely indissociable. The other example I would take is the example of what I oppose as 'law' and 'justice'; in French, 'le droit et la justice'. Justice cannot be reduced to the right, to the law, 'Recht'. The law can be improved, can be changed, the legislation can go through revolutions and transformations and so on and so forth and because it is in constant transformation, this means it never reaches pure justice. Justice is the goal, if you want, but it can never be reached by the law. You can find a number of examples in which doing justice to someone implies that you transgress the law. Let's take the example of the respectable American tradition of civil disobedience, when you disobey the law in order to obey a higher justice, a higher law. To be just you have to disobey the civil law. So, justice and law have nothing to do with one another. Now, if you want the justice to be concretely determined or incorporated or incarnated or effective, then you have to transform the law in a certain direction rather than in another direction so that justice has to become, to take the form of law, to become as legal as possible. That is, when you transform a society through a revolution in the name of justice then you make new laws that you consider more just than the previous ones. So, to that extent, justice and law are indissociable, otherwise justice would remain an abstract regulative ideal. So, justice cannot remain totally outside the law and the law cannot remain totally unjust. When we make the law, when we improve the law, it's in the name of justice, of raw justice, OK? So the two concepts are absolutely heterogeneous and, nevertheless, meddle, that is, indissociable [*sic*]. And we always have to do with this impure relation between two things or two concepts or two meanings, two values which are totally different, radically different and that's politics, that's ethics. When we take a political responsibility, we have to be as just as possible and nevertheless make laws which are necessarily imperfect and not just enough. So that's why you have this 'and/or' – justice and law, justice or law, at the same time. 'And/or'. Now, of course, Nick started with this meddling of languages, Latin, French, English and so forth. If I could speak French, I mean pure French, I would refer to another meaning of 'or', meaning 'gold'. 'Or', meaning 'now'. In the wake of Mallarmé, I wrote a long, endless footnote around the small word 'or' in French, as 'gold', 'now'.[48] And while I was exploring these various possibilities of 'or' as a word, or as a piece of a word in another word – 'dehors', 'alors', 'alors' meaning having to do with the hour – while I was exploring and formalising this collection of 'ors' through a number of quotations from Mallarmé, I was at the same time using – not only mentioning – but using these 'ors' in all possible ways. So I couldn't distinguish between mention and use as the speech act theorists do or Austin also does. So 'or' in French doesn't function as 'or' in English and I am, as someone who is a native French speaker but who understands some English, I am in this meddling of an 'or' or . . . [*sic*] and so on and so forth.

Notes

1. Jacques Derrida, 'Living On', trans. James Hulbert, in Harold Bloom et al., *Deconstruction and Criticism* (New York: Seabury Press, 1979), p. 82.
2. Eric Partridge, *Shakespeare's Bawdy*, 3rd edn (1968; London: Routledge, 2001), pp. 190–1.
3. All references to Shakespeare are to *The Norton Shakespeare: Based on the Oxford Edition*, eds Stephen Greenblatt, Walter Cohen, Jean E. Howard

and Katherine Eisaman Maus (New York and London: W. W. Norton, 1997), unless otherwise stated.

4. 'Deconstruction: A Trialogue in Jerusalem', *Mishkenot Sha'ananim Newsletter*, no. 7 (December 1986), p. 6.

5. *Monolingualism of the Other; or, The Prosthesis of Origin*, trans. Patrick Mensah (Stanford, CA: Stanford University Press, 1998) [*Le monolinguisme de l'autre: ou la prosthèse de l'origine* (Paris: Galilée, 1996)]; 'Afterw.rds: or, at least, less than a letter about a letter less' ['Afterw.rds: ou, du moins, moins qu'une lettre sur une lettre en moins'], trans. Geoffrey Bennington, in *Afterwords*, ed. Nicholas Royle (Tampere, Finland: Outside Books, 1992), pp. 197–217.

6. Jacques Derrida, 'Et Cetera . . . (and so on, und so weiter, and so forth, et ainsi de suite, und so überall, etc.)', trans. Geoffrey Bennington, *Deconstructions: A User's Guide*, ed. Nicholas Royle (Basingstoke: Palgrave, 2000), pp. 282–305: here, p. 262. Further page references appear parenthetically in the main body of the text. Where appropriate, page numbers for quotations from the French text (*Et cetera . . .* [Paris: L'Herne, 2005]) are also given parenthetically, following a slash: here, in particular, see pp. 7–8.

7. For some examples of the 'or again' in this context, see J. L. Austin, *How to Do Things with Words* (Oxford: Clarendon Press, 1962), pp. 20, 24, 28, 41, 44, 47 and 66.

8. 'Typewriter Ribbon: Limited Ink (2)', trans. Peggy Kamuf, in *Without Alibi* (Stanford, CA: Stanford University Press, 2002), pp. 71–160: here, p. 123. Further page references appear parenthetically in the main body of the text, abbreviated 'TR' where appropriate.

9. *How to Do Things with* Words, p.150.

10. 'Limited Inc a, b, c . . .', trans. Samuel Weber and Jeffrey Mehlman, in *Limited Inc* (Evanston, IL: Northwestern University Press, 1988), p. 54.

11. Ibid., pp. 54–5.

12. J. L. Austin, 'Performative Utterances', in *Philosophical Papers*, 3rd edn, eds J. O. Urmson and G. J. Warnock (Oxford: Oxford University Press, 1979), pp. 233–52.

13. Ibid., p. 235.

14. Ibid., p. 235, cited in 'Typewriter Ribbon', pp. 127–8.

15. 'Border Lines', trans. James Hulbert, in Harold Bloom et al., *Deconstruction and Criticism*, p. 80.

16. 'Différance', in *Margins of Philosophy*, trans. Alan Bass (Chicago: Chicago University Press, 1982), p. 12. Cf. *Positions*, trans. Alan Bass (Chicago: Chicago University Press, 1981), p. 14.

17. '"Le Parjure", *Perhaps*: Storytelling and Lying ("abrupt breaches of syntax")', trans. Peggy Kamuf, in *Without Alibi*, p. 201.

18. 'Living On', p. 107.

19. E. K. Sedgwick, 'Around the Performative: Periperformative Vicinities in Nineteenth-Century Narrative', in her *Touching Feeling: Affect, Pedagogy, Performativity* (London: Duke University Press, 2003), p. 70.

20. 'Performative Utterances', p. 235.

21. '"There is No *One* Narcisissm" (Autobiophotographies)', trans. Peggy Kamuf, in *Points . . . Interviews, 1974–1994*, ed. Elisabeth Weber (London and New York: Routledge, 1995), pp. 200–1.

22. 'Living On', pp. 83–4 (tr. sl. mod.); 'Survivre', in *Parages* (Paris: Galilée, 2003), pp. 118–19.

23. See 'Che cos'è la poesia?', trans. Peggy Kamuf, in Jacques Derrida, *Points*, especially pp. 295, 299.

24. 'Border Lines', pp. 82–3.

25. 'The Time is Out of Joint', trans. Peggy Kamuf, in *Deconstruction is/in America: A New Sense of the Political*, ed. Anselm Haverkamp (New York: New York University Press, 1995), p. 30.

26. 'Border Lines', pp. 93–5, tr. mod.; 'Journal de bord', in *Parages* (Paris: Galilée, 2003), pp. 130–1.

27. Ibid., p. 95.

28. Ibid., p. 100; 'Journal de bord', p. 136.

29. The posing of this question concerns the fact that this text was originally written for translation and publication in French ('Ou encore, interférence', trans. Pierre Vitoux) as part of a collection of essays, edited by René Major, provisionally entitled *Mélanges*, in homage to Jacques Derrida. Derrida's death interposed. The collection consequently appeared as a commemorative volume entitled *Derrida pour les temps à venir* (Paris: Stock, 2007). Pierre Vitoux chooses to let the original be: '"Meddling sentences." Qu'est-ce qu'un traducteur français pourra faire de cette improbable phrase de deux mots? Phrases en interference?' (p. 267).

30. 'Border Lines', p. 101.

31. See 'Living On', p. 77; *Monolingualism of the Other*, p. 25.

32. 'La loi du genre', in *Parages* (Paris: Galilée, 2003), p. 233.

33. *The Ear of the Other: Otobiography, Transference, Translation*, trans. Peggy Kamuf, ed. Christie V. McDonald (New York: Schocken Books, 1985), p. 87.

34. See 'Psychoanalysis Searches the State of Its Soul', trans. Peggy Kamuf, in *Without Alibi*, p. 246.

35. *Positions*, p. 93.

36. See, for example, Ruth Parkin-Gounelas, 'Anachrony and Anatopia: Spectres of Marx, Derrida and Gothic Fiction', in *Ghosts: Deconstruction, Psychoanalysis, History*, eds Peter Buse and Andrew Stott (Basingstoke: Macmillan, 1999); Jodey Castricano, *Cryptomimesis: The Gothic and Jacques Derrida's Ghost Writing* (Montreal: McGill-Queen's University Press, 2001); and Julian Wolfreys, *Victorian Hauntings: Spectrality, Gothic, the Uncanny and Literature* (Basingstoke: Palgrave, 2002).

37. See *Cryptomimesis*, p. 149, n. 8.

38. Horace Walpole, *The Castle of Otranto*, ed. W. S. Lewis, with an introduction and notes by E. J. Clery (Oxford: Oxford University Press, 1998). Further page references are to this edition of the novel, abbreviated 'CO' where appropriate.

39. E. J. Clery, Introduction, *The Castle of Otranto*, p. xv.

40. Ibid., p. xv.

41. Permit me to refer here to *The Uncanny* (Manchester: Manchester University Press, 2003), especially 'Night Writing: Deconstruction Reading Politics', pp. 112–32.

42. See 'The Law of Genre', trans. Avital Ronell, in *Acts of Literature*, ed. Derek Attridge (London and New York: Routledge, 1992), pp. 227, 225.

43. See *Spectres of Marx: The State of the Debt, the Work of Mourning, and the New International*, trans. Peggy Kamuf (London: Routledge, 1994), p. 18.
44. See, in particular, *The Castle of Otranto*, pp. 42, 83.
45. *How to Do Things with Words*, pp. 23–4.
46. See William Shakespeare, *Measure for Measure*, ed. N. W. Bawcutt (Oxford: Oxford World's Classics, 1991), p. 209.
47. See 'I Have a Taste for the Secret', Jacques Derrida in conversation with Maurizio Ferraris and Giorgio Vattimo, in Derrida and Ferraris, *A Taste for the Secret*, trans. Giacomo Donis (Cambridge: Polity, 2001), p. 43.
48. [N.R.:] Derrida is referring here to the footnote that appears in 'La double séance', in *La dissémination* (Paris: Éditions du Seuil, 1972), pp. 295–7; 'The Double Session', in *Dissemination*, trans. Barbara Johnson (Chicago: Chicago University Press, 1981), pp. 262–4.

Derrida's Event

'Derrida's event': won't that have been the transformation of everything? I feel tense, to the point of trembling. Trembling is already the signal, symptom or experience of a strangeness of 'event', upsetting time, uncertainly concerning something that has already happened or is about to happen or happen again. As we find written in *The Gift of Death*: 'the event that makes one tremble portends and threatens still'.[1] Tension's *tense*: there is something untranslatable about this word which, in English, is haphazardly double, a homophone that refers to being stretched tight, strained or producing strain (from the Latin *tendere*, to 'stretch') as well as the grammatical sense of 'tense' as 'time', a translation or rather a deformation of the French word *temps*. In what tense should we speak of Derrida or of 'Derrida's event'? I have felt myself stretched by this strange *tense* since 9 October 2004 (but doubtless also before this), when I was in the midst of dealing with the proofs of an essay I had written called 'Blind Cinema', due to be published as the introduction to the-book-of-the-film *Derrida*, by Kirby Dick and Amy Ziering Kofman.[2] Within a few days of his death I heard from the US publishers that they wanted me to change the tense: I was to go through the essay (an essay which Derrida himself had seen 'in the present tense') and change it to past tense 'as and where appropriate'. One of the unexpected and less intolerable aspects of attempting to respond to this bizarre yet apparently realistic and commonsensical request was finding my revised version of the proofs actually transpired to contain a higher number of instances of the present tense. 'Derrida writes', 'Derrida remarks in an interview', 'Derrida argues', and even 'Derrida thinks'. This convention of the so-called present tense, in the context of philosophical as well as literary writing and (even more perhaps) in the context of film, is at once quite familiar and strange. It tends towards, it portends spectrality. Derrida's work, the 'event' of his *œuvre*, perhaps calls for a new *ghost tense*.

Let's not be so naive as to suppose that he cannot speak. Moreover, we have to attempt to answer for the fact that – for Derrida, which is also to say *from* Derrida – a ghostly response is always possible. That much is perhaps already legible in the 'for' of 'For Derrida': it is a 'for', as he himself says in the context of the poetry of Paul Celan, 'whose rich equivocation remains ungraspable ("in the place of", "on behalf of", "destined for")'.[3] Writing of Freud in *Archive Fever* Derrida comments: 'Naturally, by all appearances, we believe we know that *the phantom does not respond*. He will never again respond . . . Freud will never again speak.'[4] And what Derrida says here about Freud, we can also say about Derrida. As his text knows – and knows also that things are not so simple. In order to illustrate this, he calls up the example of the telephone answering machine. We know that Freud is dead, and Derrida is dead. Derrida writes:

> Now in spite of these necessities, these obvious facts and these substantiated certitudes, in spite of all the reassuring assurances which such a knowing or such a believing-to-know dispenses to us, through them, the phantom continues to speak. Perhaps he does not respond, but he speaks. A phantom speaks. What does this mean? In the first place or in a preliminary way, this means that without responding it disposes of a response, a bit like the answering machine whose voice outlives its moment of recording: you call, the other person is dead, now, whether you know it or not, and the voice responds to you, in a very precise fashion, sometimes cheerfully, it instructs you, it can even give you instructions, make declarations to you, address your requests, prayers, promises, injunctions. Supposing, *concesso non dato*, that a living being ever responds in an absolutely living and infinitely well-adjusted manner, without the least automatism, without ever having an archival technique [such as that of the answering machine] overflow the singularity of an event, we know in any case that a spectral response (thus informed by a *technē* and inscribed in an archive) is always possible. There would be neither history nor tradition nor culture without that possibility. It is this that we are speaking of here. It is this, in truth, that we must answer for. (AF, pp. 62–3)

The voice of the dead person, cheerful at the end of the telephone line, is not alone: as Derrida has noted elsewhere (for example, in *Mémoires*), the voice-from-beyond-the-grave 'already haunts any said real or present voice'.[5] Derrida stresses the 'substantiated certitudes' but also affirms a 'perhaps', a perhaps that will have haunted these certitudes. The phantom speaks. *Perhaps* the phantom does not respond; but a spectral response is always possible. This possibility is inscribed in the singularity of an event. There would be no history otherwise, no tradition, no culture.

Derrida's concern in *Archive Fever* is to explore the fact that 'archivisation produces as much as it records the event' (p. 17). What goes into (and is left out of) an archive, how what goes in goes in, how it is named (or not), ordered (and disordered), framed and described (or not), is part of the production of the event. This is what leads Derrida to his remarkable question: 'How can one prove an absence of archive? How can one not, and why not, take into account *unconscious*, and more generally *virtual* archives?' (p. 64). 'There is no meta-archive' (p. 67), he remarks. 'The structure of the archive is *spectral*' (p. 84), he argues. The archive is not something done and dusted, a thing of the past. On the contrary, for Derrida (and for all of us), 'the archive is never closed. It opens out of the future' (p. 68). This corresponds with his conception of inheritance, as he describes it in an interview entitled 'The Deconstruction of Actuality', specifically in relation to Marx and Shakespeare, and above all in relation to the Ghost in *Hamlet*, 'perhaps the main character of [*Spectres of Marx*]': 'To inherit is not essentially to *receive* something, a *given* which one then *has*. It is an active affirmation, a response to an injunction, but it also presupposes initiative, the endorsement or counter-signing of a critical choice. To inherit is to select, to sift, to harness, to reclaim, to reactivate.'[6] To inherit is thus also indissociably bound up with a sense of the secret, the logic of 'an undecidable reserve'.[7]

An event is never over and done with. And the happening of an event is never pure or absolutely assured: 'An event cannot be reduced to the fact of something happening . . . it is what may always fail to come to pass.'[8] '*Never quite* taking place' is part of the alleged 'success' of 'an event'.[9] Everywhere in Derrida's writing there is the implicit, sometimes explicit injunction to submit the concept of event to 'systematic questioning'.[10] Attentive as always to the etymology and history of a word, Derrida's 'event' (itself of course already a translation of the French '*événement*' and therefore already a quite other kind of 'event') tenses, if I may put it like this, it *tenses* with the force of a 'come': 'event', like '*événement*', comes from the Latin *ēvenīre*, to come out (from), to happen. To reckon with the 'event' in Derrida it is necessary to engage with the question and experience of the 'come', the coming in and of the event and indeed the 'to come', the opening of the future ['*l'avenir*']. As he asks in the essay 'Psyche: Inventions of the Other', apropos the 'unique structure of an event' and invention: 'What does it mean, *to come?*'[11] The 'come' does not come after the event: it is the condition of an event. Thus he remarks in 'The Deconstruction of Actuality':

> The event must be considered in terms of the 'come', not conversely. 'Come' ['*viens*', implying the intimate form '*tu*': 'come', 'come hither'] is said to another, to others who are not yet defined as persons, as subjects, as equals (at least in the sense of any measurable equality). Without this 'come' there could be no experience of what is to come, of the event, of what will happen and therefore of what, since it comes from the other, lies beyond anticipation . . . There would be no event, no history, unless a 'come' opened out

> and addressed itself to someone, to someone else whom I cannot and must not define in advance – not as subject, self, consciousness, not even as animal, God, person, man or woman, living or dead. (It must be possible to *summon* a spectre, to appeal to it for example, and I don't think this is an arbitrary example: there may be something of the revenant, of the 'come again' ['*reviens*'], at the origin or conclusion of every 'come'.)[12]

The evocation of a ghost tense, once again: the differential tensing of a spectre at the origin and conclusion of every 'come'.

In an interview in April 1989, four years before delivering the lectures that became *Spectres of Marx*, Derrida speaks of Shakespeare: 'I would very much like to read and write in the space or heritage of Shakespeare, in relation to whom I have infinite admiration and gratitude; I would like to become (alas, it's pretty late) a "Shakespeare expert"; I know that everything is in Shakespeare; everything and the rest, so everything or nearly.'[13] The rest is silence, the secrecy of inheritance, the desire to affirm and to countersign. How does one go about trying to become a 'Shakespeare expert'? (Who would ever dare to describe themselves as a 'Shakespeare expert' or indeed as a 'Derrida expert'? Derrida's phrase 'Shakespeare expert' appears between the tweezers of quotation marks, suggesting a characteristic sense of irony and comedy, but also as if to draw attention to the connotations of trying, testing and experimentation that belongs with the word 'expert', the sense of 'trying thoroughly'. Derrida, like Shakespeare, can be so trying.) How does one go about trying to countersign Shakespeare, to countersign the event called *Hamlet*, for example, or even some minuscule aspect of such an event?

Incapable of doing justice here to the scope and complexity of such questions, permit me simply to offer a few brief remarks about the word 'event' (or 'events') in Shakespeare, in particular in the context of *Hamlet*. The first thing to say is that its appearances are consistently associated with a sense of strangeness. To conjure with the name of 'event' in Shakespeare is to conjure with strangeness. So, for example, we find the 'event' as 'wondrous strange' (in *3 Henry VI*: II, i, 32), 'that obscene and most preposterous event' (in fact a provoking reference to the act of writing itself, in *Love's Labour's Lost*: I, i, 245), the 'event' as that which is not 'customed' (in *King John*: III, iv, 155), 'strange events' (in *As You Like It*: V, iv, 133), 'strange event' (in *Timon of Athens*: III, iv, 17), 'strange and terrible events' (in *Antony and Cleopatra*: IV, xv, 3), 'events' that are 'not natural' and increase '[f]rom strange to stranger' (in *The Tempest*: V, i, 230–1), and life itself described in *As You Like It* (by Jacques, no less, or Jaques) as 'this strange eventful history' (II, vii, 164).[14] (This last case, by the way, is uniquely eventful, the only occasion in Shakespeare's writings where the word 'eventful' appears and the earliest recorded appearance of the word 'eventful' in English: yes, strange history, to invent the eventful . . .)

As I remarked a moment ago, 'event' comes from the Latin, it has to do with what comes from or comes out. In English the word 'event' indeed used to signify 'outcome'. In *Hamlet*, for example, when Hamlet speaks in the soliloquy at the end of Act IV of 'thinking too precisely on th'event' (IV, iv, 41), the word 'event' is generally understood to have the primary meaning of 'outcome', 'result', 'consequence'.[15] (This might lead us away into a dreamy, impassioned and perhaps interminable digression on Derrida's 'outcome' or 'outcomes', above all the 'learning outcomes' of reading Derrida.) But in the same soliloquy, within ten lines, Hamlet is also contemptuously invoking that 'delicate and tender prince, / Whose spirit, with divine ambition puff'd, / Makes mouths at the invisible event' (IV, iv, 48–50). Here is the sense of outcome again, but it is at the same time emphatically a question of what is 'invisible', unforeseeable. Too precise, too trying or not, Hamlet's thinking thus corresponds with Derrida's stress on the event as necessarily bound up with the unforeseeable, the unpredictable and unprogrammable. As he declares near the start of his compellingly hazardous essay on chance (an essay that is in part about Shakespeare and in particular the strange workings of 'nature' in *King Lear*), 'My Chances': 'unforeseeability conditions the very structure of an event'.[16]

Among the innumerable things to which Derrida seems drawn in his various readings of and remarks on *Hamlet*, we might think most immediately of the time being out of joint, anachronicity, inheritance and spectrality. Here are five lines from *Hamlet*. They come in the opening scene. Derrida, so far as I am aware, does not cite them anywhere. Indeed they may not seem much to warrant citation: they are awkward and convoluted and there's not a lot, apparently, going on in them. They tend to be excluded from many editions of the play and from most stage performances. They are lines that appear in the Second Quarto (1604) but are absent from the First Folio (1623). They are of interest here, however, first because they contain the only other instance in the play (beside the two from the soliloquy in Act IV scene iv that I have just mentioned) of the word 'event' (or 'events'); and second, on account of the fact that they immediately precede or precurse the second appearance of the Ghost. Let us then listen in to Horatio, the first one in the play who seeks a response from the Ghost, demanding that the Ghost speak. Horatio has just been evoking the time preceding the death of Caesar when 'The graves stood tenantless and the sheeted dead / Did squeak and gibber in the Roman streets' (I, i, 115–16). He then goes on:

> And even the like precurse of feared events,
> As harbingers preceding still the fates
> And prologue to the omen coming on,
> Have heaven and earth together demonstrated
> Unto our climatures and countrymen.
>   *Enter* GHOST
> But soft, behold, lo where it comes again! (I, i, 121–6)

This sentence preceding the entry of the Ghost (which is already a coming back, the second entry of the Ghost in this opening scene) is strange, as if the scholar Horatio is rambling, still or already again a bit distracted: we can't be sure finally whether or not he has finished his sentence when the Ghost appears. There is a sense that he perhaps has more to add, additional material regarding what is 'demonstrated' ('Have heaven and earth together demonstrated / Unto our climatures and countrymen . . .'). For this sentence, effectively ushering in the Ghost, the tense is out of joint.

Along with the syntax, the language likewise is complex and peculiar, above all in so far as it effects a sort of anacolouthon of 'event' or 'events'. If Horatio's statement constitutes a completed grammatical sentence (in the absence of an archived manuscript, and relying on the mixed evidence of the Second Quarto and First Folio, many critics suppose that Shakespeare wanted these lines deleted, and even that he had given up – in other words that we are dealing here with a 'composition-cut', not a 'theatre-cut' – before finishing the sentence), if Horatio's lines are to make sense as they stand, it would be in the form of a formidably convoluted, multiply chiasmatic inversion: what 'heaven and earth [have] together demonstrated' to Horatio and his fellow 'countrymen' would be 'the like precurse of feared events, / As harbingers preceding still the fates / And prologue to the omen coming on'. 'Feared events' are events anticipated with fear, yet 'precurse' in the sense of 'advance warning' (literally something 'running ahead', a word that occurs or recurs nowhere else in Shakespeare) seems to anticipate what is anticipated, running ahead of what is nevertheless already 'feared'. 'Harbingers' are likewise forerunners, those telling of something or someone that is coming: 'harbingers preceding still [always going before] the fates'. Correspondingly contorted, 'fates' means bizarrely both 'events that are fated to happen' and 'the Fates that ordain them'. We cannot tell how this syntax is 'coming on': 'As harbingers preceding still the fates / And prologue to the omen coming on . . .' The 'and' invites us to construe 'prologue' as conjoined with 'fates', at the same time as dividing and strangely repeating this image or figure of something coming before coming, a 'prologue to the omen coming on'. Shakespeare does not use the word 'omen' anywhere else and here, in this singular instance, its sense is antithetical, strangely double. 'Omen' is, in the words of the Arden editor Harold Jenkins, 'strictly, that which foreshadows an event, but here the event foretold'.[17] Strictly undone: tense and tension dissolved.

What to make of this extraordinary sentence (if it is one) about the 'coming on' of the event, that marks the coming again of the Ghost ('But soft, behold, lo where it comes again!')? If we can speak here of a kind of ghost tense in Shakespeare, a spectralisation of the 'coming' or 'coming on', conjoined and disjoined in the coming again of the Ghost, it would perhaps serve to evoke that strangeness of the event that Derrida calls 'literary'. As he describes it in an interview:

> The literary event is perhaps more of an event (because less natural) than any other, but by the same token it becomes very 'improbable', hard to verify. No *internal* criterion can guarantee the essential 'literariness' of a text. There is no assured essence or existence of literature. If you proceed to analyse all the elements of a literary work, you will never come across literature itself, only some traits which it shares or borrows, which you can find elsewhere too, in other texts, be it a matter of the language, the meanings or the referents ('subjective' or 'objective').[18]

Derrida's interest when reading a text is in trying to respond to a ghostly 'come'. If the 'event' of his *œuvre* calls for a new *ghost tense* or ghost tenses (for let's not forget, the ghost is always 'numerous'[19]), this would have to do with how his writing responds to or countersigns the ghostly and anachronistic dimensions of the literary (the coming or the coming again, the *revenance* of its ghosts) without, however, becoming ('only') literary itself. He is concerned to countersign, to produce writing events of his own. As he puts it in an essay on James Joyce's *Ulysses*: 'we must write, we must sign, we must bring about new events with untranslatable marks'.[20] There is here what he calls 'distress', 'the distress of a signature that is asking for a *yes* from the other, the pleading injunction for a countersignature'.[21] As the divided syntax suggests, the distress is on both sides. Thus he concludes: 'Only another event can sign, can countersign to bring it about that an event has already happened. This event, that we naively call the first event, can only affirm itself in the confirmation of the other: a completely other event.'[22]

Postscript

Distress, yes, I would add, but also desire. For let's remember that Derrida's work, these writing events that still await us, are also about what he calls 'the greatest possible pleasure'.[23] The connotations of the 'come' and 'coming' in his writings consistently include the sexual. Perhaps his most intensive account of the operations of signing and countersigning would be *Signsponge*, his little book on the poetry of Francis Ponge. His engagement with Ponge turns, in part, around something dared or ventured: 'What I am risking here ought to be an event,' he says near the beginning.[24] At one moment in the book Derrida seeks to describe the double and radically fictive or poematic figure of a 'single countersigned signature': it would be an 'event [that is] idiomatic every single time', 'the momentary singularity of a certain coitus of signatures'.[25] Intrigued by this sexual reference I once asked him if he would say a little more. In a wordprocessed letter dated 13 July 1991, below the 'Jacques' with which he signs himself, there is a postscript in which he writes: '"Coitus", which can have the sense you know, signifies first of all the experience that consists in going (*ire*) towards the other, to the other, with the other. A coitus of signature signifies all that, in other words the crossing of this event crossed with the sense you know.' In a short handwritten stroke he underlines the 'with' ('towards the other, to the other, with the other').[26]

14 February 2005

Notes

1. Jacques Derrida, *The Gift of Death*, trans. David Wills (Chicago: Chicago University Press, 1995), p. 54.
2. See 'Blind Cinema', Introduction to *Derrida: Screenplay and Essays on the Film* (Kirby Dick and Amy Ziering Kofman, Directors) (Manchester: Manchester University Press, 2005), pp. 10–21.
3. Jacques Derrida, *Demeure: Fiction and Testimony* (with Maurice Blanchot's *The Instant of My Death*), trans. Elizabeth Rottenberg (Stanford, CA: Stanford University Press, 2000), p. 31. ('For Derrida' was the title of the commemorative series of talks at Tate Modern, London, organised by the Forum for European Philosophy, in the Spring of 2005, of which this text originally formed a part.)
4. Jacques Derrida, *Archive Fever: A Freudian Impression*, trans. Eric Prenowitz (Chicago: Chicago University Press, 1996), p. 62. Further page references are given parenthetically in the text, abbreviated 'AF' where appropriate.
5. Jacques Derrida, *Mémoires: for Paul de Man*, trans. Cecile Lindsay, Jonathan Culler and Eduardo Cadava (New York: Columbia University Press, 1986), p. 26.
6. 'The Deconstruction of Actuality: An Interview with Jacques Derrida', trans. Jonathan Rée, in Martin McQuillan (ed.), *Deconstruction: A Reader* (Edinburgh: Edinburgh University Press, 2000), p. 548.

7. Ibid., p. 548.
8. Ibid., p. 536.
9. See Jacques Derrida, 'Limited Inc a, b, c . . .', trans. Samuel Weber and Jeffrey Mehlman, in *Limited Inc* (Evanston, IL: Northwestern University Press, 1988), p. 90.
10. Ibid., p. 58.
11. Jacques Derrida, 'Psyche: Inventions of the Other', trans. Catherine Porter, in *Psyche: Inventions of the Other*, vol. 1, eds Peggy Kamuf and Elizabeth Rottenberg (Stanford, CA: Stanford University Press, 2007), p. 6.
12. 'The Deconstruction of Actuality', p. 535, tr. mod. (The original French version of this passage can be found in Jacques Derrida and Bernard Steigler, *Échographies de la télévision: Entretiens filmés* (Paris: Galilée-INA, 1996), pp. 19–20.)
13. Jacques Derrida, 'This Strange Institution Called Literature' (interview with Derek Attridge), trans. Geoffrey Bennington and Rachel Bowlby, in *Acts of Literature*, ed. Derek Attridge (London and New York: Routledge, 1992), p. 67. In the original French version of this interview, Derrida glides into English: 'un "Shakespeare expert"'.
14. All Shakespeare quotations and references (apart from *Hamlet*) are here based on *The Norton Shakespeare*, eds Stephen Greenblatt, Walter Cohen, Jean E. Howard and Katherine Eisaman Maus (New York: Norton, 1997).
15. *Hamlet* quotations and references are based on the updated edition of the New Cambridge Shakespeare text, ed. Philip Edwards (Cambridge: Cambridge University Press, 2003).
16. Jacques Derrida, 'My Chances/*Mes Chances*: A Rendezvous with Some Epicurean Stereophonies', trans. Irene Harvey and Avital Ronell, in *Psyche: Inventions of the Other*, vol. 1, eds Peggy Kamuf and Elizabeth Rottenberg (Stanford, CA: Stanford University Press, 2007), p. 349.
17. See Harold Jenkins (ed.), *Hamlet* (London: Methuen, 1982), p. 174.
18. 'This Strange Institution Called Literature', p. 73.
19. See Jacques Derrida, *Spectres of Marx: The State of the Debt, the Work of Mourning, and the New International*, trans. Peggy Kamuf (London: Routledge, 1994), p. 138.
20. Jacques Derrida, 'Ulysses Gramophone: Hear Say Yes in Joyce', trans. Tina Kendall and Shari Benstock in *Acts of Literature*, ed. Derek Attridge (London and New York: Routledge, 1992), p. 282.
21. Ibid., p. 283.
22. Ibid., p. 309.
23. 'This Strange Institution Called Literature', p. 56.
24. Jacques Derrida, *Signéponge/Signsponge*, trans. Richard Rand (New York: Columbia University Press, 1984), p. 18.
25. Ibid., pp. 48–50.
26. The original French of Derrida's letter runs as follows: '"Coït", qui peut avoir le sens que vous savez, signifie d'abord l'expérience qui consiste à aller (*ire*) vers l'autre, à l'autre, <u>avec</u> l'autre. Un coït de signature signifie tout cela, c'est-à-dire le croisement de cet événement croisé avec le sens que vous savez.'

Woo't

What to call Jacques Derrida's writings on mourning, writings that meddle, so lovingly, with all established conceptions of mourning? And what to call some writing, after him, for him, in eulogy, mourning, tribute and memory?

This question of naming is addressed by Pascale-Anne Brault and Michael Naas, the editors of *The Work of Mourning*, in their remarkable introductory essay to the English publication of that text.[1] It is a strange book, *The Work of Mourning*, published as a collection in English in 2001, and only later in French, under the title *Chaque fois unique, la fin du monde*, with an additional foreword (*Avant-propos*) and short texts on Gérard Granel and Maurice Blanchot, in 2003.[2] The would-be shift, gap, alteration between these titles is striking: there is no other book by Derrida that has been so differently named, at least between French and English, in this fashion. As he comments in the foreword to *Chaque fois unique, la fin du monde*, it is 'a strange artefact: the translation or the return of this book in French [*un étrange artéfact: la traduction ou le retour de ce livre en français*]'.[3] Derrida notes that he would never have dared to take the initiative of such a collection in France and proposes that the book is the work of Brault and Naas, it is *their* book.[4] And at the end of the foreword he invokes another book, the conditional dare and virtual artefactuality of a grafting of one book onto or before another: 'If I dared to propose a true introduction to this book, it would be the essay I am publishing simultaneously with Galilée, *Béliers. Le dialogue ininterrompu: entre deux infinis, le poème* [Rams: Uninterrupted Dialogue – Between Two Infinities, the Poem].'[5] 'If I dared . . . it would be': I stress this tense and this word, 'would', in English. (We will come back to it, and to 'Rams'.)

The alien nature of this book or of these books, turning or returning, between English and French, between being the work of Derrida and being (at least according to him) the work of Brault and Naas, the split or double titling (*The Work of Mourning, Chaque fois unique, la fin du monde*), has to do, perhaps above all, with the persisting difficulty of what to call the texts therein. In their Introduction to *The Work of Mourning*, Brault and Naas stress the variety of these texts: there are 'letters of condolence addressed to family members', 'eulogies read at the grave site', 'words of tribute first published in newspapers' and 'memorial essays read at colloquia a few or even many months after the death'. They remark that all of these texts are nevertheless 'part of a recognisable genre, even if there is no single apt term to describe it' (p. 18). And indeed they go on to provide a superbly measured and lucid account of this 'recognisable genre'. They put aside 'the dangers of the genre' in order to affirm and explore the 'rhetorical gestures' that these 'texts of mourning' share with 'other eulogies or words of remembrance' (p. 20). There is nonetheless perhaps something slightly curious about this moment, this moving away from the question of the absence of the 'apt term' in order to focus on 'the generality of the genre'. Brault and Naas cite this last phrase from the letter that Derrida writes to the widow of his friend Max Loreau: 'the discourse of mourning is more threatened than others, though it should be less, by the generality of the genre' (p. 95).

Some of the pieces in *The Work of Mourning* bear titles that are simply descriptions, such as 'Letter to Francine Loreau', 'Letter to Didier Cahen' or 'Text Read at Louis Althusser's Funeral'. Others are more explicitly marked, and self-remarking, as texts without titles, texts for which any title would be inept and even unbearable. The text on Sarah Kofman, for example, is presented under the heading of a series of dots (eight in the English version, six in the French): '. . . . . . .'. The text begins: 'At first, I did not know, and still I do not know what title to give to these words. What is the gift of a title?' (p. 168). Derrida goes on to suggest that the best title would be 'Sarah Kofman', but immediately retracts this, confessing that he is 'afraid of being unable to measure up to it'. And then he proposes that it is with the question of the gift that he is most preoccupied, thus proceeding to specify: 'The title would then be "The Gifts of Sarah Kofman [*Les dons de Sarah Kofman*]"' (pp. 168/207). But he does not in fact make this the title. The text is titled without title, elliptically, so many dots like so many little stones: . . . . The title remains of the order of the 'would', of what 'would be [*serait*]'. And elsewhere in the book, in the case of Derrida's text on Lyotard, 'Lyotard and *Us*' ('Lyotard et *Nous*'), likewise there was initially no title. Brault and Naas note: 'The title was chosen after the talk was first given; it was originally delivered without a title' (p. 116). As they make clear in their introductory essay, the texts gathered together in *The Work of Mourning* are not only painful, moving and powerful expressions *of* mourning, but also remarkable meditations *on* the 'discourse of mourning'. Yet these texts are, in addition, consistently, lingeringly preoccupied with this question of the difficulty or impossibility of titling, with the desire or need to 'protest' (as Derrida deploys that word, in memory of Kofman (p. 169)), to refuse or refute the 'recognisable genre'.

What to call these texts? It is as if there were a constant, ongoing allusion to the title of one of his texts on the subject of titles, 'Title (to be specified)', or rather perhaps 'Title (not to be specified)'.[6] In the texts published in *The Work of Mourning*, perhaps more markedly than anywhere else in Derrida's *œuvre*, there is a sense of what he calls 'the madness of the title', an unease regarding the processes by which (as he puts it) 'a title always has the structure of a name, it induces effects of the proper name and, under this title, it remains in a very singular fashion foreign to language as discourse, in the very way it introduces an abnormal referential function and a violence'.[7] Above all in the context of words offered in the form of some kind of funeral oration, there is even something rather 'indecent' about a title. As he suggests in his untitled words on Sarah Kofman, a title 'would imply the violent selection of a perspective, an abusive interpretative framing or narcissistic reappropriation' (p. 168).

◆

What to say, how to speak about the friend or loved one who has died? Being alive is being lost, at a loss, being at a loss for words not only to describe the loss but also to say something, anything, that would *not* appear fundamentally indecent, even obscene. As Derrida remarks at the beginning of his originally titleless text on the death of Jean-François Lyotard: 'From now on bereft of the possibility of speaking or addressing oneself to the friend himself, one is condemned merely to speak *of* him . . . But how can the survivor speak in friendship of the friend without a "we" indecently setting in, without an "us" incessantly slipping in?' (WM, p. 216). And yet silence would be no solution. 'To silence or forbid the "we" would be to enact another, no less serious violence. The injustice would be at least as great as that of still saying "we"' (p. 216).

Impossible to speak, impossible not to speak. It is characteristic of the extraordinary force of affirmation in Jacques Derrida's work that this apparently paralysing double-bind is submitted to a turn, or indeed appears to have taken place thanks to a turn, in the very thinking of the 'we'. By the end of the third paragraph of 'Lyotard and *Us*' (as this text later came to be called), he has sketched a sense of 'thinking' that will occupy not only the rest of his discourse but the rest of *us*, 'we' the survivors. He addresses the trembling strangeness of this 'we' through a play on words, across languages, between French and English, and beyond: 'we' [*oui*] is 'yes'. How can he, the surviving friend, sign a 'we' for himself and Jean-François Lyotard, the friend who has died? *Unless*, he says – releasing one of those casts or jetties of thought and feeling that will have solicited, affected, altered everything – 'unless a certain experience of "surviving" is able to give *us*, beyond life and death, what it alone can give, and give to the "we", yes [*oui*], its first vocation, its meaning or its origin. Perhaps its thought, *thinking* itself' (p. 216). 'We': *yes*. What would be the 'first vocation' of this vocation, this vocable? How hear or say 'we'?

His sentence doubles and divides the sense and origin of the 'we/ *oui*'. Perhaps, he says, perhaps thinking itself, the very thought of 'we' is launched by 'a certain experience of "surviving"' or living on. This has to do with giving, he suggests, in other words with what might appear a terrible gift: the verb 'to give' (*donner*) occurs three times, a donging of *donner*, like a knell, in the first of these sentences.[8] 'Unless a certain experience of "surviving" is able to give *us*, beyond life and death, what it alone can give, and give to the "we", yes [*oui*], its first vocation, its meaning or its origin.'

'Learn to live': this 'strange watchword', as he calls it, watches over *Spectres of Marx*.[9] This is not something you do by yourself, it is to be learnt 'only from the other and by death', 'from the other at the edge of life' (p. xviii). To learn to live is 'to learn to live *with* ghosts, in the upkeep, the conversation, the company, or the companionship, in the commerce without commerce of ghosts' (p. xviii). This preliminary allusion to something spectral without or beyond commerce connects with what is perhaps the most crucial flight of thought passing across *Spectres of Marx*, namely justice. 'To be just' is linked to that notion of 'unconditional dignity' that he cites from Kant, a value of dignity that is beyond 'any market price' (p. xx). Justice 'must carry beyond *present* life, life as *my* life or *our* life'. The obligation or commitment of justice 'carries life beyond present life or its actual being-there, its empirical or ontological actuality: not toward death but toward a *living-on* [sur-vie], namely, a trace of which life and death would themselves be but traces and traces of traces, a survival whose possibility in advance comes to dis-join or dis-adjust the identity to itself of the living present as well as of any effectivity' (p. xx). To be just with Derrida (with his writing and thinking) is, as much as anything else, to be just with, to try to do justice to this thought of justice, and living on.

♦

To be specified: no normal mourning. That's life. To queer oneself, queer on oneself, queer oneself on, thinking on, on 'on', on living on.

♦

Disappearing into flowers, as if for a phantom wreath, for that and for the other, for the rest of us, anonymous fors, here is a passage from Elizabeth Bowen's *A World of Love*:

> Life works to dispossess the dead, to dislodge and oust them. Their places fill themselves up; later people come in; all the room is wanted. Feeling alters its course, is drawn elsewhere or seeks renewal from other sources. When of love there is not enough to go round, inevitably it is the dead who must go without: we tell ourselves that they do not depend on us, or that they do not have our requirements. Their continuous dying while we live, their repeated deaths as each of us die who knew them, are not in nature to be withstood. Obstinate rememberers of the dead seem to queer themselves or show some signs of a malady; in part they come to share the dead's isolation, which it is not in their power to break down – for the rest of us, so necessary is it to let the dead go that we expect they may be glad to be gone. Greatest of our denials to them is a part to play; it appears that they now cannot touch or alter whatever may be the existent scene – not only are they not here to participate, but there would be disorder if they *were* here. Their being left behind in their own time caused estrangement between them and us, who must live in ours.
>
> But the recognition of death may remain uncertain, and while that is so nothing is signed and sealed. Our sense of finality is less hard-and-fast: two world wars have raised their query to it. Something has challenged the law of nature: it is hard . . . not to sense the continuation of the apparently cut-off life, hard not to ask, but *was* dissolution possible so abruptly, unmeaningly and soon? And if not dissolution, instead, what?[10]

With him (and recalling his suggestion that 'living' is always 'living with'[11]) we should seek to establish a sense of the context for these remarks. Absent without leave, or absent without official leave: Bowen's novel, published in 1955, plays on the acronym of its title. It summons up, without ever specifying it as such, the strangeness of that phrase. AWOL: to be specified. 'Leave' is liberty or permission to depart or be absent, but it is the time of this absence as well, and of course it can also signify the farewell itself, as in taking one's leave.[12] The passage I have just cited from Bowen's novel seems to articulate and disarticulate all of these senses of leave, extending to the figure indeed of taking leave of one's senses.

The novel is about a young man called Guy who died in the First World War. He is absent, ghostly, at the strange heart of the work: he has died before the narrative begins. The novel is set in Ireland, at the house he has left behind, and the narrative focuses on the women who loved him, in particular his cousin Antonia and his fiancée Lilia, and on a twenty-year-old girl (Lilia's elder daughter) called Jane, not yet living at the time of Guy's death. How to live on? That is the question the novel poses and explores vis-à-vis these women who knew Guy. But Bowen also foregrounds a transgenerational logic, that is to say the life of the survivors of survivors, living on beyond those who live on, and above all thanks to the possibilities of writing. Guy has left behind, in the attic of the house, some love letters, which Jane finds and reads. Bowen thus offers a compelling account of the haunting, generative effects of writing itself, of how it is possible, in the context of letters without specified addressee, to identify oneself with and in writing, fall in love with letters, literally, fall in love through a bundle of letters or *envois*, like so many postcards. You can fall in love through reading him. He comes back, or perhaps *comes for the first time*, there, in the reading of those who survive the survivors.[13]

An attempt at a few *quick* remarks about the passage quoted. There is a provocation here, I believe, to think about the analytical force of literary fiction, to *think on* the ways in which a work of literature can, for example, both inscribe itself historically and analyse that history, here above all perhaps as a history *of* ghosts and mourning. Bowen is one of the greatest twentieth-century writer-analysts of mourning in the English language.[14] As *A World of Love* brings forcefully into focus, two world wars (the first of course also marked, not by chance, by the writing and publication of what is arguably the first explicit attempt to theorise this topic, namely Freud's essay 'Mourning and Melancholia', written in 1915 and first published in 1917) have altered our thinking about mourning and living on.[15] 'Our' thinking: what is perhaps especially enigmatic about this Bowen passage is the shifting shadowy delineation of the 'we', 'us' and 'our'. The narrative perspective entails a kind of 'omniscience-in-mourning'.[16] The fiction of omniscient narration itself appears broken up by these wars. It is no longer a matter of figuring narratorial omniscience as at once useful and an object of satirical fun (a strategy more familiar in the writings of, for example, Henry James), but rather of a gravely caught up, strangely divided 'we'. Those who 'queer themselves' might look to be distinct from the narratorial 'we', in other words from 'the rest of us'. (This 'rest' suggests primarily those who are not 'rememberers', of course, though also carries a more cryptic intimation of what, as a result, is left of them, the remains.) But the 'signs of a malady', the sense of attentiveness to 'obstinate remember[ing]', the suggestion of the 'us' as necessarily 'queer[ed]', increase as the passage unfolds.[17] The queerness is perhaps already intimated in the eerie inversions of the first sentence, in which life is defined by its work on death, in a knell-like series of d-sounds and insistent sibilants (*dispossess, dead, dislodge, oust*): it is the dead, not the living, who are to be – but are not yet – dispossessed, moved on, ousted. The queerness is there in the strange manner in which the dead figure as still carrying on, in 'their continuous dying' and in 'their repeated deaths'. And above all it is there in the 'But' that ushers in the second paragraph, the sense of a 'recognition [that would] remain uncertain', a signature or countersignature unfinished, a fundamental 'query[ing]' of 'our sense of finality'. As readers we, yes, we too perhaps find ourselves here queerly, queryingly suspended and divided.

I have been meddling with the context of Bowen's sentences: that is the law of citation. As we may recall from Derrida's 'Border Lines', to present another text to be read – especially if it is just an *extract* of another text – is inevitably to mess with it.[18] No citation without the violence of tearing out of context and imposing, however fleetingly, a recontextualisation. The passage I have quoted from the opening of Chapter 4 of *A World of Love* is in fact preceded by a single sentence, constituting a stand-alone paragraph:

> Antonia thought, so there *is* more to happen. (p. 44)[19]

The sentence refers to the end of the preceding chapter (Bowen's writing ousts, breaks down, jumps the borders of chapter-divisions – 'everywhere is a frontier' (p. 79), as we read later – just as it seems endlessly to be up to something shady with syntax and the structure of words). There we learn that Antonia chances to see Jane 'disappearing into the flowering elder', in other words to realise where the young girl is hiding the love letters.[20] So: Bowen sows and sews this 'so', leading us to think, at first perhaps, that what follows is *also* what 'Antonia thought'. 'Antonia thought, so there *is* more to happen. Life works to dispossess the dead, to dislodge and oust them . . .' But, at the same time, the paragraph break and the alteration in tone and style (from the informality of the transcribed thought – 'so there *is* more to happen' – to the formality of 'Life works to dispossess the dead . . . Feeling alters its course, is drawn elsewhere . . . When of love there is not enough to go round . . .') comport with the sense of another voice. These are no longer simply the transcribed thoughts of a character (themselves presented to us by virtue of that structure of telepathy or magical thinking which is at the very heart, the *mysterious core* of literary fiction), but rather of the figure of the narrator whose queer 'we' is uncertainly more and other than that of a fictional character. More and other, but at the same time sowed, sewn up, in a space of thinking, or *thinking on*, both literary and analytical, fictive and historical, spectral and real.

A query has been raised: Bowen's phrase ('raised their query') recalls the queerness or self-queering of the preceding paragraph at the same time as evoking spectrality (wars raise ghosts). If a query has been raised, this has to do with a new kind of writing in which telepathy is at once acknowledged ('Antonia thought . . .') and encrypted; voice and narrative perspective disseminate; and the question of history (the catastrophes of two world wars and their consequences for thinking about mourning) becomes an analytical or theoretical focus of the literary work. There is no final gathering up in the alleged unity of some Christianised or Christianising 'omniscience', but rather a new, queer construal of the telepathic in writing (between a narrator and a character, between the living and the dead, strange distances and disjunctions *within* the 'we'; *tele-pathos*: suffering, feeling, thinking in and of distance), engaging an unprecedented attentiveness to death and signing alike as uncertain, not recognisable, not yet, not now.

♦

Not so quick, then, says the novel. *A World of Love* is about the 'not-dead' (p. 45). 'You're far too quick to assume people are dead' (p. 37), as one of the characters comments. (How quickly should one read 'quick', its ironies and abeyances, in the work of Elizabeth Bowen?) The passage cited earlier concludes with the question: 'And if not dissolution, instead, what?' But then Bowen's text goes on: 'This had been so, so far, for Antonia in the case of her cousin Guy: yes, though a generation was mown down his death seemed to her an invented story' (pp. 44–5). *Sown*: mown down. A magical so-and-so, this writing, weaving 'we', reaving bereaving, the Bowen narrator, Antonia, omniscience-in-mourning, history-in-telepathy: 'This had been so, so far . . .' *So*: the 'invented story' is of Guy's death – as if there would be, from now on, no story of someone's dissolution without a knotting or notting of now, without (in other words) another thinking of invention and remembering, love letters, death and dying, mourning and being queer. So many nots, to be or not to be read: 'not enough to go round', 'do not depend', 'have not our requirements', 'not in nature', 'not in their power', 'they now cannot touch or alter', 'not only are they not', 'hard not to sense', 'not to ask', 'if not dissolution'. The name of the author of these letters with whom the survivor falls in love is not legible, we are told, beyond the 'squirl' of a 'knot' (pp. 41–2). The signature is still to come: 'nothing is signed and sealed'. In the knot or net of these homophones, rhyming and half-rhyming, from 'not' to 'what' ('And if not dissolution, instead, what?'), instead of dissolution there is a *what* for *we*, for us, the *obstinate* ('obstinate rememberers of the dead'): obstinet and knot, obstinotted wot.

◆

What would, or who, without word, wot watch, witless, to say not? Not goodbye, letting go, denying a part to play: not concerning someone to whom one will never stop speaking, or never stop wishing to speak. How speak or write about someone who is dead, obstinately dead (for that is also what Bowen's sentences insist on, obstinate remembering is *of the dead* themselves, being in memory of the dead, 'shar[ing] the dead's isolation'), but someone without whose thinking, speech and writing, without whose continuing colloquy, however spectral, living on is not imaginable? Woo't? For a long time I have been in love with this word, if it is one. These four letters make up a cryptic vocable, a strange sort of portmanteau, starting with the apostrophe indicating an elision, the ghostly slipping of two words into one. What is *woo't*? It occurs in Shakespeare, specifically in *Hamlet* (*c.*1600–1) and *Antony and Cleopatra* (*c.*1606).[21] It does not seem to merit any special attention among editors. It generally elicits a cursory note in which it is glossed as a colloquial form of the second person singular of 'wilt', that is to say a condensation of 'wilt' and 'thou'. As the editor of the second series Arden *Antony and Cleopatra* (1954), M. R. Ridley, summarises: *woo't* is 'a common form = *wilt*'.[22]

  'Woo't' is *colloquial*. So say Harold Jenkins (editor of the Arden *Hamlet*), G. R. Hibbard (editor of the Oxford *Hamlet*), Philip Edwards (editor of the Cambridge *Hamlet*), David Bevington (editor of the Cambridge *Antony and Cleopatra*), John Wilders (editor of the Arden Third Series *Antony and Cleopatra*) and Michael Neill (editor of the Oxford *Anthony and Cleopatra*).[23] There is a remarkable consensus, a veritable party-line of 'colloquial' on this subject. But the widespread critical inclination to characterise 'woo't' as 'colloquial' is perhaps misleading. Indeed, there is perhaps something questionable about the idea of categorising *any* example of Shakespeare's language as 'colloquial'. For the earliest recorded instance of 'colloquial' in the sense of 'belonging to common speech; characteristic of or proper to ordinary conversation, as distinguished from formal or elevated language' (*OED*, sense 2), according to the *OED*, is in 1752, when Samuel Johnson writes of the English language and the need 'to clear it from colloquial barbarisms'. The anachronistic use of 'colloquial' to describe Shakespeare's writing, then, would go along with a similar insistence, among Shakespeare editors and critics, on the terms 'pun' and 'quibble'.[24]

There is also something at least a little ironic about the supposed colloquialism of 'woo't' in light of the fact that, in the *OED* (will, *v.*[1], section 3), its first recorded use is given as 1602, in *Hamlet*. What neater instance in the *OED* of the colloquial as the *literary*? But the critical unison about 'woo't' as 'colloquial' is doubtless also resonant and suggestive in other ways. These Shakespeare editors are doubtless not so wrong after all: their colloquial colloquy, their univocal harmony would then be a response to something strangely intimate in this 'woo't', raising in turn a query about tone, about how 'woo't' sounds, how to say or hear it. In fact this word (if it is one) is rare in Shakespeare: it is an uncommon compound, a compounding of singular force and strangeness, at once a projecting and stopping of voice on the question of living on, death and mourning. *Woo't*: terrible, even unbearable, especially perhaps in so far as it would be a matter of trying to sound or hear it together, across or between the two plays in question, its occurrences in *Hamlet* and *Antony and Cleopatra* apparently opposed yet mingling.

What a woo't, already dissolving or dissolved! What a formation, in deformation!

◆

In the earlier play 'woo't' has to do with a kind of dismal violence, a sense of what Gertrude refers to as absolute or 'mere madness' (V, i, 251). It is a sort of knell, a 'bringing home of bell and burial' (V, i, 201–2) marking the appalling moment at or in Ophelia's grave, when Hamlet challenges Laertes on the subject of mourning. Hamlet has just realised whose burial he is witnessing: 'What, the fair Ophelia!' (V, i, 209). He says nothing else until he approaches the grave, now addressing Laertes: '*What* is he *whose* grief / Bears such an emphasis? *whose* phrase of sorrow / Conjures the wandering stars, and makes them stand / Like wonder-wounded hearers?' (V, i, 221–4, my emphases). He has been roused to this fury by Laertes' speech ('O treble woe . . .': V, i, 213) and his leaping into his sister's grave. Subject of mourning: O woe, of *what* or *whose*? Appearing nowhere else in Shakespeare's writings (or, according to the *OED*, in anyone else's writings) until this point, 'woo't' bursts in, or out, as if bursting its speaker, bursting its cerements, five times in two lines. 'Woo't' thus sounds and resounds through what is perhaps the most egregious and distasteful passage in Shakespeare's play. As George MacDonald remarked in 1885: 'Perhaps this is the speech in all the play of which it is most difficult to get into a sympathetic comprehension.'[25] It is the 'theme' on which Hamlet declares he will fight with the dead woman's brother, 'Until my eyelids will no longer wag' (V, i, 234). 'Wag' here has the sense of flickering, the last sign of life in a dying man. A wonder-wounded wandering, then, from 'woe' to 'what' to 'wag' to 'wilt' to 'woo't':

HAMLET	I loved Ophelia; forty thousand brothers
	Could not with all their quantity of love
	Make up my sum. What wilt thou do for her?
CLAUDIUS	Oh he is mad Laertes.
GERTRUDE	For love of God forbear him.
HAMLET	'Swounds, show me what thou't do.
	Woo't weep, woo't fight, woo't fast, woo't tear thyself?
	Woo't drink up eisel, eat a crocodile?
	I'll do't. Dost thou come here to whine,
	To outface me with leaping in her grave?
	Be buried quick with her, and so will I.

                                                          (V, i, 236–46)

Hamlet's questions run counter to his own earlier declaration that grief entails 'that within which passes show' (I, ii, 85); it is 'not alone [his] inky cloak' and other 'trappings and . . . suits of woe' that 'denote [him] truly' (I, ii, 77–86). In the earlier part of the play it is precisely not, for Hamlet, a question of what Claudius coolly calls 'mourning duties' (I, ii, 88).

Thanks to Jacques Derrida we now have new formulations, new ways of thinking about this strange, quasi-oxymoronic conjunction or disjoining of 'mourning' and 'duty'. As he puts it in the essay on *Hamlet* entitled 'The Time is Out of Joint', in 1993: the idea of putting an end to mourning 'presumes (but this is one of the enigmas of [Shakespeare's] play, as it is of mourning) that mourning depends on us, in us, and not on the other in us'.[26] If there are 'mourning duties' they would include a duty *not* to mourn, a duty moreover that can never be simply dutiful but, on the contrary, beyond any and all duty, like justice. Lovingly, obstinately, mourning would entail the refusal to mourn or, phrased less negatively perhaps, a fidelity to *not* mourn, an interminable affirmation of being unable to be done with one's mourning. Fidelity and infidelity double up. As he comments in an interview with Anne Berger in 1983:

Is fidelity mourning? It is also the contrary: the faithful one is someone who is in mourning. Mourning is an interiorisation of the dead other in oneself; to complete one's mourning is to keep [*faire le deuil, c'est garder:* to complete or

be done with one's mourning is to keep, to guard, watch over or look after],
it is an experience of fidelity, but it is also the contrary. Hence the impossibility of completing one's mourning, and even the will not to mourn, is also a
form of fidelity. If to mourn and not to mourn are two forms of fidelity and
two forms of infidelity, the only thing remaining – and this is where I speak
of semi-mourning [*demi-deuil*] – is an experience between the two; I cannot
complete my mourning for everything I lose, because I want to keep it, and at
the same time, what I do best is to mourn, is to lose it, because by mourning,
I keep it inside me. And it is this terrible logic of mourning that I talk about
all the time, that occupies me all the time, whether in 'Fors' or in *Glas*, it is
this terrible fatality of mourning: semi-mourning or double mourning. The
psychoanalytic discourse, despite its subtlety and necessity, does not go into
this fatality, this necessity. This is the double constraint of mourning.[27]

What is the time of this double or portmanteau mourning? Or to put
it perhaps another way: what is the time of 'woo't'? From *Hamlet* to
Antony and Cleopatra, between these two plays, 'woo't' prompts us
to think, to think *on*, the possibilities of a new ghost tense or, rather
perhaps, new ghost tenses.[28]

As if he has completely forgotten what we know he knows, then,
Hamlet demands that Laertes 'show' – and vie with him in showing –
what is irreducible to showing, what goes beyond the 'actions that a
man might play' (I, ii, 84). In this agonistic irruption of sui-homicidal
homo-fraternal violence, Hamlet's attempts to learn to live appear literally to be in the grave. What is additionally sickening about his speech
to Laertes no doubt has to do with its indecency in interrupting the time
of inhumation, intensifying the already pervasive sense of 'maimèd rites'
(V, i, 186). Coming between the time of death and burial, it calls to mind
some of the more tasteless or disgusting statements that were published
in the supposedly serious and responsible British press shortly after 9
October 2004.[29]

'Woo't weep, woo't fight, woo't fast, woo't tear thyself? / Woo't drink
up eisel, eat a crocodile? / I'll do it': if the movement of these challenges
is increasingly nauseating, it is also increasingly burlesque. Weeping,
fighting, fasting, and tearing or cutting oneself lead seemingly seam-
lessly on to drinking vinegar (epitomising bitterness as well as carrying
Christ-like sacrificial connotations) and eating a crocodile. This last is
perhaps one of the most disturbing instances of the indefinite article in
Shakespeare – not 'eat crocodile' as in 'eat chicken', but eat an entire,
entirely unappetising, uncertainly dead or alive crocodile. At the same
time, however, Hamlet's 'woo't' speech, perhaps more shockingly
than any other in the play, compels us to acknowledge the singularity
of mourning and to sense the immeasurable: to face what cannot be
'outface[d]', what is alien to comparisons in terms of 'quantity' (whether

in love or mourning, love and mourning). This passage illustrates the force of the proposition Derrida makes in 1984, in the essay about the Cold War and the threat of nuclear conflict, entitled 'No Apocalypse, Not Now': 'There is no common measure able to persuade me that a personal mourning is less grave than a nuclear war.'[30]

More violently perhaps than anywhere else in Shakespeare's death-laden play, the realisation of death ('What, the fair Ophelia!') and the demonstration of mourning ('Woo't . . .?') are thrown together, in collision, two in one and one in two. It is a matter of speed, of the traumatic impact on the realisation of the present (that the beloved is dead: hallucination or memory?) of a strange second-person inflexional form. As the *OED* suggests, 'woo't' has numerous variants including 'wilt', 'wult', 'wolt', 'w'oot', 'wot' and 'wut' (*OED*, will, $v.^1$, section 3). The Second Quarto text (1604–5) of *Hamlet*, indeed, prints not 'woo't', but 'woul't', glossed by Ann Thompson and Neil Taylor as 'wouldst thou (colloquial)'.[31] But 'woo't' is neither exactly a 'wilt' nor a 'wouldst (thou)'. It is as if the 'what' ('What, the fair Ophelia!'), the exclamation of incredulity that the beloved is dead, were still resonating in the 'woo't'. 'Woo't': Shakespeare's cryptic foreshortening or verbal deformation for the experience of posthuming while you breathe.[32] It is as if all grief and mourning were doubled up, arrested and encrypted in the iteration of this ghostly performative, at once question, defiance, challenge or dare, a querying of life, 'buried quick'.

♦

The association between 'woo't' and being buried alive provides one link between the passage in *Hamlet* and the – in some respects contrasting – 'woo't' of *Antony and Cleopatra*. In both cases, however, it is a matter of recognising the fact, apparently overlooked by all of Shakespeare's editors, that 'woo't' is not 'wilt' or 'wouldst (thou)'. 'Woo't' is 'woo't':

> ANTONY   The miserable change now at my end
> Lament nor sorrow at, but please your thoughts
> In feeding them with those my former fortunes,
> Wherein I lived the greatest prince o'th'world,
> The noblest . . .
>   . . . Now my spirit is going;
> I can no more.
> CLEOPATRA   Noblest of men, woo't die?
> Hast thou no care of me? Shall I abide
> In this dull world, which in thy absence is
> No better than a sty? O see, my women:

[Antony dies]

The crown o'th'earth doth melt. My lord!
O, withered is the garland of the war;
The soldier's pole is fall'n! Young boys and girls
Are level now with men; the odds is gone,
And there is nothing left remarkable
Beneath the visiting moon. *[She starts to faint]*

(*Antony and Cleopatra*, IV, xv, 53–70)

'Woo't' is 'woo't', a querying vocable, of separation and elision, going and remaining, neither simply futural ('will', 'will you', 'wilt thou die?') nor conditional ('would', 'would you die?'), a portmanteau of times in which sound and sense breaks up, as if carrying in the cloak of its clock 'woe', 'woo', 'wound' and 'wood' (the word for 'mad' we find, for example in *Venus and Adonis*, in 'Life-poisoning pestilence, and frenzies wood'), and 'why', and 'what' (precisely as if anticipating Cleopatra's own last words, the seemingly ungrammatical, extraordinary aposiopesis, 'What should I stay –': V, ii, 307), and 'wot' (earlier she uses the questioning phrase 'wot'st thou?', in other words 'do you know?', 'do you think?': I, v, 23), and 'world', all withered, all *whithered*.[33] Woo't: it is also, of course, an anagrammatic question of the two ('o two?'), jumbling two in one, two in 'o'. You become a letter ('t'), words out of joint, melting, falling, discandying. No, not now: it would be the end of the world.

'Noblest of men, woo't die?', asks Cleopatra. 'Woo't' has already been sounded in the play: in Act IV, scene ii Antony asks Enobarbus, 'Woo't thou fight well?' (IV, ii, 7). (In the First Folio of 1623, the only authoritative text for the play, these words are not followed by an interrogation mark, as if again suggesting the way that Shakespeare's 'woo't' unsettles the distinction between a question and a challenge or dare: 'Woo't thou fight well', says Antony.) Cleopatra is present on stage and may or may not hear it: she cites her Antony, in any case, when she puts her insupportable question to him: 'woo't die?' *Woo't*: it is as if she were giving the word back to him, at the last, to the last. But she is also, without her knowledge, beyond any simulacrum of knowledge attributable to a character in the theatre, citing Hamlet. And Hamlet no doubt, in the strange space of Shakespeare's iteraphonia, will have been citing or calling forth Cleopatra. One 'woo't' communicates with the other, calling us to an experience *between the two*, returning to neither one nor the other, a posthuming 'woo't' beyond being. Woo't: an apparitional word that would thus acknowledge death and its unbearable, immeasurable impact, and at the same time, in a fleeting time without time, figure the to-come, still, before death, a querying, on the side of life, as to whether death could really happen.

He hasn't died yet. When does he die? There are various editorial suggestions for the moment of death: the New Cambridge has the stage direction '*Antony dies*' three lines later, just before Cleopatra says, 'The crown o'th'earth doth melt' (IV, xv, 65). Other editions (such as the Arden Second Series and the Oxford) place this stage direction *after* 'The crown o'th'earth doth melt'. The Arden Third Series has it two words later, following 'The crown o'th'earth doth melt. My lord!' The Norton Shakespeare has it a line or so earlier, after 'No better than a sty?' and immediately before 'O see, my women'. There is no such stage direction in the First Folio. The absence of such a stage direction is hardly unusual in that work, but it does perhaps help to underscore the precariousness, the quasi-miraculous temporality of Cleopatra's question. 'Noblest of men', she says, and pauses: Do you have to die? Would you? Will you? Must you? Surely not? You wouldn't now, please, no, not yet, would you, not now? Of course she doesn't say any of this, she just says: 'woo't die?' Recalling Antony's word to Enobarbus, and recalling yet also reversing, traversing and reinscribing all the raging grief and madness of Hamlet's iteration of the word (if it is one) *after death* (though not perhaps, strictly speaking, not yet, *posthumously*), it is a question of how to respond to or countersign the cryptic singularity of Cleopatra's 'woo't'. For whom, to whom is 'woo't?' said? And who says it? Does 'woo't' have a sex? In how many voices, in what tone, with what ear should we hear it? What is its time?

By way of trying to let these queries resonate more clearly, let us turn finally to Derrida's remarkable discussion of poetry, in the context of Hans-Georg Gadamer and Paul Celan, in the essay that he suggests 'would be' the 'true introduction' to the French edition of *The Work of Mourning*, namely (in its English translation) 'Rams: Uninterrupted Dialogue – Between Two Infinities, the Poem'. Originally delivered as a lecture in memory of Gadamer at the University of Heidelberg in February 2003 and published as a separate book in French later that year, this is one of the last essays Derrida was to write. In it he fore-grounds the importance of a notion of dialogue, not only between his work and Gadamer's for example, but also within speech and writing in general and, most of all perhaps, in what we call poetry. With dialogue, he suggests, there is always interruption and the sense of 'a missed encounter', an 'active and provocative trace', a 'promising trace', that carries with it something '*unheimlich*' or uncanny (pp. 136–7). Does one ever talk to oneself, Derrida wonders. He writes: 'One speaks often and too easily of interior monologue. Yet an interior dialogue precedes it and makes it possible. Dividing and enriching the monologue, such dialogue commands and orients it' (p. 138).

'Rams' focuses on the poetry of Celan, and is concerned above all to explore and respond to a single line, the last line of the poem entitled 'Grosse, Glühende Wölbung' ('Vast, Glowing Vault'). The line runs: 'Die Welt ist fort, ich muß dich tragen' ('The world is gone, I must carry you') (p. 141). It is in 'Rams' that we encounter some of Derrida's most lucid and terrible remarks on the proposition that death is 'each time unique, the end of the world' (*chaque fois unique, la fin du monde*). For example, he writes:

> Death puts an end neither to someone in the world nor to *one* world among others. Death marks each time, each time in defiance of arithmetic, the absolute end of the one and only world, of that which each opens as a one and only world, the end of the unique world, the end of the totality of what is or can be presented as the origin of the world for any unique living being, be it human or not. (p. 140)

It is in this essay too, between two infinities, that he speaks of the poem as 'the best example of untranslatability', especially as regards the experience of 'an idiom that forever defies translation and therefore demands a translation that will do the impossible, make the impossible possible in an unheard-of event' (p. 137). The dialogue, as Derrida imagined it, is not finished, either in 'Rams' or here. And perhaps this is to be picked up, as if in an unprecedented whisper or sigh, in Cleopatra's 'woo't'. In uncanny dialogue, as I have tried to suggest, not only with Antony ('woo't' was his word, and he is still alive, addressed at this moment in the single letter, 't') but also with Hamlet, Cleopatra's lips spill or slip forth a vocable that can be repeated over and over, each time unique in the theatre, and yet still to be heard, perhaps, as never before. To what will have been Antony's last words, 'Now my spirit is going; / I can no more', she responds: 'Noblest of men, woo't die?' (IV, xv, 60–1). It is about 'the world after the end of the world' (p. 140), to borrow Derrida's phrasing; and nowhere, perhaps, is this more gently or more powerfully voiced, in Shakespeare's work, than in the 'woo't'.

It is like 'the hiatus of a wound whose lips will never close', to adopt another of Derrida's formulations in 'Rams' (p. 153). Not now, protesting the now, but also resisting the future as death, neither 'wilt (thou)' nor 'wouldst (thou)', at once desiring and querying, incredible, beyond belief, 'woo't' has, perhaps, something of the 'brief' and 'elliptical' character of the poematic, as Derrida describes it in 'Che cos'è la poesia?'[34] Cleopatra's 'woo't' inscribes a world of love in defiance of the end of the world, a will or wish, neither futural nor conditional, at once appealing and abandoned to the other.[35]

Notes

1. Jacques Derrida, *The Work of Mourning*, eds Pascale-Anne Brault and Michael Naas (Chicago: Chicago University Press, 2001). Further page references are given parenthetically in the main body of the text, abbreviated 'WM' where appropriate.
2. Jacques Derrida, *Chaque fois unique, la fin du monde*, Textes présentés par Pascale-Anne Brault and Michael Naas (Paris: Galilée, 2003).
3. *Chaque fois unique, la fin du monde*, p. 10.
4. He writes: '*Ce livre est donc* leur *livre: avant tout leur* œuvre *à tous deux*' (p. 10).
5. Derrida writes: '*Si j'osais proposer une véritable introduction à ce livre-ci, ce serait l'essai que je publie simultanément aux Éditions Galilée, Béliers . . .*' (p. 11). *Béliers* appears in English as 'Rams: Uninterrupted Dialogue – Between Two Infinities, the Poem', trans. Thomas Dutoit and Philippe Romanski, in *Sovereignties in Question: The Poetics of Paul Celan*, eds Thomas Dutoit and Outi Pasanen (New York: Fordham University Press, 2005), pp. 135–63. Further page references to 'Rams' are given parenthetically in the main body of the text.
6. Jacques Derrida, 'Title (to be specified)', trans. Tom Conley, *SubStance*, 31 (1981), 5–22. The French text, 'Titre à préciser', is published in *Parages*, Nouvelle édition revue et augmentée (Paris: Galilée, 2003), pp. 205–30.
7. 'Title (to be specified)', tr. mod., pp. 11, 7; 'Titre à préciser', pp. 216, 210. To give just one example of the foreignness and referential waywardness of a title. A recent review of the English publication of Derrida's *Psyche* volumes and Joanna Hodge's *Derrida on Time* (London: Routledge, 2008), in the pages of the *Times Literary Supplement* (22 and 29 August 2008, Nos. 5499/5500, pp. 30–1), appears under the title 'Farewell to him'. I wrote the review but did not supply the title: anyone who troubles to read beyond the first paragraph (and thus take on board the advice Jacques Derrida himself once gave apropos articles in the *TLS*, namely 'always, always "*venture beyond the beginning*"': see 'Reading "beyond the beginning"; or, On the Venom in Letters: Postscript and "Literary Supplement"', in *Demeure: Fiction and Testimony*, trans. Elizabeth Rottenberg (Stanford, CA: Stanford University Press, 2000), p. 106) will discover that the review in question is about precisely the untimeliness and even impossibility of saying 'farewell to him'.
8. The original French is: '*À moins qu'une certaine expérience du survivre puisse nous donner, au-delà de la vie et de la mort, ce qu'elle serait seule à donner, à donner au nous, oui, à savoir sa première vocation, son sens ou son origine. Sa pensée peut-être, la pensée même*' (*Chaque fois unique, la fin du monde*, pp. 259–60).
9. *Spectres of Marx: The State of the Debt, the Work of Mourning, and the New International*, trans. Peggy Kamuf (London: Routledge, 1994), p. xvii. Further page references are given in the main body of the text.
10. Elizabeth Bowen, *A World of Love* (Harmondsworth: Penguin, 1983), p. 44. Further page references are given in the main body of the text.

11. See Jacques Derrida, *Politics of Friendship*, trans. George Collins (London and New York: Verso, 1997), p. 20.

12. This last phrase in turn perhaps inevitably also brings to mind the idiomatic expression 'to take French leave', to depart without notice or permission, to disappear suspiciously.

13. On this notion of 'the first coming of the other', see Jacques Derrida, *Mémoires: for Paul de Man*, trans. Cecile Lindsay, Jonathan Culler and Eduardo Cadava (New York: Columbia University Press, 1986), where he is meditating on 'the being "in us" of the other, in bereaved memory' (p. 21) and the ways in which this 'other' constitutes a kind of foreign body within the self. He writes: 'Already installed in the narcissistic structure, the other so marks the self of the relationship to self, so conditions it that the being "in us" of bereaved memory becomes the *coming* of the other, a coming of the other, and even, however terrifying this thought might be, the first coming of the other' (p. 22, tr. sl. mod.).

14. For more on this, see Andrew Bennett and Nicholas Royle, *Elizabeth Bowen and the Dissolution of the Novel* (Basingstoke: Macmillan, 1995), and Maud Ellmann, *Elizabeth Bowen: The Shadow Across the Page* (Edinburgh: Edinburgh University Press, 2003).

15. Sigmund Freud, 'Mourning and Melancholia', *Pelican Freud Library*, vol. 11, ed. Angela Richards (Harmondsworth: Penguin, 1984), pp. 245–68.

16. Cf. *Elizabeth Bowen and the Dissolution of the Novel*, p. 113 ff.

17. Cf. Derrida's phrasing at the beginning of 'Title (to be specified)': 'But this malaise lasts', 'this malady lingers on' (*Mais ce malaise dure . . .*). See 'Titre à préciser', p. 207 (my translation).

18. As Derrida puts it, rhetorically and even a touch maniacally (in a text, 'Border Lines', that is palpably playing on its bordering another text, 'Living On', printed directly above it on the page): 'How can one text, assuming its unity, give or present another to be read, without touching it, without saying anything about it, practically without referring to it?' See 'Living On: Border Lines', trans. James Hulbert, in Harold Bloom et al., *Deconstruction and Criticism* (New York: Seabury Press, 1979), p. 80.

19. As will perhaps also have been noticed, there is an ellipsis in the main passage quoted: I have cut off Bowen's text, produced a cut-off life of the text by discreetly omitting a few words in which the narrator makes it clear that the 'cut-off life' refers in particular to those who have died young in war. I leave that as it is, by leave of this passage.

20. See *A World of Love*, pp. 43–4.

21. Unless otherwise stated, quotations from these two plays are based on *Hamlet*, ed. Philip Edwards, updated edition (Cambridge: Cambridge University Press, 2003), and *Antony and Cleopatra*, ed. David Bevington (Cambridge: Cambridge University Press, 1990). G. R. Hibbard, editor of the Oxford World's Classics *Hamlet*, supposes that 'woo't' occurs also in *Henry IV Part 2* (II, ii, 55–6), and on this basis contends that '["woo't"] seems to have been associated with challenges and the like in Shakespeare's mind': see *Hamlet*, ed. Hibbard (Oxford: Oxford World's Classics, 1994), p. 333. The identification of 'woo't' in *Henry IV Part 2* is, however, contentious. The 'woo't' form does not appear at this point in the First Folio version; it is 'wilt'. The 1600 Quarto, on the other hand, gives 'wot'. Most

editors thus offer this moment in Act II, where Mistress Quickly is confronting Falstaff and his page boy, evidently challenging them to strike her: 'Thou wot, wot thou, thou wot, wot ta?' (II, i, 55–6).

22. See *Antony and Cleopatra*, Arden 2nd series, ed. M. R. Ridley (London: Methuen, 1954), p. 146.

23. See Harold Jenkins, *Hamlet* (London: Methuen, 1982), p. 392; G. R. Hibbard, *Hamlet* (Oxford: Oxford World's Classics, 1994), p. 333; Philip Edwards, *Hamlet*, updated edition (Cambridge: Cambridge University Press, 2003), p. 236; David Bevington, *Antony and Cleopatra* (Cambridge: Cambridge University Press, 1990), p. 230; John Wilders, *Antony and Cleopatra*, Arden 3rd Series (London: Thomson Learning, 2003), p. 268; Michael Neill, *Anthony and Cleopatra* (Oxford: Oxford University Press, 1994), p. 262.

24. I discuss the anachronistic critical reliance on the 'pun' and 'quibble' in more detail in *How to Read Shakespeare* (London: Granta, 2005).

25. George MacDonald, *The Tragedy of Hamlet*, quoted in *Hamlet*, ed. Philip Edwards, updated edition (Cambridge: Cambridge University Press, 2003), p. 235.

26. Jacques Derrida, 'The Time is Out of Joint', trans. Peggy Kamuf, in *Deconstruction is/in America: A New Sense of the Political*, ed. Anselm Haverkamp (New York: New York University Press, 1995), p. 20. (This text was originally delivered as a lecture at New York University in 1993.)

27. Jacques Derrida, 'Dialanguages', trans. Peggy Kamuf, in *Points . . . Interviews, 1974–1994*, ed. Elisabeth Weber (Stanford, CA: Stanford University Press, 1995), p. 151, trans. mod.; 'Dialangues', *Points de suspension: Entretiens*, ed. Elisabeth Weber (Paris: Galilée, 1992), p. 161.

28. See 'Derrida's Event' (above, and *passim*).

29. For two examples of such statements, published before the person in question had even been buried, including the very morning of the day of the funeral (12 October 2004), see Amelia Hodsdon's 'What to say about . . . The death of Derrida', in *The Guardian*, 12 October 2004, which begins: 'So, you quip, joining headline writers the world over, the father of deconstructionism has himself deconstructed'; and the editorial in *The Times* (London), for 11 October 2004, entitled 'Is Derrida Dead? A conceptual foundation for the deconstruction of mortality'. Cf. also Johann Hari's violent, enraged and similarly inane article, 'Why I won't be mourning Derrida', published the following day in *The Independent* (13 October 2004). And finally, as a sort of counter to the thinking of the portmanteau we are concerned with here, let us cite a Humpty-Dumpty-related statement, another piece of nonsense that we might variously consider shocking, laughable, irresponsible, abject or else just drearily ignorant, that appeared in the *Daily Telegraph*, another British publication (like the London *Times* and *The Independent*) ordinarily identifying itself as a 'serious' newspaper that purports to adhere to acknowledged standards of responsible journalism and statements of factual truth: 'The French philosopher Jacques Derrida, whose obituary appeared yesterday, taught a generation of academics to "deconstruct" a text. Rather than take the trouble to grasp what an author was trying to say, readers could make it

up. Derrida and his disciples treated texts like Humpty-Dumpty: when they used a word, it meant just what they chose it to mean' (Editorial, 'Deriding Derrida', *The Daily Telegraph*, 12 October 2004).

30. Jacques Derrida, 'No Apocalypse, Not Now (Full Speed Ahead, Seven Missiles, Seven Missives)', trans. Catherine Porter and Philip Lewis, in *Psyche: Inventions of the Other*, vol. 1, eds Peggy Kamuf and Elizabeth Rottenberg (Stanford, CA: Stanford University Press, 2007), p. 403.

31. See Ann Thompson and Neil Taylor, *Hamlet*, Arden 3rd series (London: Thomson Learning, 2006), p. 430.

32. I am here recalling Derrida's remarkable words: 'I posthume as I breathe [*je posthume comme je respire*].' See his 'Circumfession', trans. Geoffrey Bennington, in Bennington and Derrida, *Jacques Derrida* (Chicago: Chicago University Press, 1993), p. 26; 'Circonfession', in *Jacques Derrida* (Paris: Éditions de Seuil, 1991), p. 28. This phrase has to do as much with the future or future perfect as with any present declaration of 'death-in-life'. As Hélène Cixous notes:

> . . . feebly but still, everything can call itself future, future perfect for the one who declares – will have declared – 'I posthume as I breathe' brilliantly inventing the verb to posthume, for his own personal usage as a 'survivor' who wants to make liars of life and death. There you have him then he who dies at the top of his lungs, a buried-alive supernatural, who gets wind of a new definition of immortality through the magic of writing. A frenzy of activity. [*Une activité folle.*] He'd like to believe in it, his substitute of a lie. He writes live right in the nick of time. [*Il écrit-vit au saut du temps.*] There you have him, he who comes to life at the sound of a pun, who sniffs out and revives the verb *respire*, he mocks and swaps hats at the drop of a word [*Voilà donc celui qui se revit de calembours, qui hume et ranime le verbe* respirer, *il se moque et se troque au moi*] – knowing we'll call him a liar just when he's telling the truth, for *respire* respirare, it really is re- or post-humous, come back from the dead [*revenir à la vie*]; but then he never lies. Here's one liar who always never ceases to tell the truth and perfectly naturally, or at least so he writes. He writes as he posthumes. The writing is his survivor, she [*l'écriture, f.*] survives him.

See Hélène Cixous *Portrait of Jacques Derrida as a Young Jewish Saint*, trans. Beverley Bie Brahic (New York: Columbia University Press, 2004), pp. 58–9; *Portrait de Jacques Derrida en jeune saint juif* (Paris: Galilée, 2001), pp. 56–7.

33 For 'wood' as 'mad', see *Venus and Adonis* in William Shakespeare, *Complete Sonnets and Poems*, ed. Colin Burrow (Oxford: Oxford University Press, 2002), p. 214, l. 740. 'Wots', 'what' and 'watch' come together in *Henry V*, when the King speaks of the slave who 'little wots / What watch the king keeps to maintain the peace': see *Henry V*, ed. Andrew Gurr, updated edition (Cambridge: Cambridge University Press, 2005), IV, i, 255–6.

34. See Jacques Derrida, 'Che cos'è la poesia?', trans. Peggy Kamuf, in *Points*, pp. 288–99. As he puts it: 'A poem must be brief, elliptical by vocation' (p. 291). For more on 'Che cos'è la poesia?' see 'Forgetting Well' (below).

35. In this context 'woo't' would also seem to prefigure what Derrida has to say, apropos Hélène Cixous's work and 'the mighty power of the "might"',

the 'grammatical alchemy' of a 'would that you might live', 'that this might happen', 'would that you might hear me', would that you might not die, not now, not yet. See Jacques Derrida, *H.C. for Life, That Is to Say . . .*, trans. Laurent Milesi and Stefan Herbrechter (Stanford, CA: Stanford University Press, 2006), p. 70. 'Woo't' might thus bear witness to the necessity of 'rethink[ing]' desire as being able 'to reach where the distinction between phantasm and the so-called actual or external reality does not yet take place and has no place to be' (p. 108). I explore this *might* further, in terms of queerness and the work of E. M. Forster, in 'Impossible Uncanniness' (below).

Jacques Derrida's Language (Bin Laden on the Telephone)

— At the beginning of an essay entitled 'The Great Hoax' (first published in 1957), Maurice Blanchot writes:

> That we live in a fraudulent world where our gestures, our words and thoughts – our writings too, of course – come to us supplied with a deceptive meaning which we do not detect, which not only gets accepted by us as our own, as if it came naturally from ourselves, but which within us and by means of us dodges and divides and changes form, with the result that we ourselves employ this duplicity, sometimes for our own, barely conscious purposes, sometimes in the service of greater powers whose accomplices or victims we are: none of this, presumably, should surprise us, since Montaigne, Pascal and Montesquieu, then Hegel, Marx and Freud, in short, an impressive number of thinkers and learned men have pointed it out and demonstrated it to us, sometimes with a precision well able to dispel all doubts.[1]

There is so much in this extraordinary opening sentence which comes to us, no doubt, dodging and dividing and changing form. One could, to borrow a formulation from Jacques Derrida, spend years on it.[2] But in order to try to reckon with this 'great hoax' of which Blanchot speaks, we should also have to grasp the much shorter second sentence of his essay. He immediately starts a new paragraph: 'Yet we are not really aware of it' (p. 157). This has the violent contrariness of a turn of description in a story by D. H. Lawrence. Like Lawrence's, Blanchot's writing is intimate with psychoanalysis, at once close and counter to it, in ways that have hardly begun to be explored.[3]

— I don't know what he's talking about. It's a hoax, isn't it? He sounds like a sort of clown to me.

— A clown, yes, funny. This is precisely how Blanchot goes on to describe it:

> Thus I am a sort of clown of language who thinks he is master of what he says, all the while speaking exactly the way a greater master causes him to. Should I happen to sense this, I come upon a strange, fantastic scene which

gives me the impression of a glinting void: I suspect another who is, however, me, of fooling me incessantly; I am ready to extend this duplicity, simulation and dissimulation to everything and make it the basis of thought until, in this excessively general view of consciousness ever foreign to itself, I unexpectedly encounter the very ideology most apt to mask reality and stabilise mystification. Whence a certain anger, the idea that only action and violence will put an end to this trickery and that, if there is mystification, it is because there are mystifiers and one must deal with them first. (p. 160)

There is, in Blanchot's terms, 'another language', another speech which 'necessarily accompanies my own', even if 'I am not always aware [of it]' (p. 160). What kind of 'action and violence' could put an end to this trickery? And what has happened to Blanchot's perception in the decades since it was articulated in this little masterpiece, 'The Great Hoax'?

– One of the most obvious things, surely, is a massive shift towards focusing on the integral or constitutive place of language in determining what goes on, in cultural, social and political life, in public and in private, nationally and internationally (to use terms and distinctions that have themselves come to sound more and more archaic). This movement has been given various names – structuralism, the linguistic turn, poststructuralism, etc. It is in some respects as much in evidence in Richard Hoggart's *The Uses of Literacy* (1957) as in the essays by Roland Barthes, *Mythologies* (1957), about which Blanchot writes in 'The Great Hoax'.

– All of this is so 'obvious' that we have to suspect another fold. In recent years the dominance of so-called new technology with all its special effects, in TV, film and DVD, the speed and evanescence of e-mail and digital camera photography, mobile phones and so-called personal music systems and the Internet, has tended to elide the question of language. We don't have to trouble ourselves with questions of language so much anymore, we're too busy on our mobiles (or 'cells' as they're rather eerily known in the US), watching TV, thinking about spectaculars.

– I'm sorry: I didn't catch that.

– 'Jacques Derrida's Language (Bin Laden on the Telephone)': what kind of title is that? Some sort of joke?

– In the dialogue with Elisabeth Roudinesco published in English as *For What Tomorrow . . .*, Derrida talks a lot about psychoanalysis in terms that enable us, I think, to elaborate further on what might be called the continuing experience of the great hoax. 'We proceed', he says, 'as if psychoanalysis had never existed . . . In an entire zone of our life, we proceed as if, at bottom, we believed in the sovereign authority of the ego, of consciousness, etc., and we speak the language of this "autonomy".[4] Derrida affirms his belief in 'the ineluctable necessity of the psychoanalytic *revolution*' (p. 179), the necessity of reckoning with the 'nearly unimaginable earthquake' produced by psychoanalysis and its impact on this language of 'autonomy'. 'For', as he emphatically remarks, 'the "logic of the unconscious" remains incompatible with what defines the identity of the ethical, the political, and the juridical in its concepts, but also in its institutions, and therefore in its human experiences' (p. 179). 'In our life, as we well know, we know it too well, we keep up discourses that are equivocal, hypocritical, in the best of cases ironic, structurally ironic' (p. 179, tr. mod. / pp. 290–1). It is in terms of this sense of what is 'structurally ironic', perhaps, that we can understand something of Derrida's legacy or legacies (there is no *one* legacy).

— Come again?

— This dialogue with Roudinesco is about Derrida's language, about the way he writes as compared with certain other contemporaries. He talks about his feeling that Foucault, Lévi-Strauss, Deleuze, Althusser and Lyotard, 'despite [all their] differences in style . . . maintained a common relation to the French language, one that is at bottom very placid, very sedentary. They all write "a certain French"; they have the respect not of an academic or conventional attitude, but of a certain classicism. Their writing does not make the French language tremble' (pp. 13–14). He goes on to suggest that his own relation to the French language is that of 'a turbulent but *primordial* hand-to-hand struggle; I mean one in which the entire stakes are set, in which the essential is at stake' (p. 14, tr. mod.).[5] In these respects, he says, he 'feel[s] . . . closer to Lacan than to any of the others' he has just named. Derrida's love for the French language is 'anxious, jealous, and tormented': '[Lacan], too, has a way of *meddling with* [*toucher à*] the French language, or of *letting himself be meddled with* by it . . . I share with him a constant attention to a certain movement of the sentence, to a work, not of the signifier, but of the letter, of rhetoric, composition, address, destination, mise-en-scène' (p. 15, tr. mod. / p. 31).

— Touching, tampering or meddling with language: it is not enough to propound revolutionary ideas or theses. Mingling, in meddling voice, with Walter Benjamin, in *The Truth in Painting* (1978) Derrida suggests that an author should not 'be content to take up a position, through discourse, *on the subject* of society': he or she should 'never, even with revolutionary theses or products, stock up an apparatus of production without transforming the very structure of that apparatus, without twisting it, betraying it, attracting it out of its element.'[6] It is a question of the experience of a sort of '*faux-bond*' (a phrase also sounding as *faux-bon*, and suggestive of fake bond or title, forgery, false well-doing, leaving in the lurch, false jump, and so on[7]). As he puts it in the interview '*Ja*, or the *faux-bond* II', in 1975: 'One must meddle with *the* code', one must tamper with the 'homogeneity and the singularity of the system that orders and regulates languages and actions'.[8] It is not enough just to elaborate apparently radical or revolutionary arguments or ideas, it's a matter of how to deal with the hoax, starting with the programming or fake-bonds of language. To recall Blanchot in 'The Great Hoax', once again:

> In everything we say there is a thickness of language, a sediment of words always supplied in advance, in which ours establish themselves comfortably and almost silently. We hardly ever say anything; we just move like fugitives into a prearranged communications system, speaking a language that is already spoken, not even speaking it, but letting ourselves be spoken in it or simply letting it speak in our stead. (pp. 163–4).

— Education, education, education.

— I'm sorry. The line's breaking up.

— 'Language [is] a machine for undoing urgency', Derrida says in the 1975 interview.[9] How should we read that statement? At what speed? Here is the thinker some people still seem to want to characterise as a 'linguistic philosopher', the one who claims or believes (or so it is claimed or believed) that everything-is-language, there's nothing-outside-the-text, and so forth, here he is invoking something outside language, apparently beyond it. Urgency. Derrida's thinking is so urgent it might be more apt to speak of him as the first radically non-linguistic philosopher. Try that.

— Sometimes I have images cropping up in my head of Jacques Derrida's language. A spectral machine, yes, a mad line drawing, with remarkable hatching, done blind, or else, but this is not an alternative, a luscious, furiously green grass field featuring molehills with, in places, see-through cross-sections.

— To meddle with language, with a national language, to meddle with one's own language because it is never one's own, in order to produce a counter-signature to that language, as Derrida speaks of Celan doing to the German language, for example. 'Language can never be appropriated', Derrida remarks: 'language is never owned'.[10] And it is precisely on this account that we have what he calls the desire for idiom. This is what gives rise to those kinds of writing which, in their very idiomaticity, modify the language. He comments on this as follows:

> It is of the essence of language that language does not let itself be appropriated. Language is precisely what does not let itself be possessed but, for this very reason, provokes all kinds of movements of appropriation. Because language can be desired but not appropriated, it sets into motion all sorts of gestures of ownership and appropriation. What is at stake here politically is that linguistic nationalism is precisely one of these gestures of appropriation, a naïve gesture of appropriation . . . [P]aradoxically, what is most idiomatic, that is to say, what is most proper to a language, cannot be appropriated.[11]

No countering, we might say, no counter-institution, no countersigning of language without an idiomatic meddling. It is a question, still, of that 'structural irony' you were talking about a few moments ago.

– 'Jacques Derrida's Language (Bin Laden on the Telephone)': I have picked it up now. There is an echo on the line. This title alludes to a brief text called 'Language (*Le Monde* on the Telephone)', published in *Le Monde* in 1982.[12] This text was presented as the transcription of a telephone conversation between Derrida and the editor, but actually it is a hoax. You read the text and perhaps wonder. Or alternatively perhaps you don't. Will it have been a hoax? (This is a question that we can pretend to leave to one side, perhaps return to, but never finish thinking about: what is the time of a hoax?) When the text is republished some years later, there is a footnote which states: 'The remarks attributed to Christian Delacampagne are obviously fictive, and since certain commentators at the time thought otherwise, it is better to make clear that their author is Jacques Derrida.'[13] 'Language (*Le Monde* on the Telephone)' calls and resonates in a space of structural irony. This is not, in case anyone is wondering, a space of play that would be tantamount simply to frivolity or having fun. It is a question of trying to reckon with the force of Derrida's language in terms of what we might provisionally call the counter-hoax. It is here too that we can perhaps begin to construe the strange place and significance (in all its apparent feebleness and impertinence) of literature, of what Blanchot calls 'literature as literature', namely 'its perpetual opposition, its violent contrariness, its refusal of itself and of all natural legitimacy' (GH, p. 165). The structural irony of which Derrida speaks, then, is political: as he makes clear in *Rogues*, it is democracy that 'gives the right to irony in the public space . . . for democracy opens public space, the publicity of open space, by granting the right to a change of tone (*Wechsel der Töne*), to irony as well as to fiction, the simulacrum, the secret, literature, and so on'.[14]

– To whom should I address myself in public? To whom does a national newspaper editor wish me to address myself? Who is the addressee of a text (such as an essay or interview) in a national newspaper? In a formidable rhetorical question Derrida asks: 'Does [this addressee] exist *before* a reading which can also be active and determinant (in the sense that it is only then that the reader *would determine himself or herself*)?' (p. 172). Derrida's fictive telephone call at once evokes and affirms the logic according to which a text can in some way alter or even invent its addressee. This performative dimension of writing (whereby a text can produce unforeseeable effects, up to and including the very identification of its reader, the kind of phenomenon that is perhaps most easily grasped in relation to the experience of reading a horoscope and determining oneself as its addressee, the one to whom the words of the horoscope singularly apply, a phenomenon which Derrida explores in complex, strange and fascinating ways in another of his peculiarly 'fake' texts, 'Telepathy', focused on Freud's so-called 'fake lectures' on telepathy and occultism[15]), this performative dimension is at once mimed and ironised in the text's creation of its interlocutor, the fictional discourse of the editor. In his fictive conversation, Derrida is very clear. The editor is in fact so seduced by this clarity that he says: 'you have indeed been speaking to me about language and it's clearer than what you usually write. I'll give you some advice: dictate your books over the telephone' (p. 174).

– Of course that is just what Derrida does. All of his work is 'over the telephone'. As he demonstrates, in a series of texts over many years (I am thinking for example of all the phone-calls, including the apparent hoax phone-call from someone called Martini Heidegger, in the 'Envois'; the connections between Derrida and Freud, and between telephony and telepathy, in the text called 'Telepathy'; the telephonic network of voices in the essay on apocalyptic tone; the explorations of telephone, being and voice in 'Ulysses Gramophone'; or the insected intersections with Hélène Cixous in 'Ants' or again, in *H.C. for Life*[16]), the telephone participates in a deconstructive transformation of the 'question of the subject', of notions of auto-affection and hearing-oneself-speak, distinctions between public and private, conscious and unconscious, and the nature of being as such. Derrida's description of Leopold Bloom in James Joyce's *Ulysses* thus opens onto a more generalised theory of being: Bloom's being, we are told, is 'being-at-the-telephone. He is hooked up to a multiplicity of voices and answering machines.'[17] There is what Derrida calls 'a telephonic interiority': 'before any appliance bearing the name "telephone" in modern times, the telephonic *technē* is at work within the voice.' It is this 'mental telephony which, inscribing remoteness, distance, *différance*, and spacing [*espacement*] in the *phonē, at the same time* institutes, forbids, and interferes with the so-called monologue.'[18]

— Hello? Lost you there. So there's no monologue, no monological voice in Bakhtin's sense.[19] Is that what you're saying? Hello? OK: ignore me.

— Derrida concludes his counter-hoax call by advocating a 'pragmatics' of language, an attentiveness to 'the "performative" – its fictions and its simulacra', that would include a critical reading of psychoanalysis, a trying or testing out in which psychoanalysis and pragmatics alike would be differently construed, in particular a pragmatics which would be removed from 'an axiomatics of intentional consciousness and of the "self" present to itself' (p. 179).

— 'Some singular utterance, whispered like a secret, can still, incalculably, over the centuries . . . Hello?' (p. 177). I am quoting again. All of Derrida's thinking is to be traced here, in this abyssal 'telephonic "hallo"', this 'primary *yes*' as he calls it, in this thought of 'some singular utterance' the effects of which we have still to hear.[20]

— I remember once inviting Jacques Derrida to come to Scotland to talk about football. I knew it was a long shot (sorry), but I had a feeling that, given his well-known early love of football, he might be intrigued. (As he is quoted as saying in the book with Geoffrey Bennington: 'We used to play until it was pitch dark. I dreamt of becoming a professional footballer.'[21]) This was for a seminar at the University of Stirling called Foreign Body, in 1993.[22] He regretted that he was unable to accept, being so busy with other commitments. I have very little sense of what he might have said: that was one of the reasons I suggested the topic. But then this was – and is – one of the most remarkable, and ironically consistent, things about Derrida's work, the relationship that each of his texts seems to forge with surprise.[23] It is a matter of the unforeseeable, of a certain engagement with the law of necessity that is chance, with the surprising, indeed dispossessing ways in which (to recall a stickily compelling formulation from *Glas*) 'The glue of chance [*alea*] makes sense'.[24] I will always wonder, then, what he might have said, and indeed about how he might have changed the way we think and talk about football. I imagine a piece called 'The Rhetoric of Football' (a companion piece to his remarks on 'the rhetoric of drugs'[25]).

— He refers to football in his published writings very seldom. One such reference comes up, however, in 'Limited Inc', at a point at which he thinks John Searle (in his celebrated 'reply' to Derrida's 'Signature Event Context' ['SEC']) has perhaps somehow wrong-footed him. An underlying desire here would seem to be that Derrida would actually like Searle to *take* him, to trick and pass him, to wrong-foot him with a step-over, a side-step or even perhaps a nutmeg, for the sheer pleasure of the thing, for the sheer delight of such an exhibition of counter-logic and non-mastery. It is a beautiful moment of deconstructive fantasy football. Searle declares, in a formulation that is offered as a gloss on Derrida's argument in 'SEC': 'intentions must all be conscious'.[26] Does Searle mean to say that Derrida is claiming that 'intentions must all be conscious'? Derrida writes:

> Confronted with this assertion I must confess that I had to rub my eyes. Was I dreaming? Had I misread? Mistranslated? Was the text suddenly becoming sarcastic? Or even, as I had just wished, ironic? Was it all a joke? Was the patented theoretician – or theoreticians – of speech acts calling us to task for forgetting the existence of the unconscious? What a *contre-pied*, leaving me flat-footed in the camp of those insufficiently aware of the unconscious! I always love to watch a good *contre-pied*, even if it's at my expense. But my delight, unfortunately, is short-lived. I cannot imagine how Sam Weber is going to translate '*contre-pied*'. For his benefit let me specify that, ever since my adolescence, I have understood the word above all as a football term, denoting an active ruse designed to surprise one's opponent by catching him off balance. Littré, however, lists the following, which can be used as necessary: CONTRE-PIED 1. Hunting term. The trail followed by the prey and which the dogs, led astray, take instead of the new trail upon which the animal continues. To follow the *contre-pied* is to follow tracks in the wrong direction. 2. Fig. The contrary of something. 'People have taken precisely the *contre-pied* of the will.' La Fontaine.[27]

Derrida wonders if he is hallucinating. He refers to Searle as the 'patented theoretician' or 'theoreticians [plural]'. Earlier in his essay he has highlighted Searle's proprietorial attitude to his ideas and has wondered, with a mixture of amusement and intellectual gravity, what it means to impose a 'Copyright © 1977 by John R. Searle' on a work of philosophy: see pp. 29–30). He questions, satirises and unsettles the authenticity of Searle's particular *brand* of 'speech act theory' as true to the legacy of J. L. Austin, author of *How To Do Things With Words* and ostensive founder of the aforesaid theory. Derrida's essay is a sustained and often very funny critique as well as an active, even violent displacement of what is allegedly 'patent' or 'patentable', as well as of what is 'genuine', 'serious', 'authentic' or 'inauthentic' vis-à-vis speech act theory and the praxis or pragmatics to which it may appear to give rise.

– How would you translate *contre-pied*? Samuel Weber gives 'fake-out'. *Contre-pied*: literally, counter-foot; a foot against or in place of. Contretemps of the *contre-pied*: when does this trick, fake-out or wrong-footing take place? Derrida loves a good *contre-pied*. But his delight, unfortunately, is short-lived. [*Hélas! la jubilation n'aura pas duré*: p. 138.] More literally, 'Alas, the jubilation will not have lasted.' His deployment of the future anterior is perhaps significant, suggesting a strange counter-time, delight or jubilation out of joint.

— Not wanting to muscle in, but a word, if I may, in passing (sorry), about 'Anglo-American'. It is a vexed term. As Derrida remarks in *The Other Heading*, Anglo-American 'both is and is not a language'; as a strange yet familiar, increasingly ubiquitous silhouette-language, it is nonetheless 'destined to overtake or dub all the idioms of the world'.[28] As he says in an interview in 2001, 'this Anglo-American does violence not only to other languages but also to a certain English or American genius'.[29] Samuel Weber's translation of *contre-pied* as 'fake-out' is a little piece of American genius, an Americanisation that shifts the English of Derrida's remarks into a more North American context where the word is used not only in soccer but also, for example, in basketball and ice hockey. 'Fake-out' has a condensed elegance and wit all of its own, drawing together the sense of playing a game with the experience of a hoax or fake. But as the passage makes clear, it is specifically soccer (or 'football' in British English) – *le football* – that Derrida has in mind. (As he puts it, in a passing glance or glancing pass to his translator: '*Je précise à son intention que je l'entends d'abord, depuis mon adolescence, dans le code du football . . .*' (p. 138).)

— British English? That always makes me smile. Isn't it a term that came into existence just at the point of having to acknowledge its disappearance? As Derrida says in his hoax phone call, 'There is a war raging for and by means of the property of language, among philosophers and between them and others' (p. 178), and it seems to me that the aspirations and fighting chances of any 'English genius' (Derrida occasionally speaks of 'English' when he should, I think, say 'British') are up against the wall. To write about deconstruction in terms of 'linguistic nanoterrorism',[30] for example, as you have done: is that *glorifying terrorism*, would you say? In which case, we are all in trouble. I mean Tony Blair as well. Perhaps especially him. Or the next vicar. The substitute. Of whichever party. The next one who comes on to the field. I think we have to dig deep, keep elaborating the possibilities of what is 'in' English, trying to read the astonishingly rich and strange texts of the tradition that are there for all to see or hear while working away in some subterranean resistance movement still perhaps without a name. Not in the cause of some mad project of rebuilding 'British English' (a veritable folly), but of preserving memory while opening onto the elsewhere of what is *plus d'une langue* (in other words, concerning Derrida's succinct definition of deconstruction as what is at once 'more than a language and no more of *a* language'[31]). This is a task of 'critical reading', as Derrida would say.[32]

– Shakespeare's *Hamlet*: now there's an example of British English. Isn't it? I mean, wasn't it? I mean, would it have been?

– You are not being serious.

– I'm struck by the fact that the *contre-pied*, in the mix of hunting sense and La Fontaine's ostensibly more figurative sense of 'exactly the opposite', appears in Shakespeare's play in the more abbreviated or elliptical form simply of 'counter'. As the Danish 'rabble', led on by Laertes who himself leads, break into the chamber containing the false king Claudius and his false queen, Gertrude exclaims: 'How cheerfully on the false trail they cry. / O, this is counter, you false Danish dogs.'[33] Editors often proffer a gloss from Dr Johnson: 'Hounds run *counter*, when they trace the trail backwards.'[34] 'Counter' is and is not the same as 'false'. In some sense there is nothing at all 'false' about what these 'Danish dogs' seem to have picked up – an impression heightened by Gertrude's insistent, apparently superfluous repetition of the word 'false', the suspiciously inept transferred epithet ('false trail', 'false Danish dogs'). She evidently means, or wants to say, that Hamlet has already left the court. But the trail of the 'counter' in *Hamlet* engulfs everything. 'O, this is counter': O, this little world, is moving backwards, out of joint, against itself. 'Counter' is a sort of shibboleth, a spectral portal for the play. Everything is counter – the dead man returning, the incestuous criminal become king, son turned against mother, lover against lover, friends transpiring to be murderous enemies and, more generally, in Horatio's closing words, 'purposes mistook / Fall'n on th'inventors' heads' (V, ii, 389–90). As the Player King asserts, in a formulation that encapsulates the wilful madness of the play: 'Our wills and fates do so contrary run / That our devices still are overthrown' (III, ii, 206–7). Because 'our wills and fates' run so counter, our devices or designs are always defeated. The Player King's phrasing allows us to construe 'wills' and 'fates' as running at once counter to one another and counter to themselves. The conjunctive 'and' ('our wills and fates') runs the 'our' into 'fates', countering any straightforward sense that our fates are not our own. What is false and what is the trail? What is counter in *Hamlet* is never simply true or false. It runs away with thinking, onto another trail, another scene of the scent. To be sent, and to scent. 'But soft, methinks I scent the morning air: / Brief let me be' (I, v, 58–9), says the Ghost (in the only instance in Shakespeare of the word 'scent' as a verb: I think I scent, I scent I think, I think scenting, I scent therefore I am), thereby interrupting himself, interrupting the cryptic unfolding of the tale out of which the tale of *Hamlet* itself erupts, interrupting his description of how 'the will of [his] most seeming-virtuous queen' (I, v, 46) was won, as if counter to her will, and just before announcing that he himself has been sent – 'sent to my account', as he puts it, 'With all my imperfections on my head' (I, v, 78–9). What is it to be sent to one's account? Who has been sent or sent for? That is the question – not only as regards Rosencrantz and Guildenstern (Hamlet: 'be even and direct with me whether you were sent for or no' . . . Guildenstern: 'My lord, we were sent for' (II, ii, 287–92)), but also as regards the Ghost and Hamlet himself. Who sent the Ghost? Who or what is not sent? What does it mean to be sent? And to scent? 'Sent' scents English mad. Who is Hamlet? As the Grave-digger says: 'he that is mad and sent into England' (V, i, 143–4). To season Beckett's phrase: in the beginning was the pong.[35] Follow your nose. The nose knows, or not: nose not known, not now. Where, for example, to 'send' to for Polonius, whether or not 'you shall nose him as you go up the stairs into the lobby' (IV, iii, 33, 36–7)? The question of the scent takes us back, or forwards, to the question of where 'we must begin', as Derrida describes it in *Of Grammatology*: 'the thought of the trace', he writes, 'cannot not take the scent [*le flair*] into account'.[36] '*O, this is counter*' . . .

– I want to say something more about football. Sometimes things happen in a football match for which there appears no adequate or apposite language. Do you know what I mean? I'm thinking, for instance, of the astonishing moment in Arsenal's 7–0 whupping of Middlesbrough (14 January 2006) when Thierry Henry on the right-hand side of the pitch moving towards the Middlesbrough penalty area looks for all the world as if he is going to sweep the ball into the box with his right foot but apparently fluffs the kick completely. The ball goes forward to his right, felicitously into the path of another Arsenal player, Robert Pires, who then crosses. Only in the action-replay do we see that Henry doesn't fluff it at all. It's an extraordinary football *trompe-l'œil*, in which he pretends to play the ball with his right foot but actually passes it, perfectly into the path of Pires, with his left. What name to give this singular moment, this singularly inventive feint or dummy or dummy-switch? I would be tempted to call it an exemplary *contre-pied*, a *contre-pied* in a sense *against* nobody. There is a cross here perhaps with the sort of *contre-pied* that is evoked in Derrida's football fantasy.

— As regards this *contre-pied* with Searle, Derrida puts the wrong-footing (his own sense of dreaming or having to rub his eyes, as well as Searle's having been left standing) down to Searle's misleading, fundamentally incoherent sense of 'unconsciousness' as 'a kind of implicit or potential reserve of consciousness', a 'lateral virtuality' (pp. 73/139, tr. mod.). In response to Searle paraphrasing Derrida as saying that 'intentions must all be conscious', Derrida declares that '[t]o claim that for *Sec all* intentions are conscious is to read *à contre-pied*' (pp. 73/139, tr. mod.). On the contrary, *on the counter*, *Sec* argues not only that intentions need not be conscious, but that '*no* intention can *ever* be fully conscious, or actually present to itself' (p. 73). Derrida is concerned with a thinking that is at once closer to and more general than a Freudian conception in this respect. (We may here recall Freud's 'Note on the Unconscious' of 1912 in which he declares: 'We have no right to extend the meaning of this word ["conscious"] so far as to make it include a consciousness of which its owner himself is not aware. If philosophers find difficulty in accepting the existence of unconscious ideas, the existence of an unconscious consciousness seems to me even more objectionable.'[37]) Derrida is concerned with acknowledging the radicality of Freud's thought while also displacing and transforming it in terms of what 'Limited Inc' calls a 'structural unconsciousness' (p. 73; cf. p. 18). It is a question of the mole-like work of the trace, the incessant grafting without origin, as well as 'the Unconscious' as the undecidably comical and frightening 'giant Parasite' (*le Grand Parasite*, pp. 73/139) that subverts or outsmarts [*déjoue*] (pp. 74/140) everyone and everything, including every traditional notion of parasitism. It is a question of trying to think (as Derrida put it in the great essay 'Freud and the Scene of Writing' in 1966) 'in other terms than those of individual or collective psychology, or even of anthropology'.[38]

— So we come back to that primary telephonic yes, a yes 'more ancient than knowledge', then, yes? Derrida frequently recalls Freud's proposition that there are no contradictions in the unconscious. Or as he phrases it in 'Ulysses Gramophone': 'the unconscious knows nothing of *no*'.[39] How to reckon with the strange *non-counterability*, the *non-contradictatability* of the unconscious?

— Yes, but at the same time he is consistently circumspect around this word or concept 'the unconscious'. As in the case of the figure of 'the giant Parasite', which appears in 'Limited Inc' but which, as far as I am aware, doesn't show up again in his writings under this name, he is always affirming and searching for another language.[40] He often glosses the word 'unconscious' as 'what is still designated by this name in psychoanalysis' (p. 73). He repeatedly emphasises this provisionality, just as his laughter haunts any attempt to speak seriously about the unconscious in terms of the proper, property or ownership, Derrida's unconscious, my unconscious, Bin Laden's unconscious. As he says in 'Telepathy': 'I feel like laughing every time I write this word ["unconscious"], especially with a possessive mark.'[41] But Derrida also consistently affirms the necessity of the unconscious being 'taken seriously, *in (as) a manner of speaking*, up to and including its capacity for making jokes' (p. 74). It is impossible to construe 'Jacques Derrida's language' without reckoning with the place of the so-called unconscious. But this place is also the site of those transformative effects generated by his writings, including another thinking of *contre-pied*, a certain new openness to jokes and humour, and the elaboration of a new vocabulary, new languages, in the name of what he calls 'a new psychoanalytic Enlightenment'.[42] This would be what we might call Derrida's psychoanalytic *contre-pied*, his countersigning of psychoanalysis.

— Standing outside 10 Downing Street on 21 July 2005, the British Prime Minister Tony Blair commented on those who had that day attempted to detonate bombs in London, exactly two weeks after the bus and underground bombings that became known as '7/7' (in memory, recollection and imitation of '9/11'): 'Everyone is canny enough to know what these people are trying to do.' How canny is Tony Blair? How canny was he when he committed himself and the British people to go to war in Iraq with President George W. Bush and the people of the United States? What is 'canny'? What is 'canny enough'? I imagine, however fleetingly, a strange kind of counter-discourse, even a counter-institution, in the logic of the *contre-pied* or the exactly opposite, in other words the spectral figure of the 'counter'. Perhaps this is all I have been trying to think about for a quarter of a century or more, ever since I first began reading Jacques Derrida. It would be as if when Martin Jay asserted in 1997, in his rather fake intellectual-historian mode, that 'the uncanny' was a 'master trope' of the 1990s (a bizarre claim not least because the decade in question still had several years to run and because of the vague supposition that this apparent tropological dominance, if it is possible to speak of a 'master trope' here or indeed anywhere else, would fade away, as if upon the crowing of the millennial cock, at midnight on 31 December 1999), everything was to have been working in the other direction at the same time, throughout that period and up to this very moment, it would be as if it were really a question of 'the canny', as if all of Derrida's work, for example, could and should be rethought, relaunched, reread and newly disseminated under the rubric of 'the canny'.[43]

– 'Everyone is canny enough to know what these people are trying to do.' Is the British Prime Minister's remark constative or performative? We're all perhaps canny enough to know this, aren't we? We all *know*, in any case: he is only telling us what we all already know. But what is it that we know? What is going on when someone seeks to assure us (but also doubtless to assure himself), to confirm that we are (and also of course that he himself is) 'canny enough to know'? Tony Blair's invocation of the canny is no doubt, in many respects, canny. 'Everyone is canny enough to know what these people are trying to do.' There is 'everyone' (and that includes us) and then there are 'these people', i.e. *those* people (not us). We, ordinary good decent British citizens, etc., we are 'canny enough'. There is something odd about this Blairite 'canny'. What strikes a funny chord perhaps has to do with the incongruity of 'canny' as an attribute of 'everyone'. Margaret Thatcher's most notoriously insane remark may have been that 'There is no such thing as society', but it could reasonably be supposed that there is no such thing as a canny society. There is something distinctive about the word 'canny' that perhaps tends to be effaced, suppressed or forgotten as regards its alleged counterpart 'uncanny', namely that 'canny' is about the singular, about a singular knowledge, luck, shrewdness or ability. 'Canny' would seem to be of the one, the *anyone*, but not the *everyone*. There is, perhaps, a loneliness of the 'canny' that corresponds to Derrida's contention that deconstruction is lonely.[44] It is by way of a certain wrong-footing, perhaps, that the 'uncanny' can be understood to have been at work in what Jay calls 'cultural semantics'. It is all to do with what is 'canny', with this word that can mean 'knowing', 'lucky', 'fortunate', 'good', 'innocent', 'sly', 'shrewd', apparently from Old English *cunnan*, to know, to be able. 'Canny' *can* mean, canny can *can*. The can of canniness, like knowing your nose: it would be a matter of reckoning with the uncanny first of all in English, from an Anglophone or Anglish angle, and where it must be sharply distinguished from the *heimlich* or *unheimlich*, specifically in the ways that the 'canny' is a question of knowledge and of action or potential, of being able. There are strange epistemological dimensions in this English or Scottish word 'canny' that call for our attention in quite different ways from the so-called German equivalent.

– I miss Jacques Derrida.

– With his death in October 2004, what have we lost? I believe that we have lost, among so many other things, the most canny, the most knowing, shrewd, lucid and insightful analyst of the world situation. The dialogue that took place in New York on 22 October 2001 with

Giovanna Borradori, published under the title 'Autoimmunity: Real and Symbolic Suicides. A Dialogue with Jacques Derrida', remains, I believe, the most profound as well as the most urgent account of '9/11' to date.[45] How would Tony Blair, or George W. Bush, or their vicars or substitutes, the next ones on the field, read 'Autoimmunity: Real and Symbolic Suicides'? How would Osama Bin Laden read it, or how would it be read by 'these people' as Blair calls them, these people who may be taken to represent what Derrida calls 'the Bin Laden effect'?

— I'm sorry. What did you say?

— It's the future. Trauma has to do with the future, with the sense of 'what might or perhaps will take place, which will be *worse than anything that has ever taken place*' (PTT, p. 97). 'Traumatism is produced by the *future*, by the *to come*, by the threat of the worst *to come*, rather than by an aggression that is "over and done with"' (p. 97). This is why, for Derrida, the current situation is worse than the Cold War. As he puts it: 'From now on, the nuclear threat, the "total" threat, no longer comes from a state but from anonymous forces that are absolutely unforeseeable and incalculable' (p. 98). What is at risk is 'world order, the very possibility of a world and of any worldwide effort [*mondialisation*] (international law, a world market, a universal language, and so on)' (p. 98).

— In 'Autoimmunity' Derrida not only offers an extremely incisive analysis of the world situation, of what is happening 'on the ground', after Ground Zero, but also insists on the need to engage with what might appear more abstract or philosophical questions, such as the definition of 'trauma' and 'event', the meaning of 'terror' and 'terrorism', and the role and significance of the unconscious. The text remains true to Derrida's evocation of the future in *Of Grammatology* in 1967: 'The future can only be anticipated in the form of an absolute danger.'[46] But at the same time it has a canniness that, already in October 2001, can look back on the immediately preceding weeks with a sort of scary clarity:

> One day it might be said: 'September 11' – those were the ('good') old days of the last war. Things were still of the order of the gigantic: visible and enormous! What size, what height! There has been worse since. Nanotechnologies of all sorts are so much more powerful and invisible, uncontrollable, capable of creeping in everywhere. They are the micrological rivals of microbes and bacteria. Yet our unconscious is already aware of this; it already knows it, and that's what's scary. (PTT, p. 102)

A thinking of the canny, in other words, must include the giant Parasite or, more bizarrely perhaps, the nanoparasite, a nanoparasitism. As he notes a little earlier on in the dialogue: 'we do not know what an event *of* the unconscious or *for* the unconscious is (though we must nonetheless take it into account)' (p. 99).

— 'Everyone is canny enough to know what these people are trying to do.' Of course Blair is talking about people who want to destroy Western democracy, terrorise us, even if they destroy themselves in the process. Canny enough to kill oneself or let oneself be killed? What is one trying to do? Where is the future in that? The dialogue with Borradori called 'Autoimmunity' (it's all about the deadly logic whereby someone or something destroys itself through the process of seeking to protect itself) illustrates the extraordinary mobility of Derrida's discourse: as those who heard him talk at seminars or conferences may readily recall, his spoken improvisations possessed a lucidity and precision, and a capacity for surprise, scarcely different from his written texts. Thus, for example, at one point in the discussion with Borradori he starts multiplying questions about the meaning of the word 'terrorism' and seems, as if by chance, to stumble on what might be deemed crucial to a contemporary understanding and political reading of 'the great hoax', namely *unconscious terrorism*:

> [D]oes terrorism have to work only through death? Can't one terrorise without killing? And does killing necessarily mean putting to death? Isn't it also 'letting die'? Can't 'letting die', 'not wanting to know that one is letting others die' – hundreds of millions of human beings, from hunger, AIDS, lack of medical treatment, and so on – also be part of a 'more or less' conscious and deliberate terrorist strategy? We are perhaps wrong to assume so quickly that all terrorism is voluntary, conscious, organised, deliberate, intentionally calculated: there are historical and political 'situations' where terror operates, so to speak, as if by itself, as the simple result of some apparatus, because of the relations of force in place, without anyone, any conscious subject, any person, any 'I', being really conscious of it or feeling itself responsible for it. (p. 108)

If there is a moment in the 'Autoimmunity' text where Derrida offers a distillation, a telegrammatic formulation concerning what it might mean to be at least minimally canny (for who could ever, sensibly, speak of being 'canny enough' and know or convince anyone else of what they are talking about?), it is perhaps when he remarks, concerning what 'we now know', a month after September 11:

> What will never let itself be forgotten is . . . the perverse effect of the autoimmunitary itself. For we now know that repression in both its psychoanalytical sense and its political sense – whether it be through the police, the military, or the economy – ends up producing, reproducing, and regenerating the very thing it seeks to disarm. (p. 99)

The irony of this remark in the context of what continues to unfold around us, in the wake of the US and British response or responses to '9/11' – autoimmunitary suicidal logic, *contre-pied* of the political – makes the line tremble, breaks up the *polis* in different voices.[47]

– It is the canninesss of Derrida's sense of 'the worst *to come*', the urgency of the absolutely unforeseeable, but also and at the same time of an extraordinarily patient, long-term 'pragmatics' that recognises both the ineluctable necessity of the psychoanalytic revolution and of transformations that will 'take centuries'. (Regarding this last point, I am thinking in particular of his various remarks in the book *For What Tomorrow* about the centuries ahead, the future of human rights, international law and democracy, the human and other animals, the concept of the family, and so on.[48])

– I recall a sort of interrupted, interminably disjunctive conversation I had with him shortly after the 'Autoimmunity' dialogue, on 10 November 2001. This was on the occasion of a seminar at the University of Loughborough entitled 'life.after.theory'.[49] On the morning of the seminar Sarah Wood, Christopher Norris and I were having breakfast in the hotel when Jacques came in to join us. He was due to give the lecture that morning, a version of the text later published as '"Le Parjure", *Perhaps*: Storytelling and Lying ("abrupt breaches of syntax")'.[50] He appeared, as he often did before giving a lecture, rather nervous and agitated. He said good morning to us and then: 'Bin Laden may have a nuclear device.' There was nothing about this in the British newspapers in the hotel that morning. He had heard about it via his mobile phone from Paris. Later he delivered his lecture, the usual two or more hours' remarkable performance, and then before lunch, amid the hundreds of other people milling around, he was on his mobile again. He then came towards me. I asked: 'Any more news of Bin Laden?' What was I thinking? Or not thinking? Was I fearing or expecting him to say calmly, yes, Paris has been attacked? He looked at me directly and said simply: 'I am not in personal communication with him, Nick.' He was, evidently, translating my 'of' as a 'de' in French: any more news of Bin Laden? Any more news from Bin Laden?

– I miss Derrida's humour, his sense of irony, of structural irony, his extraordinary thinking of the serious and non-serious.

– Consciously or not, you might imagine that Bin Laden is always on the telephone. As *The Guardian* reports, in phrasing perhaps uncomfortably reminiscent of the Monty Python sketch describing the police tracking the movements of Doug Dinsdale and the Piranha Brothers by reading the colour supplements of the Sunday papers, in its front-page story following the release of the latest audio tape (20 January 2006): 'Bin Laden closely follows the media and has attempted to intervene directly in the past to influence political events in the West, putting messages out on the eve of the US presidential election and the Spanish parliamentary election.'[51]

– Let's be clear about the argument in 'Autoimmunity'. For all his 'very strong reservations . . . about the "international antiterrorist" coalition, despite all the de facto betrayals, all the failures to live up to democracy, international law [and so on]' (PTT, pp. 113–14), Derrida is committed to democracy, above all perhaps because 'the inherited concept of democracy is the only one that welcomes the possibility of being contested, of contesting itself, of criticising and indefinitely improving itself' (p. 121). On the subject of 'Bin Laden', on the other hand, he remarks:

> What appears to me unacceptable in the 'strategy' (in terms of weapons, practices, ideology, rhetoric, discourse, and so on) of the 'Bin Laden effect' is not only the cruelty, the disregard for human life, the disrespect for law, for women, the use of what is worst in technocapitalist modernity for the purposes of religious fanaticism. No, it is, above all, the fact that such actions and such discourse *open onto no future and, in my view, have no future.* If we are to put any faith in the perfectibility of public space and of the world juridico-political scene, of the 'world' itself, then there is, it seems to me, *nothing good* to be hoped for from that quarter. What is being proposed, at least implicitly, is that all capitalist and modern technoscientific forces be put in the service of an interpretation, itself dogmatic, of the Islamic revelation of the One. Nothing of what has been so laboriously secularised in the forms of the 'political', of 'democracy', of 'international law', and even in the nontheological form of sovereignty (assuming, again, that the value of sovereignty can be completely secularised or detheologised, a hypothesis about which I have my doubts), none of this seems to have any place whatsoever in the discourse 'Bin Laden'. (p. 113)

By way of trying to tie things together I would just like to propose . . .

– Do what?

– . . . that in order to be canny enough to read Derrida it would first be necessary to get beyond the notion that his writing or his thinking, his language, if you will, takes on an increasingly political character, starting perhaps with 'The Force of Law' in 1989 or *Spectres of Marx* in 1993. It's political all the way down the line. For instance concerning the question of Israel and Palestine and what, in *Spectres*, he calls the world war that is going on around the appropriation of Jerusalem. Derrida's remarks, at the Royal National Hotel in London on 1 March

2004, about the suicidal character of Israel, its autoimmunity destroying itself through its own defences, should be tracked back, in the manner of what I would like to call (with another ear, or other tone) a counter-reading, for example to what he says about 'the Palestinian struggle' in the '*faux-bond*' interview in 1975 and about the Palestinian friend in *Glas* (1974), in other words about what in that early interview he calls '[that] place [i.e. Jerusalem] that still gives place today to so much of our discourse, our history, our politics that we cannot be assured of having any distance on it'.[52]

– I would like to close with another evocation of Derrida. It is an alleged transcription of what he says on the phone to a stranger. It's a funny pedagogical scene in which he receives a call from a parent, the mother of a student at the Sorbonne (in other words not even one of his own students). The woman asks him about his views on Israel, in a so-called improvisation that he recounts, improvising once more, in *For What Tomorrow*. It is as if he were already inscribed within, the telephonic interview within the interview, dictating another book over the telephone:

> . . . although the conditions of the foundation of the state of Israel remain for me a tangled knot of painful questions that I could not possibly address over the phone (and even if it is considered a given that every state, that every foundation itself is founded in violence, and is by definition unable to justify that), I have a great many reasons to believe that it is *for the best*, all things considered, and in the interests of the greatest number of people, including the Palestinians, including the other states in the region, to consider this foundation, despite its originary violence, as henceforth irreversible – on the condition that neighbourly relations be established *either* with a Palestinian state endowed with *all* its rights, in the fullest sense of the term 'state' (at least insofar as anything remains of this full sense and of sovereignty in general; another very serious question which I must leave aside for now while briefly relating, in an interview, a telephone interview), *or*, at the centre of the same 'sovereign' and binational 'state', with a Palestinian people freed from all oppression or from all intolerable segregation. I have no particular hostility in principle toward the state of Israel, but I have almost always judged quite harshly the policies of the Israeli governments in relation to the Palestinians. I have often said so publicly, in particular in Jerusalem, for example, in a lecture I gave quite a long time ago, which was published in more than one language, during the period when one spoke of 'occupied territories', etc. After a few more sentences along these lines, I heard on the other end of the line: 'I see. Well, that's what I suspected [*Ah bon, je m'en doutais*].' (FWT, pp. 118–19/192–3)

– No more. The end of the line.

– And yet of course there is the 'spectral machine', a listening machine that can also answer.[53] It can. To be read and to be heard. And you can even, elsewhere, see him, for instance in that beautiful film about 'elsewhere' (*D'ailleurs Derrida*, dir. Safaa Fathy, 1999) in which he speaks so hauntingly about the braid of voices of which a voice is made up and of the importance for a responsible political attitude and the democracy to come of listening well to the unconscious.

– I miss Jacques Derrida.

– Me too. In almost every sense, I miss him, keep missing him.

– We do. Yes.

– Yes.

Notes

1. Maurice Blanchot, 'The Great Hoax', trans. Ann Smock, in *The Blanchot Reader*, ed. Michael Holland (Oxford: Blackwell, 1995), pp. 157–66. Further page references are given parenthetically in the main body of the text, abbreviated 'GH' where appropriate. I would like to record here a special note of thanks and indebtedness to Jinan Joudeh for rich and stimulating discussions on the topic of the hoax.
2. Derrida says this apropos a sentence in Blanchot's 'The Instant of My Death': see Jacques Derrida, *Demeure: Fiction and Testimony* (with Maurice Blanchot's *The Instant of My Death*), trans. Elizabeth Rottenberg (Stanford, CA: Stanford University Press, 2000), p. 54.
3. We might recall here Deleuze and Guattari's pointed exhortation: 'Let us keep D.H. Lawrence's reaction to psychoanalysis in mind, and never forget it.' See Gilles Deleuze and Félix Guattari, *Anti-Oedipus: Capitalism and Schizophrenia*, trans. Robert Hurley, Mark Seem and Helen R. Lane (London: Athlone Press, 1984), p. 49.
4 Jacques Derrida and Elisabeth Roudinesco, *For What Tomorrow . . . A Dialogue*, trans. Jeff Fort (Stanford, CA: Stanford University Press, 2004), pp. 179–80. Further page references are given parenthetically in the main body of the text. All references to the original French text, *De quoi demain . . . Dialogue* (Paris: Fayard/Galilée, 2001), will be given in parenthesis, following a slash.
5. The French here reads: '*un corps-à-corps turbulent mais* primordial, *je veux dire où tout l'enjeu se fixe, où l'essentiel est en jeu*' (pp. 30–1). The phrase '*corps-à-corps*' is well translated as 'hand-to-hand', though the original of course has a full-bodied quality the English version cannot match. It is in keeping with Derrida's concern, to be found everywhere in his work, with the body and feeling, with the desire to 'experience [the impossible] in [his] body'. (See, for example, '*Ja*, or the *faux-bond* II', trans. Peggy Kamuf, in *Points . . . Interviews, 1974–1994*, ed. Elisabeth Weber, trans. Peggy Kamuf and others (London and New York: Routledge, 1995), p. 49.) Correspondingly, the English translator Jeff Fort renders 'primordial' as '*primal*', which has the virtue of underscoring the psychoanalytically

attuned ambience of Derrida's remarks (we might think, for example, of a primal scene of language here), while in the process, however, effacing a more phenomenological resonance. In this hand-to-hand struggle with language everything, for Derrida, is at stake. Again, the English effaces the tricky play of the '*enjeu*'/'*en jeu*' in Derrida's phrasing: '*je veux dire où tout l'enjeu se fixe, où l'essentiel est en jeu*'. What is at stake, the essential, is at once at work and in play: the '*enjeu*' drifts apart before our eyes, spacing out.

6. Jacques Derrida, *The Truth in Painting*, trans. Geoff Bennington and Ian McLeod (Chicago: University of Chicago Press, 1987), pp. 151–2.
7. See Peggy Kamuf's note on this, in *Points*, p. 460.
8. '*Ja*, or the *faux-bond* II', p. 58, tr. sl. mod.
9. Ibid., p. 34.
10. See Jacques Derrida, 'Language Is Never Owned: An Interview', trans. Thomas Dutoit and Philippe Romanski, in *Sovereignties in Question: The Poetics of Paul Celan*, eds Thomas Dutoit and Outi Pasanen (New York: Fordham University Press, 2005), pp. 99–100.
11. Ibid., p. 101.
12. Jacques Derrida, 'Language (*Le Monde* on the Telephone)', in *Points*, pp. 171–80. Further page references are given parenthetically in the main body of the text.
13. See *Points*, p. 468.
14. Jacques Derrida, *Rogues: Two Essays on Reason*, trans. Pascale-Anne Brault and Michael Naas (Stanford, CA: Stanford University Press, 2005), pp. 91–2.
15. Jacques Derrida, 'Telepathy', trans. Nicholas Royle, in *Deconstruction: A Reader*, ed. Martin McQuillan (Edinburgh: Edinburgh University Press, 2000), pp. 496–526.
16. See 'Envois', in *The Post Card: From Socrates to Freud and Beyond*, trans. Alan Bass (Chicago: Chicago University Press, 1987), pp. 3–256; 'Telepathy' (see preceding note); 'Of an Apocalyptic Tone Recently Adopted in Philosophy', trans. John P. Leavey, Jr, *Oxford Literary Review*, 6: 2 (1984), 3–37; 'Ulysses Gramophone: Hear Say Yes in Joyce', trans. Tina Kendall and Shari Benstock, in *Acts of Literature*, ed. Derek Attridge (London and New York: Routledge, 1992), pp. 256–309; 'Ants', trans. Eric Prenowitz, in *Reading Cixous Writing*, ed. Martin McQuillan, special issue of *Oxford Literary Review*, vol. 24 (2002), 17–42; *H.C. for Life, That Is to Say . . .*, trans. Laurent Milesi and Stefan Herbrechter (Stanford, CA: Stanford University Press, 2006).
17. 'Ulysses Gramophone', p. 273.
18. Ibid., pp. 271–2.
19. Cf. Timothy Clark's remarks on literature, testimony and voice, concerning Bakhtin, in *The Poetics of Singularity: The Counter-Culturalist Turn in Heidegger, Derrida, Blanchot and the Later Gadamer* (Edinburgh: Edinburgh University Press, 2005), p. 178, n. 29.
20. See 'Ulysses Gramophone', p. 298.
21. See Geoffrey Bennington and Jacques Derrida, *Jacques Derrida*, trans. Geoffrey Bennington (Chicago: Chicago University Press, 1993), p. 341. Cf. Derrida's remarks in an interview, on the subject of being at school and

starting to read Gide, Nietzsche and Rousseau: 'even as I withdrew into this reading or other solitary activities, well, in a dissociated, juxtaposed way, I also led the life of a kind of young hooligan, in a "gang" that was interested more in soccer or track than in studying' (*Points*, p. 342).

22. For more on this seminar, permit me to refer to 'Foreign Body: "The deconstruction of a pedagogical institution and all that it implies"', in *After Derrida* (Manchester: Manchester University Press, 1995), pp. 143–58.

23. It is in the context of the always 'surprising' character of the supplement, for example, that we can see the proximity or overlap between *Of Grammatology* (1967) and 'The Great Hoax'. As Derrida puts it:

> We should begin by taking rigorous account of this *being held within* [*prise*] or this *surprise*: the writer writes *in* a language and *in* a logic whose proper system, laws, and life his discourse by definition cannot dominate absolutely. He uses them only by letting himself, after a fashion and up to a point, be governed by the system. And [a] reading must always aim at a certain relationship, unperceived by the writer, between what he commands and what he does not command of the patterns of the language that he uses.

See *Of Grammatology*, trans. Gayatri Chakravorty Spivak (Baltimore, MD: Johns Hopkins University Press, 1976), p. 158.

24. Jacques Derrida, *Glas*, trans. John P. Leavey, Jr and Richard Rand (London: University of Nebraska Press, 1986), p. 140.

25. See 'The Rhetoric of Drugs', trans. Michael Israel, in *Points*, pp. 228–54.

26. John R. Searle, 'Reiterating the Differences; A Reply to Derrida', *Glyph*, 2 (1977), 202.

27. Jacques Derrida, 'Limited Inc a b c . . .', trans. Samuel Weber, in *Limited Inc* (Evanston, IL: Northwestern University Press, 1988), p. 73 (tr. sl. mod.). Further page references will be given in brackets in the main body of the text. All references to the French text, *Limited Inc*, Présentation et traductions par Elisabeth Weber (Paris: Galilée, 1990), will be given in parenthesis, where appropriate, following a slash.

28. See Jacques Derrida, *The Other Heading: Reflections on Today's Europe*, trans. Pascale-Anne Brault and Michael B. Naas (Bloomington, IN: Indiana University Press, 1992), p. 23. I discuss the question of language and the 'Anglo-American' at greater length in *The Uncanny* (Manchester: Manchester University Press, 2003), pp. 121–2, and *passim*.

29. Jacques Derrida, 'Language Is Never Owned: An Interview', p. 103.

30. The allusion here is to 'Nanotext', *Imprimatur*, 2: 1 & 2 (1996), 13–19.

31. Jacques Derrida, *Mémoires: for Paul de Man*, trans. Cecile Lindsay, Jonathan Culler and Eduardo Cadava (New York: Columbia University Press, 1986), p. 15.

32. *Of Grammatology*, p. 158.

33. Shakespeare, *Hamlet*, ed. Harold Jenkins (London: Methuen, 1982), IV, v, 109–10. Further references to *Hamlet* are to this edition, unless otherwise stated.

34. See, for example, *Hamlet, Prince of Denmark*, ed. Philip Edwards, updated edn (Cambridge: Cambridge University Press, 2003), p. 210.

35. 'In the beginning was the pun': see Samuel Beckett, *Murphy* (London: Picador, 1973), p. 41.

36. *Of Grammatology*, p. 162.
37. Sigmund Freud, 'A Note on the Unconscious', in *Pelican Freud Library*, vol. 11, ed. Angela Richards (Harmondsworth: Penguin, 1984), p. 53.
38. Jacques Derrida, 'Freud and the Scene of Writing', in *Writing and Difference*, trans. Alan Bass (London: Routledge & Kegan Paul, 1978), p. 229.
39. 'Ulysses Gramophone', p. 288.
40. In 'Freud and the Scene of Writing' he does, however, note Freud's use of 'the image of the feeler [*l'antenne*]' in connection with the unconscious (as well as with the ego): see pp. 225–6, and 331, n. 32.
41. Jacques Derrida, 'Telepathy', p. 506.
42. 'Psychoanalysis Searches the States of Its Soul: The Impossible Beyond of a Sovereign Cruelty (Address to the States General of Psychoanalysis)', in Jacques Derrida, *Without Alibi*, trans. and ed. Peggy Kamuf (Stanford, CA: Stanford University Press, 2002), pp. 276–7.
43. See Martin Jay, 'The Uncanny Nineties', in his *Cultural Semantics: Keywords of Our Time* (Amherst, MA: University of Massachusetts Press, 1998), pp. 157–64. (The essay was originally published in *Salmagundi* in 1995.) Jay's piece also makes reference to the 'canny'. In a rather hasty and misleading summary of Derrida's *Spectres of Marx*, he declares: 'Ultimately, then, the alternative between the uncanny and the canny is, for Derrida, undecidable' (p. 160). This generalising remark about the 'ultimately . . . undecidable' perhaps inclines too easily toward an equation of Derrida's work with indeterminism. It also misleadingly suggests that Derrida explicitly discusses this 'alternative': in fact, his account of the uncanny focuses on Heidegger and Freud, in other words on the German term 'unheimlich' (as in Freud's essay 'Das Unheimliche'). Nowhere, so far as I am aware, does Derrida talk about 'the canny' as such. But neither does Jay himself give any detailed critical or philosophical consideration to the term in his essay. He concludes by proposing: 'It is now the height of canniness to market the uncanny' (p. 163). This formulation, evoking the specifically business-and-marketing associations of the word 'canny', perhaps suggests more about Jay's commercialist conception of intellectual life than about the cultural and political possibilities of strangeness (canny-uncanny) in writing. As author of a book on the uncanny that did not appear until some time after the 'uncanny nineties' were over, I humbly acknowledge the ineptitude of my marketing *nous*.
44. As Derrida puts it: 'If only you knew how independent deconstruction is, how alone, so alone, all alone!' By way of counter, in the same essay, he also foregrounds and elucidates the contention that 'nothing is less lonely and thinkable on its own'. See 'Et Cetera . . . (and so on, und so weiter, and so forth, et ainsi de suite, und so überall, etc.)', trans. Geoffrey Bennington, *Deconstructions: A User's Guide*, ed. Nicholas Royle (Basingstoke and New York: Palgrave, 2000), pp. 282 and 288 ff.
45. 'Autoimmunity: Real and Symbolic Suicides. A Dialogue with Jacques Derrida', trans. Pascale-Anne Brault and Michael Naas, in Giovanna Borradori, *Philosophy in a Time of Terror: Dialogues with Jürgen Habermas and Jacques Derrida* (Chicago and London: Chicago University Press, 2003), pp. 85–136. Further page references are given parenthetically in the main body of the text, abbreviated 'PTT' where appropriate.

46. *Of Grammatology*, p. 5.
47. I am thinking here of Dickens's *Our Mutual Friend*, of course, but also of Derrida's provoking remarks about civil disobedience in his 'History of the Lie: Prolegomena', in the context of his questioning a certain kind of 'totalitarianism with a democratic face', in particular concerning that 'political agency, most often in the figure of state sovereignty or even of reason of state, [which] summons everyone to behave first of all and in every regard as a responsible citizen before the law of the *polis*'. See Jacques Derrida, 'History of the Lie: Prolegomena', trans. Peggy Kamuf, in *Without Alibi*, pp. 63–4.
48. See, for example, *For What Tomorrow*, pp. 18–19, 37, 73–4, 87, 96–7.
49. Discussions from this seminar were published in *life.after.theory*, ed. Michael Payne and John Schad (London: Continuum, 2003).
50   Jacques Derrida, '"Le Parjure", *Perhaps*: Storytelling and Lying ("abrupt breaches of syntax")', trans. Peggy Kamuf, in *Without Alibi*, pp. 161–201.
51. Brian Whitaker and Ewen MacAskill, 'Bin Laden talks of truce but threatens US with new attacks', *The Guardian*, 20 January 2006, p. 1. In the same article US Vice-President Dick Cheney is reported as saying that the offer of truce in the latest audio tape 'sound[s] like a "ploy"'. How canny is *that*?
52. See '*Ja*, or the *faux-bond* II', pp. 67–8, and cf. *Glas*, pp. 36–8.
53. On the 'spectral machine', see Jacques Derrida, 'Typewriter Ribbon: Limited Ink (2)', trans. Peggy Kamuf, in *Without Alibi*, p. 160.

Impossible Uncanniness:
Deconstruction and Queer Theory

What can this ciphered letter signify, my very sweet destiny, my immense, my very near unknown one? Perhaps this: even if it is still more mysterious, I owe it to you to have discovered homosexuality, and ours is indestructible.[1]

Queer's not just a queer word but belongs, if it belongs, to a queer time. I would like to think of that sentence as a tiny installation, a snowflake of sound, around which one might take one or more queer turns, or sketch a few queer footnotes. There is perhaps a queer theory of the First Sentence. In a dreamy, radical passivity, I imagined an encounter of 'deconstruction and queer theory' in relation to the writings of Leo Bersani, starting with the falling into place of the First Sentence. What is the character of a first sentence? How, along what paths and with what effects does the tone adopt you as much as you it (to borrow Derrida's formulation)? How does it commit or even (in the strongest sense) determine you? Bersani is fascinated by what happens, like lightning, by what is struck or striking in first sentences. 'There is a big secret about sex: most people don't like it.' 'The vagina is a logical defect in nature.' 'Psychoanalytically speaking, monogamy is cognitively inconceivable and morally indefensible.' These are three of his first sentences, the opening words of 'Is the Rectum a Grave?', 'Merde alors' (an essay co-authored with Ulysse Dutoit) and 'Against Monogamy', respectively.[2] I could envisage devoting a separate essay to each of these sentences, in homage to the thinker who, it seems to me, first elaborated, a good while before Judith Butler and others, the theoretical and political dimensions of deconstruction and queer theory. But in the limited time I have here, this will have to be signalled as a bypath – a bypath that inevitably takes in *Billy Budd*, a path by Billy, a billy by-blow, proceeding and even coming into bud, by way of the opening of Chapter 4 of that masterpiece in which Melville's narrator declares:

> In this matter of writing, resolve as one may to keep to the main road, some
> paths have an enticement not readily to be withstood. I am going to err into
> such a bypath. If the reader will keep me company I shall be glad. At the
> least, we can promise ourselves that pleasure which is wickedly said to be
> in sinning, for a literary sin the divergence will be.[3]

Does *Billy Budd* have a main road? What would it mean to keep its narrator company? How should we construe the pleasure of literary sinning
and what might be discovered on its bypaths?

◆

'Queer's a queer word': that is a quotation, as some might recognise,
from two men, co-authors, indulgers or 'collaborators', as Wayne
Koestenbaum calls them, in 'doubletalk' or 'double writing'.[4] Who came
out with this phrase (and in doing so deliberately omitted the quotation
marks around queer)? Is it to be read or heard in the voice of Andrew
Bennett or of his co-author? Of an authorial double-voice or double-
double-voice? Queer is instilled at the very quick of quotation, queer
would be in the ear, like a bypath in the voice. It falls outside the scope
of this essay to discuss my love of Andrew Bennett, or my collaboration
with him. But no doubt, as in the case of *Billy Budd*, I shall be addressing this, even or especially when I appear not to be doing so, or when I
am most firmly convinced that I am not doing so, tacitly immersed in the
kinds of logic and experience that Kostenbaum discusses in his fascinating book about 'the erotics of male literary collaboration', starting with
his contention that 'double authorship attacks not primarily our dogmas
of literary propriety, but of sexual propriety' (pp. 8–9) and examin-
ing how, for example in the case of the novel called *Romance* (1903)
that Joseph Conrad wrote in collaboration with Ford Madox Hueffer
(almost twenty years his junior), double-writing entails a queer mixing
of voices or rather (as I would like to designate it here) a magical thinking writing in which voice is queer. Koestenbaum quotes the narrator
Kemp recalling his sense of being one 'I' and simultaneously another,
Kemp's queer, queerly unkempt self-division in the act of speaking: 'in
a queer way, the thoughts of the one "I" floated through into the words
of the other'.[5]

◆

Queer belongs, if it belongs, to a queer time. In a number of texts,
perhaps most notably 'Freud and the Scene of Writing' and *Archive
Fever*, Jacques Derrida suggests that one of Freud's greatest discoveries

is, or was, or will have been, *Nachträglichkeit*, deferred effect, delayed action, delayed or deferred sense or meaning, after-effect or effect of deferral, deferred event, event in deferral, and so on.[6] It seems to me that comparatively little has been made of this discovery, as yet, in the context of queer theory. Deferred effect is, I just said, or was or will have been and even, I would like to add, might be one of Freud's most extraordinary and most disruptive discoveries, still might be, might have been or might be. There is a necessary *might* that, I think, comes into play or comes out here, as if by a mole-like progression, through the supplementing of Derrida's reading of Freud (in 'Freud and the Scene of Writing' and *Archive Fever*, for example) with his reading of Hélène Cixous and the 'might' of literature (in later texts such as *H.C. for Life* and *Geneses, Genealogies, Genres and Genius*).[7] I am referring here to what Derrida says about 'the strange tense of [the] *puisse* [might] or *puissiez-vous* [would that you might]' that is to be found, in an exemplary fashion, in the writings of Cixous.[8] It is the question of a strange tense, a mighty optative that 'would attest to unpower, vulnerability, death', even as it affirms a certain omnipotence, an omnipotence that is 'in league with the im-possible' and that 'would do the impossible', in short an optative that would respond to the fact that 'desire [can] reach where the distinction between phantasm and the so-called actual or external reality does not yet take place and has no place to be'.[9] This 'might', I would like to suggest, is intimately related to what Cixous and Derrida have to say about sexual differences in the plural, to their singular but shared affirmations of the polysexual, 'a sexuality without number' (as Derrida calls it), 'beyond the binary difference that governs the decorum of all codes, beyond the opposition feminine/masculine, beyond bisexuality as well, beyond homosexuality and heterosexuality which come to the same thing'.[10]

♦

Here is an apparently straightforward, if not straight, example of deferred effect or event in deferral. In an essay published in *Radical Philosophy* in 2000 called 'Wishful Theory and Sexual Politics', originally given as a talk at a conference (in the same year) entitled '30 years of Radical Politics and Philosophy', Jonathan Dollimore reflects on the state of queer theory, writing as follows:

> the more fashionable Queer became, the more it was appropriated by those who wanted to be fashionable and the more inclusive and meaningless the term became. As I write, an anthology of literary theory arrives on my desk which reprints work of mine as representative of queer theory even

though that work was written before queer was a glint in anyone's eye. A few days before that another book arrived, an introduction to the work of E. M. Forster, in which the author, Nick Royle, boldly explores the idea that Forster wrote not one queer novel but six. Somehow Nick, I don't think so. But then, when the deco boys start to out-queer queer, maybe it's time to move on.[11]

For me, the deferred effect here consists first of all, perhaps, in the fact that I only became aware of Dollimore's essay some five years after it was published. If you thought you were queer, even a little bit, if you thought what you were *writing* was queer, even a little bit, or even if you thought only that you were writing *about* queer, if you were hoping or imagining (the cheek!) that you might have had some very slight contribution to make to elaborating on the nature of queer or queer theory, for example in the context of E. M. Forster's work and the relationship between queer and literature staged there, you were wrong, boy. But the scene and logic of deferred effect is also more complicated. Indeed, as with the question of how one translates *Nachträglichkeit* into English, it is about irreducible multiplicity from the beginning.

Queer's is a queer time. Jonathan Dollimore testifies to this in more than one way, and not only when he appears to resist or reject it. Thus, for example, towards the end of his essay, he will explicitly propose that 'desire, and perverse desire most acutely, is at once an effect of history, and a refusal of history'.[12] It is of course part of the purpose of Andrew Bennett and the other man's account of the queerness of queer in their chapter entitled 'Queer' (first published in the second edition of their book, in 1999, though presumably without Dollimore's knowledge) to suggest that 'the entry of the word "queer" into the English language is itself a study in the queer ways of words', and to explore what they call the *delay* – the 'delay of more than four hundred years between the introduction of the "odd" or "singular" sense of the word into English and the introduction of its "homosexual" sense', in other words from the first recorded use of 'queer' ('Heir cumis awin quir Clerk', in William Dunbar in 1508) to its alleged first 'homosexual' use (where, as the authors note, the word 'queer' is, a little queerly, already in quotation marks) in a US government report published in 1922.[13] It's as if this 'delay' that they talk about were a feature of its usage from the beginning, as if for example pre-1922 writing (such as that of Forster, Conrad, Henry James and numerous others, going back at least as far, as we shall see, as Gerard Manley Hopkins) were concerned with establishing in advance the need to read 'queer' in quotation marks. The word 'queer', says the *OED*, is 'of doubtful origin', and this is effectively also, as the dictionary goes on to note, one of its primary meanings: 'Strange, odd, peculiar, eccentric, in appearance or character. Also, of question-able character, suspicious, dubious' (sense 1a). There can be no queer theory, we might say, without doubtful origin.

Dollimore's prose is rich and suggestive, not least in its apparent colloquialism and simplicity. Let us consider, for example, his refer-ence to the anthology that, after the fact, by deferral, reprints some of his work 'as representative of queer theory even though that work was written before queer was a glint in anyone's eye.' In this rework-ing of the phallo-paternal, heterosexual, reproductive 'twinkle' into the 'glint' that is more readily associated with the killer or with sheer lust, Dollimore's writing intimates a compelling priority of the body or of physical gesture: 'Queer' begins in the eye of a beholder; in the beginning was the glint. At the same time he also appears to want to argue for a sense of history, an orderliness and chronologism, which queer, starting perhaps with the queer history of the word itself, queers the pitch of. Not insignificantly perhaps, this double gesture (the glint and the logocentric, rectilinearist affirmation of history) is subordinate, in Dollimore's sentence, to the strange time of writing: 'As I write, an anthology of literary theory arrives on my desk which reprints . . .' The writing, the arriving and even the reprinting all seem to come together in the present, or at least under that sort of 'false appearance of a present' that Derrida so resonantly evokes in the opening pages of 'Outwork' in *Dissemination*, apropos the drawing-everything-together time of a preface.[14]

But who am I to talk? I'm *so* last week (and this was already years ago). 'A few days before that another book arrived, an introduction to the work of E. M. Forster, in which the author, Nick Royle, boldly explores . . .' I like that 'that' ('A few days before *that*'), as if Nicholas Royle arrived before writing, *avant la lettre*. Anyway, apparently (it was in the late 1990s, let's remember) I wanted to be fashionable and therefore I appropriated 'Queer'. To quote Dollimore again: 'the more fashionable Queer became, the more it was appropriated by those who wanted to be fashionable and the more inclusive and meaning-less the term became.' Is 'queer' meaningless? What does it mean to say that a word, or a concept, a proper name even (for Dollimore here gives 'Queer' a capital letter), becomes *more* 'meaningless'? What is the relation here between the 'meaningless' and 'inclusive' or, conversely perhaps, meaning and the *exclusive*? Without launching off into a full-scale 'Limited Inc' kind of response here, I would just like to suggest that, if there is or was something 'fashionable' about 'Queer', this had nothing to do with any effort on my part and, moreover, I do not believe that it is possible to appropriate anything in writing, not least when it has a capital letter, whether it be a theory or an autobiography or one's own so-called proper name. In writing, as in any work of identification, however personal or political or personal-as-political (as people used to say), whether construed as love of oneself or of the other, the very movement of appropriation is an expropriation, as Derrida makes lovingly clear in text after text. Deconstruction (if there is any) is what cannot be appropriated: it is the undoing of any movement of appropriation.

It's not a matter (as many early critical commentaries in the 1970s and 1980s supposed) of deconstruction as the blank rejection of 'presence', a dismissal of the desire for appropriation, or of feelings of identification or 'belonging'. It's a matter of rendering these things 'enigmatic' (as *Of Grammatology* explicitly states)[15] with a view to their being thought and activated *otherwise*: this is what is going on in Derrida's interest in what 'Limited Inc' calls '"literatures" or "revolutions" that as yet have no model'.[16] Deconstruction, if there is any, is first of all a deconstruction of the spontaneous, of what is supposedly immediate or of one's own free will. In this respect, Derrida's work has an affiliation with Lenin's. As Lenin nicely puts it, in the chapter entitled 'The Spontaneity of the Masses and the Consciousness of the Social-Democrats' in *What Is To Be Done?* (1901): 'There is spontaneity and spontaneity.'[17] There is a thread to be followed here as regards what Derrida refers to as 'a sort of crypto-communist legacy' in deconstruction. Deconstruction, in his view, inherits something of the 'condemnation of "spontaneism"' in Lenin. As he summarises in a discussion with Maurizio Ferraris in 1994: 'what remains constant in my thinking [is] a critique of institutions, but one that sets out not from the utopia of a wild and spontaneous pre- or non-institution, but rather from counter-institutions . . . The idea of a counter-institution, neither spontaneous, wild nor immediate, is the most permanent motif that . . . has guided me in my work.'[18] Permit me here simply to signal the importance of the question of queer theory and counter-institutions and the indissociable links, in my view, between deconstruction, queer and a certain communism. It's a question also of spectrality, and I will try to say a little more about this shortly. Suffice to recall for the moment Derrida's remark about communism in *Spectres of Marx*: 'communism has always been and will remain spectral: it is always still to come and is distinguished, like democracy itself, from every living present understood as plenitude of a presence-to-itself, as totality of a presence effectively identical to itself.'[19]

Derrida's 'crypto-communist legacy', as he calls it, also entails another thinking of the 'crypto-', of the hidden and secret. There is spontaneity and spontaneity, but there is also always going to be a secret of 'me' for 'me'.[20] This notion of the secret is crucial to the hesitation I have been trying to mark vis-à-vis the time to which queer belongs, if it belongs. Queer would have to do with a queering of time as such, and with a deconstructive thinking of the secret as what 'does not belong'.[21] It's not a question of appropriation but rather of the experience of its impossibility. It's not a question of spontaneity but of reckoning with the argument (already explicit and fundamental in *Of Grammatology*) that 'immediacy is derived' (OG, p. 157). As Derrida remarks of the logic of deferred effect, delayed sense or what Freud called *Nachträglichkeit*: 'The temporality to which [Freud] refers cannot be that which lends itself to a phenomenology of consciousness or of presence and one may indeed wonder by what right all that is in question here should still be called time [or now or delay, etc.]' (OG, p. 67). Insofar as it is a question of affirming one's identity (I am queer, or I am a queer, I will have been or I might be queer, and so on), it is also one of attending to the secrecy and non-belonging that structure all movements of identification. As Derrida says in *A Taste for the Secret*: 'The desire to belong to any community whatsoever, the desire for belonging *tout court*, implies that one *does not belong* . . . *Accounting for* one's belonging – be it on national, linguistic, political or philosophical grounds – in itself implies a not-belonging' (TS, p. 28). Derrida wants to affirm *not-belonging*, in part because 'belonging', 'the fact of avowing one's belonging' or 'putting in common', in his terms, 'spells the loss of the secret' (TS, p. 59). As he says in a related essay, 'Passions: "An Oblique Offering"': '*There is something secret*. But it does not conceal itself . . . It remains inviolable even when one thinks one has revealed it . . . It does not belong therefore to the truth, neither to the truth as *homoiosis* or adequation, nor to the promised truth, nor to the inaccessible truth.'[22] This secrecy is at issue every instant, and in every word. One name for it might be 'queer'.

♦

Permit me to add one or two further remarks concerning the passage I quoted from Jonathan Dollimore: '[Royle's book] boldly explores the idea that Forster wrote not one queer novel but six. Somehow Nick, I don't think so. But then, when the deco boys start to out-queer queer, maybe it's time to move on.' It really does look as if Dollimore doesn't approve, even if he expresses this in a touching gesture, at once patronising and affectionate as well as comical, of turning aside from his discourse in order to address me directly: 'Somehow Nick . . .' Boldly but apparently quite erroneously trying to explore the idea that Forster wrote not one but six queer novels, I am labelled as a 'deco boy'. I must admit it makes me smile, this performative moment, this embedded act of naming whereby I become a 'deco boy'. What do deco boys do? Do they get to meet deco girls or do they only meet other deco boys? Or do they get up to something else? And are there deco men as well as deco boys? Was Derrida a deco man or just another deco boy? And what would be the relation between a deco boy and a deco man or between one deco boy and another (perhaps you, my love), before or beyond, before and beyond all thinking of the filial or homo-fraternal? No one, so far as I know, has ever called me a deco boy before or since, and as the years go by the chances of it happening again no doubt continue to recede. Am I, was I, will I have been a 'deco boy'? Supposing that 'deco' refers principally not to 'deco' (as in art deco) or to 'decko' (as in having a quick look, possibly with a glint in one's eye) or to 'decoy' (despite its perhaps special aptness and allure in this context) but to 'deconstruction', I wonder about the relationship between deconstruction and queer theory that is being suggested here. It looks, at least at first decko, as if it would be antagonistic, even oppositional: 'But then, when the deco boys start to out-queer queer, maybe it's time to move on.'

I need to step sideways here, or at least note a footnote, which I believe helps to illuminate the passage in question. It comes after the sentence about Forster writing 'not one queer novel but six'. There's a footnote following 'six' in which Dollimore quotes me as saying, in the Introduction to my book: 'I hope to establish a sense of Forster's novels not only as queer . . . but also . . . queerer than queer'.[23] 'Somehow Nick, I don't think so': this brisk and witty sentence, in which my book is summarily dismissed (six words for a reading of six novels), is also, as far as I am aware, the only thing that anyone has ever said in print about the book, at least as a reading of Forster and 'queer'. So in some ways I can only be grateful. But it is also a pity, I think, that this critic couldn't have taken a little longer over the reading and, perhaps, over his assessment. First he tells me 'I don't think so', but then he says *but then*: 'But then, when the deco boys start to out-queer queer, maybe it's time to move on.' This rather curious 'but then' is more or less directly followed by another. For Dollimore at this point ends the paragraph and begins a new section under the heading 'Out-queering', which begins with another kind of 'but then', this time in the form of the phrase 'Except that'. He writes: 'Except that out-queering was always an aspect of queer, especially in relation to perversion' (p. 19). In this way his text appears to gesture in two directions – an outflanking of the 'deco boy', on the one hand, and on the other a lingering, as if uncomfortable or inadvertent suggestion that there is something to be affirmed about deconstructive thinking in this context, specifically as regards its focus on the hyperbolic or exorbitant, its attention to how queer perhaps always already exceeded itself or is indeed generated out of this very logic of out-queering. One might reasonably expect a critic as astute as Jonathan Dollimore candidly to acknowledge this, but his work's relationship with deconstruction remains uneasy: I have written elsewhere regarding its avoidance or elision of deconstructive questions.[24]

So there is something about queer that out-queers itself: this 'was always an aspect of queer'. Queer cruises new senses and directions and continues to alter. As Judith Butler noted in *Bodies That Matter*, in a passage that I also cite in the book on Forster:

> If the term 'queer' is to be a site of collective contestations, the point of departure for a set of historical considerations and future imaginings, it will have to remain that which is, in the present, never fully owned, but always and only redeployed, twisted, queered from a prior usage and in the direction of urgent and expanding political purposes.[25]

I cannot explore in detail the more intricate or twisted and perhaps unsettling dimensions of Butler's argument here except to note that 'queer theory' would have to do with deferred effect and the incalculable, with what cannot be 'anticipated in advance' as she puts it; and indeed that this can and must include the possibility of the disappearance or obsolescence of the term 'queer' itself.[26] This logic of deferred sense and the incalculable, disappearing and spectrality is, I think, one of the ways in which deconstruction and queer theory can be aligned or even be seen to merge into one another. In this context there is perhaps a further irony in Dollimore's remarks, namely that Nicholas Royle's book on E. M. Forster contains not a single explicit reference either to Derrida or to deconstruction. 'Deco boys', you can spot them a mile off: go figure.

♦

'A sudden lurch' (BB, p. 125): it's off, it's by, it's across the path, veering. 'The greasy liquid streamed just across [the] path' (BB, p. 125) of Claggart, the master-at-arms. Over and over, apparently off at a tangent, coming back to this climactic spillage, for instance, with a couple of sentences about passion at the start of Chapter 13: 'Passion, and passion in its profoundest, is not a thing demanding a palatial stage whereon to play its part. Down among the groundlings, among the beggars and rakers of the garbage, profound passion is enacted' (BB, p. 130). It's mourning, top of the mourning, highest mourning as of the beautiful queer butterflies or *papillons* about which Derrida writes in his 'Circumfession', their colourings 'a mélange of black and white',[27] with you I go down, by you, yes, neither to the woods nor Buckingham Palace, but to the municipal tip, delirious dog-days of blazing sun and streaming grief to do and have done it, we eye the totter in a *folie à deux* following flowing towards this soiled sublime blond rugged agelessly old-young creature of the dump transfixing us as we make love to his presence totting an account as if suddenly able to see shadowing sweating heaving in the blistering heat of a fire neither of us can put out, to semen the portmanteau, coming in voice, 'homosexual ventriloquy' as Derrida calls it,[28] high writing cementing, seeing men at sea, panting from the foretop, our Billy Budd, the one with whom we come, in secret, every time.

◆

In *E. M. Forster* I argue that homosexuality and queerness constitute a crucial aspect of all of his novels: in this, despite Jonathan Dollimore's 'I don't think so', I am not claiming anything particularly controversial or even new. A significant collection of essays entitled *Queer Forster* had already appeared in 1997.[29] In the case of *The Longest Journey*, for example, I examine what I refer to as 'all its queer coding, switching and multiplying of sexual identities' (p. 32). (In passing I would just remark that if *The Longest Journey* isn't a queer novel, we are still in need of inventing a critical language to respond to it. This takes us in the direction of what I tentatively refer to as 'queerer than queer', which would include above all perhaps questions of telepathy and spectrality, especially as these pertain to the anonymous, affective, burrowing, tugging strangeness of identification and disidentification in literary fiction. My text is a modest attempt to explore the sense that Forster is at once cannier and uncannier than readers generally give him credit for. There is, if you will, a Forsterian 'I don't think so' addressed to every one of his readers, waiting in the wings. This is related to the sort of mindgameful, cryptic, mole-like curiosity that is evident, for example, in a Forster diary entry from 25 October 1910: 'To work out: The sexual bias in literary criticism . . . What sort of person would the critic prefer to sleep with, in fact.'[30] End of taupological parenthesis.) I try to elucidate what seems to me a Freudian aspect of Forster's work, or at least the Freud who declares in his 1919 essay on Leonardo da Vinci:

> Everyone, even the most normal person, is capable of making a homo-sexual object-choice, and has done so at some time in his life, and either still adheres to it in his unconscious or else protects himself against it by vigorous counter-attitudes.[31]

On this basis, I contend not only that 'all men are queer', but more specifically that that queerness has to do with a time that may never be consciously experienced, a time that doesn't belong. I seek to illustrate this in various ways and indeed to let it (however anachronistically or *deferrentially*) come out in the writing, as a way of trying to countersign what I believe pervades Forster's.[32]

By way of a brief example, I would like to turn, not to one of the novels (which constituted the focus of my earlier work) but to one of Forster's short stories, his unpublishable 'sexy stories' as he called them.[33] 'Ansell' (written probably in 1903) is narrated by a 23-year-old man called Edward who is supposed to be writing 'a dissertation on the Greek optative'.[34] Forster's marvellous little text works and plays with, along and through the bypaths of this word 'optative', defined in two principal current senses in the *OED* as 'adj. '*Grammar.* Having the function of expressing wish or desire' (sense 1); and 'Relating to choice, or expressing desire; relating to the future and to the decisions it involves' (sense 2a). The 23-year-old has just a month in which to complete his dissertation, and then he'll get 'a Fellowship' (p. 29) (those were the days). He leaves Cambridge to stay with his cousin in the country, accompanied by a hefty box containing the relevant books and a mass of notes – 'editions interleaved and annotated, and pages and pages of cross-references and criticisms of rival theories' (p. 30). 'The optative,' as the narrator puts it, 'does not admit of very flowing treatment' (p. 30). On this visit to his cousin's the main focus of Edward's attention is Ansell, the former 'garden and stable boy' (p. 28), 'now gamekeeper . . . and only occasional gardener and groom' (p. 29). In their youth, the narrator tells us, they had been 'on the most intimate footing' (p. 28). As Ansell drives him from the railway station, along a road high above a river, the horse is sent wild by 'clegs' and, in the ensuing 'bang[ing]' and 'back[ing]' and 'crack[ing]' (p. 31), the box containing the narrator's books and thesis-notes slides and falls 'into the abyss', breaking open 'like a water-lily', disseminating its contents down 'through the trees into the river' (p. 32). They try to recover them but, as the narrator puts it, 'of the unfinished dissertation and the essential notes there was not a sign' (p. 34).

So much for academic life. The story concludes: 'Whenever we pass the place Ansell looks over and says "Them books!" and laughs, and I laugh too as heartily as he, for I have not yet realised what has happened' (p. 35). It is this extraordinary final sentence that, to my mind, most resists 'flowing treatment'. In a bizarre, impossible present, it conjoins what narratologists call a pseudo-iterative ('Whenever we pass the place'), a sense that this happens on numerous occasions and yet it is just this one time, with a shared laughter that is attributed to a future that has not yet happened, that cannot yet have happened: 'I laugh too as heartily as he, for I have not yet realised what has happened'. This is not so much the 'not yet' of homoerotic friendship at the end of *A Passage to India*, but rather the strange 'would have', 'might have' and even, in the same sweeping moment, 'did' and 'do' of *Maurice*, in particular of Clive's cryptic turn to apparent heterosexuality at the end of that novel, marked by his perception of Maurice's departure on the last page of the novel. As Forster puts it: 'To the end of his life Clive was not sure of the exact moment of departure, and with the approach of old age he grew uncertain whether the moment had yet occurred.'[35] This sense of deferred queerness or queer deferral in *Maurice* is staged at the end of 'Ansell' in the laughter of what I would like to call a deconstructive optative or, with a wink at Jonathan Dollimore, deco-optative.[36] It is the dreaming of literature, its dream-power, the strange might of a narrator (here a fictional 'I' called Edward, but just as often an anonymous 'I' or so-called 'third-person') who knows more than he or she should or could, with a strange knowingness which is perhaps too easily and too quickly organised and transposed into the familiar filters and grids of narratology. At issue here is the question of a new and altogether queerer vocabulary for flashback, retrospection or ana-lepsis, anticipation, foreshadowing or prolepsis, omniscience, point of view and focalisation, indeed for the entire workings and effects of magical thinking in literature, for its twisted impossible knowledge and knowledge-effects: 'for I have not yet realised what has happened'. I am homosexual, I am queer, from now on, without realising it, in a future that has not yet happened, that *cannot* yet and yet *must have* happened.

◆

On another little by-path, close yet almost out of the picture, I see the figure of Lee Edelman, or more specifically his provocative book *No Future: Queer Theory and the Death Drive*.[37] Though resolutely Lacanian and curiously silent on Derrida, Edelman's book has notable affinities with our concerns here. In particular, we might think of the stress he gives to a deconstructive notion of 'irony', 'that queerest of rhetorical devices' as he calls it (p. 23);[38] or his characterisation of queer theory in terms of a 'refusal . . . of every substantialisation of iden-tity . . . and, by extension, of history as linear narrative . . . in which meaning succeeds in revealing itself – *as itself* – through time' (p. 4). In other respects Edelman's argument might seem entirely contrary to what we are trying to elucidate in these pages: 'queer', for him, 'comes to figure the bar to every realisation of futurity, the resistance, internal to the social, to every social structure or form' (p. 4). Queerness, he thus comes to assert, 'promises, in more than one sense of the phrase, absolutely nothing' (p. 5). Edelman's work is predicated on the force of its polemical negative: think queer, he says, as 'no future'. Queer would be that which 'cuts the thread of futurity' (p. 30), above all insofar as that future comprises 'reproductive futurism' (pp. 4, 27). This may look quite far from Derrida's thinking, especially if one recalls the latter's repeated affirmation of the 'democracy to come' and his cautioning against 'los[ing] sight of the *excess* . . . of the future': the notion of 'no future' in this respect would be linked with totalitarianism.[39] But Edelman's polemic is, I think, considerably closer to Derrida than it may initially appear. For the force of his argument is in fact bound up with what I have just been referring to as the deconstructive optative: what is at issue is not so much 'no future' as it is a thinking of the future in terms of a *wilful* commitment to 'disturbing, [or] queering, social organisation as such' (p. 17), in terms of 'embrac[ing]' this as precisely 'the impossible' (p. 109), an 'impossible project' that we '*might* undertake' (p. 27, emphasis added). No 'no future' without deconstructive desire, without 'what is queerest', namely the '*willingness* to insist intransitively – to insist that the future stop here' (p. 31, emphasis added).

♦

Would that you might taste me. Would that you might taste my selftaste. Impossible, but desired. Such would be the deconstructive optative. In 'Justices', the late great essay on deconstruction and queer theory, apropos J. Hillis Miller and Gerard Manley Hopkins (first given as a lecture in April 2003), Derrida suggests that this is where love and friendship come from. (We may recall how profoundly his work elsewhere intertwines the two – friendship and love, love in friendship – above all, perhaps, in *Politics of Friendship*.[40]) He writes:

> Love and friendship are born in the experience of this unshareable selftaste: an unshareable experience and nevertheless shared, the agreement of two renunciations to say the impossible. As for hatred, jealousy, envy, cruelty, they do not renounce. That is perhaps why they go together more often with knowledge, inquisitorial curiosity, the scopic drive, and epistemophilia.[41]

I would like to relate this renunciation, this double renunciation 'to say the impossible', to the radical passivity to which I alluded at the beginning and to what seems to be happening at the very heart of *Billy Budd*, in other words to the force of Melville's work as 'an inside narrative' that lets us see the 'hatred, jealousy, envy [and] cruelty' embodied in Claggart alongside the declaration that what 'may have' happened in the final interview between Billy Budd and Captain Vere, 'each radically sharing in the rarer qualities of our nature', 'was never known' (BB, p. 156). But time is running out.[42] 'Justices' contains all sorts of strange and surprising treasures. It picks up Miller's picking up the remarkable phrase 'selftaste' in Hopkins, in his early book *The Disappearance of God*, linking it with a taste for the secret and a taste for deconstruction, as well as with the meaning of 'queer' and the 'unspeakable'.[43] Derrida stresses the queer character of the term (and concept of) 'inscape', Hopkins's neologism for the uniqueness of design and pattern, the singularity and even, one might say, the signature or signature-effect of his perception and experience of the world. 'All the world is full of inscape', writes Hopkins: 'looking out of my window I caught it in the random clods and broken heaps of snow made by the cast of a broom.'[44] Snowflakes of sound, fallen or still falling, falling without cease, still to fall, as in the extraordinary lines describing the storm and coming shipwreck in 'The Wreck of the Deutschland': 'Wiry and white-fiery and whirlwind-swivellèd snow / Spins to the widow-making unchilding unfathering deeps.'[45] Inscape is queer, Hopkins affirms, it becomes queer: 'Now, it is the virtue of design, pattern, or inscape to be distinctive and it is the vice of distinctiveness to become queer. This vice I cannot have escaped.'[46] As ever alert to the minuscule shifts of words, Derrida notes this slippage from 'inscape' to 'escape': 'It is [Hopkins's] destiny, his virtue, but also his vice, not to have managed to escape the inscape. He was not able to escape the becoming-vice, the becoming-queer, of this virtue' (J, p. 240). In this veering from 'inscape' to 'escape', there is a queer, vice-versing *cape* that is perhaps another way of getting at the strangeness of 'selftaste'. Inscape has to do with vice and virtue and with the absolute singularity and aloneness that is you, yourself. 'In a childlike fashion', as Derrida puts it, you wonder what it feels like to be the other, or rather how it tastes to be Hillis Miller or, let's say, Jinan Joudeh or, for example, God. Derrida argues that it is on the basis of Hopkins's 'solitude and the unspeakable singularity of [his] selftaste' that he 'speaks, addresses himself to another, and gives to be shared just that, the unshareable of his own taste' (p. 241).

Derrida asks: 'How does the word "queer" impose itself on Hopkins?' (J, p. 240). In doing so his text bears witness at once to the queer time of 'queer' and the deconstructive force of substitutability, that logic according to which the irreplaceably singular can and must be replaced on the spot.[47] For here is 'queer' in Hopkins, at least in Derrida's reading of it, long before the date of 1922 specified in the *OED*, and here is this essay 'Justices' prompting us to wonder in turn: 'How does the word "queer" impose itself on Derrida?' The author of 'Justices' declares: 'The singular says itself, but it says itself as "unspeakable". What is strange and "queer" here is that all this comes down to an experience and, in Hopkins's own words, to a sort of theory of the queer, if not to the impossible uncanniness of a "queer theory"' (J, p. 240). It is in the context of this question of impossible uncanniness and its 'unlimited' pertinence, experience of the impossible necessarily partaking of or sharing in what he calls 'the experience of thought and literary writing' (J, pp. 243–4), that Derrida arrives at perhaps his most aphoristic, haunting and haunted formulation: 'To be is to be queer' (p. 243). If Derrida's work argues for, while enacting, a queering of being, the same can be said of time: deconstruction queers being and time.

♦

I would like to conclude anecdotally, with another footnote of sorts. The brutality and brutal actuality of homophobia remains. It is an over-determined, cryptic story, no doubt, of departures and railway stations (such as the one recalled by Jonathan Dollimore at the beginning of his book *Sexual Dissidence*). The day after the 'life after theory' conference at the University of Loughborough in November 2001, early in the morning, I drove Jacques Derrida to the station ('the oldest railway station in England' as a little plaque on the wall told us), to see him off on his journey back to Paris via London. Such farewells were always strange, disturbing, touching on the uncanny. As he says in *The Work of Mourning*, precisely apropos scenes of 'parting in a train station': 'we do not know if and when and where we will meet again'.[48] We arrived at least forty minutes early and were the only people there. It was cold, so we went into the waiting room, where we talked about, among other things, the uncanny: I asked him if he would come to Sussex and speak on the subject and he agreed to do so. (This was to have been in June 2003: the seminar never happened, in fact, for by then he was ill.) By the time the train for London arrived there were quite a few people on the platform, including a corpulent railway employee with closely cropped hair, evidently the so-called station master. (Thomas the Tank Engine eat your heart out.) Having been far and away the first people waiting for the train we were somewhat slow to find the right coach, and then, still on the platform, we said farewell in our customary way. We embraced and kissed. We kissed in French style, *bises*, lovingly, cheek to cheek. And at this, it became obvious, the nearby official was incensed with disgust. I could see it clear as day in his eyes. He ordered the doors to be closed before Jacques was able to get on. I managed to stick my foot in, just in the nick of time: the official was forced to have the doors reopened and Jacques was able to board. Without a word on this subject ever being exchanged afterwards, the train departed.

Notes

1. Jacques Derrida, *The Post Card: From Socrates to Freud and Beyond*, trans. Alan Bass (Chicago: Chicago University Press, 1987), p. 53.
2. For more on Bersani and the first sentence, and his first sentences in particular, see 'Beyond Redemption: An Interview with Leo Bersani', *Oxford Literary Review*, 20 (1998), 179 ff.
3. Herman Melville, 'Billy Budd, Sailor', in *Melville's Short Novels*, ed. Dan McCall (New York: Norton, 2002), pp. 103 ff.: here, p. 113. For Billy Budd as 'by-blow', see p. 110; for the suggestive instance of a 'budding pink', see p. 170. Further page references to this text are given parenthetically, abbreviated 'BB' where appropriate.
4. Wayne Koestenbaum, *Double Talk: The Erotics of Male Literary Collaboration* (London: Routledge, 1989). Further page references to *Double Talk* appear parenthetically in the main body of the text.
5. Joseph Conrad in collaboration with Ford Madox Hueffer, *Romance* (London: Dent, 1949), p. 533; quoted in Koestenbaum, p. 172.
6. See Jacques Derrida, 'Freud and the Scene of Writing', in *Writing and Difference*, trans. Alan Bass (London: Routledge & Kegan Paul, 1978), pp. 196–231 (especially p. 203); *Archive Fever: A Freudian Impression*, trans. Eric Prenowitz (Chicago: Chicago University Press, 1996), especially p. 80.
7. Jacques Derrida, *H.C. for Life, That Is to Say . . .*, trans. Laurent Milesi and Stefan Herbrechter (Stanford, CA: Stanford University Press, 2006) and *Geneses, Genealogies, Genres and Genius: The Secrets of the Archive*, trans. Beverley Bie Brahic (Edinburgh: Edinburgh University Press, 2006).
8. See *H.C. for Life*, p. 60.
9. Ibid., pp. 107–8.
10. Jacques Derrida, 'Choreographies', trans. Christie V. McDonald, in *Points . . . Interviews, 1974–1994*, ed. Elisabeth Weber (Stanford, CA: Stanford University Press, 1995), p. 108.
11. Jonathan Dollimore, 'Wishful Theory and Sexual Politics', *Radical Philosophy*, 103 (2000), 18–24: here, p. 19. I am grateful to Alex Thomson for bringing this essay to my attention.
12. Ibid., p. 22.
13. See Bennett and Royle, 'Queer', in *Introduction to Literature, Criticism and Theory*, 2nd edn (Hemel Hempstead: Prentice Hall, 1999), p. 178 and ff.
14. See Jacques Derrida, 'Outwork', in *Dissemination*, trans. Barbara Johnson (Chicago: Chicago University Press, 1981), p. 7.

15. See Jacques Derrida, *Of Grammatology*, trans. Gayatri Chakravorty Spivak (Baltimore, MD: Johns Hopkins University Press, 1976), p. 70. Further page references to this text are given parenthetically, abbreviated 'OG' where appropriate.
16. Jacques Derrida, 'Limited Inc a, b, c . . .', trans. Samuel Weber and Jeffrey Mehlman, in *Limited Inc* (Evanston, IL: Northwestern University Press, 1988), p. 100.
17. V. I. Lenin, *What Is To Be Done?* (http://www.marxists.org/archive/lenin/works/1901/witbd/ii.htm#v05fl61h-373-GUESS). In note 16 to this chapter Lenin remarks:

> It is often said that the working class *spontaneously* gravitates towards socialism. This is perfectly true in the sense that socialist theory reveals the causes of the misery of the working class more profoundly and more correctly than any other theory, and for that reason the workers are able to assimilate it so easily, *provided*, however, this theory does not itself yield to spontaneity, *provided* it subordinates spontaneity to itself. Usually this is taken for granted, but it is precisely this which *Rabocheye Dyelo* forgets or distorts. The working class spontaneously gravitates towards socialism; nevertheless, most widespread (and continuously and diversely revived) bourgeois ideology spontaneously imposes itself upon the working class to a still greater degree.

18. Jacques Derrida, 'I Have a Taste for the Secret', in Jacques Derrida and Maurizio Ferraris, *A Taste for the Secret*, trans. Giacomo Donis (Cambridge: Polity Press, 2001), p. 50. Further page references to this text are given parenthetically, abbreviated 'TS' where appropriate.
19. Jacques Derrida, *Spectres of Marx: The State of the Debt, the Work of Mourning, and the New International*, trans. Peggy Kamuf (London: Routledge, 1994), p. 99.
20. See Jacques Derrida, 'Dialanguages', trans. Peggy Kamuf, in *Points*, p. 134.
21. Jacques Derrida, *The Gift of Death*, trans. David Wills (Chicago: Chicago University Press, 1995), p. 92. Cf. *TS*, p. 59.
22. Jacques Derrida, 'Passions: "An Oblique Offering" ', trans. David Wood, in *Derrida: A Critical Reader*, ed. David Wood (Oxford and Cambridge, MA: Basil Blackwell, 1992), p. 21.
23. Nicholas Royle, *E. M. Forster* (Plymouth: Northcote House/British Council, 1999), p. 6; quoted by Dollimore, pp. 19–20, n. 6. Further page references to *E. M. Forster* are given parenthetically in the main body of the text.
24. See, for example, *The Uncanny* (Manchester: Manchester University Press, 2003), pp. 102, n. 6, and 122–3, and the review of Dollimore's *Death, Desire and Loss in Western Culture* (London: Allen Lane, 1998) in *Textual Practice*, 13: 2 (Summer 1999), 389–94, where I discuss the 'marvellously perverse' absence of Derrida from that work.
25. Judith Butler, *Bodies That Matter: On the Discursive Limits of 'Sex'* (London: Routledge, 1993), p. 228; quoted in *E. M. Forster*, p. 87.
26. Ibid., p. 228.
27. See Jacques Derrida, 'Circumfession', trans. Geoffrey Bennington, in Bennington and Derrida, *Jacques Derrida* (Chicago: Chicago University

Press, 1993), p. 166; 'Circonfession', in *Jacques Derrida* (Paris: Éditions de Seuil, 1991), p. 156.

28. 'Circumfession', p. 160.
29. *Queer Forster*, eds Robert K. Martin and George Piggford (Chicago: Chicago University Press, 1997).
30. See Oliver Stallybrass, Introduction to E. M. Forster, *The Life to Come and Other Stories* (Harmondsworth: Penguin, 1989), p. 17, n. 12.
31. Sigmund Freud, 'Leonardo da Vinci and a Memory of his Childhood' (1910), trans. Alan Tyson, in *Art and Literature*, Pelican Freud Library, vol. 14, ed. Albert Dickson (Harmondsworth: Penguin, 1985), 191, n. 1 (note added 1919).
32. I picture the copy-editor, and then perhaps the reader, who thinks that there was an error in this sentence, supposing 'deferrentially' to be a spelling mistake. Elsewhere I hope to elaborate a more extensive account of this queer-looking neologism.
33. Quoted in Stallybrass, Introduction, p. 16.
34. 'Ansell', in *The Life to Come*, pp. 27–35: here p. 29. Further page references to this story are given parenthetically in the main body of the text.
35. E. M. Forster, *Maurice* (Harmondsworth: Penguin, 1972), p. 215.
36. This notion of the deconstructive optative would perhaps provide an illuminating point of agreement and disjunction with what Jonathan Dollimore has to say about queer theory more generally. For him, queer theory is 'wishful theory'. As he puts it: 'Queer radicals, far from liberating the full potential of homosexuality, tame and rework it in various ways.' In particular, 'they tend to represent themselves as personally immune to the subversiveness of desire' ('Wishful Theory and Sexual Politics', p. 21). Queer theory, he goes on, is

> [w]ishful as in wishful thinking. It is a pseudo-radical, pseudo-philosophical, redescription of the world according to an a priori agenda . . . In wishful theory a preconceived narrative of the world is elaborated by mixing and matching bits and pieces of diverse theories until the wished-for result is achieved . . . [T]he contrived narratives of queer theory insulate their adherents from social reality by screening it through high theory, and this in the very act of fantasising its subversion or at least its inherent instability. (p. 21)

Dollimore's is an intriguingly 'literary' version of queer theory: queer theory is characterised, at least in part, in terms of its narrative contrivances and its power of fictional or quasi-fictional redescription. I would broadly subscribe to what he has to say here, concerning the ways that critical or theoretical discourse loses sight of what he calls 'the subversiveness of desire'. Beginning with the remarkable *Sexual Dissidence: Augustine to Wilde, Freud to Foucault* (Oxford: Clarendon Press, 1991), Dollimore's work seems to me to offer admirable analyses and a powerful affirmation of the incalculable, unforeseeable, protean or (as I would like to call it) veering character of desire. At the same time, however, I wonder if his characterisation of queer theory as 'wishful' doesn't actually have the effect of eliding the question of the wish, or at least of bracketing off attention to the ways in which desire is necessarily at work in what is called 'theory'. The phrase 'wishful theory' perhaps inevitably suggests that there is also 'non-wishful theory', or indeed that theory should be not wishful but, rather, separable from wishing or desire, as if its discourse could be free of all affectivity, optativity or performative effects (whether intentional, unconscious or, more generally, *iterable* in Derrida's sense). For more on the notion of 'wishful theory', see also Dollimore's earlier essay, 'Bisexuality, Heterosexuality, and Wishful Theory', in *Textual Practice*, 10: 3 (1996), 523–39, as well as the revised version of some of this material in his *Sex, Literature and Censorship* (Cambridge: Polity Press, 2001).

37. Lee Edelman, *No Future: Queer Theory and the Death Drive* (Durham, NC: Duke University Press, 2004). Further page references to Edelman's book are given parenthetically in the main body of the text.

38. Edelman specifically invokes uncanniness when he writes: 'Queer theory . . . would constitute the site where the radical threat posed by irony, which heteronormative culture displaces onto the figure of the queer, is uncannily returned by queers who no longer disown but assume their figural identity as embodiments of the figuralisation, and hence the disfiguration, of identity itself' (p. 24). The word 'assume' is up to mischievous business in this formulation – its ambiguity (merely 'assuming') nicely sidestepping the question of 'owning' or 'appropriating'.

39. See, in particular, 'I Have a Taste for the Secret', p. 22.

40. At issue here, in particular, is the importance of the term *aimance* ('lovingness' or, in George Collins's translation, 'lovence'): see *Politics of Friendship*, trans. George Collins (London: Verso, 1997), pp. 7–8, and *passim*. I discuss 'love', 'friendship' and 'lovingness' further, in 'Forgetting Well' (below).

41. Jacques Derrida, 'Justices', trans. Peggy Kamuf, in *Provocations to Reading: J. Hillis Miller and the Democracy to Come*, eds Barbara Cohen and Dragan Kujundzic (New York: Fordham University Press, 2005), p. 238. Further page references to this essay are given parenthetically in the main body of the text, abbreviated 'J' where appropriate.

42. A sudden lurch, she is saying in my ear, into a footnote (once again, the *pas* and *démarche* of deconstruction, the footstep of the other), scarcely a whisper, concerning the Handsome Sailor or foretopman of such 'masculine beauty' but also embodying something of 'the beautiful woman' (BB, p. 111), his voice 'singularly musical' but with one 'defect', viz. 'an organic hesitancy' (p. 111), the murmur and proliferation of voices echoing (like that of each or any reader subvocalising or reading aloud as s/he goes) in the wake of the appalling benediction at the heart of Melville's text, the work so worked upon (from 1886 up until his death in 1891) and so deferred in appearance (eventually coming out in print only in 1924, but have we really even begun to read it, for example the hesitancy of its title, turning between 'Billy Budd, Sailor' and 'Billy Budd, Foretopman', into its abyssal subtitle, 'an inside narrative'?), the last words of Billy, 'delivered in the clear melody of a singing bird on the point of launching from the twig': '"God bless Captain Vere!"' (BB, p. 163). Billy Budd might seem to resemble one of the *papillons* in Derrida's *Circumfession*: the sailor's 'external apparel, white jumper and white duck trousers, each more or less soiled, dimly glimmered in the obscure light of the bay like a patch of discolored snow in early April lingering at some upland cave's black

mouth. In effect he is already in his shroud, or the garments that shall serve him in lieu of one' (BB, p. 159). As with the 'by-path' with which I began, this fragmented sentence or two might detain us sinning at literature's pleasure for an inordinately long time, among other things precisely in terms of its derangement of time, the internal shiftings or the ruinously, magically, impossibly internal-external shiftings of a narrative perspective between past ('dimly glimmered'), present ('In effect he is already in his shroud') and future ('the garments that shall serve him'). Even more intensely than *Moby-Dick*, 'Billy Budd' seems at once to emerge out of and to provoke the experience of what Leo Bersani calls 'the inability to stop reading'. (See Leo Bersani, 'Incomparable America', in his *The Culture of Redemption* (Cambridge, MA: Harvard University Press, 1990), pp. 136–54: here, p. 150.) This inability is figured perhaps most sharply in the extraordinary subtitle of Melville's last work, 'an inside narrative', a phrase that alerts us to the irreducibly and inexhaustibly telepathic or literary dimensions of this apparently 'historical' account. It may be tempting to categorise and thus effectively bracket off the question and experience of this 'inability' in terms of a principle of uncertainty that would be 'queer'-identified. This is a danger that seems to me at issue in Robert K. Martin's suggestion that the 'adoption of a queer model that proposes contingency instead of certainty seems likely to offer the best future for the study of sexuality in Melville's texts' (Robert K. Martin, 'Melville and Sexuality', in *The Cambridge Companion to Herman Melville*, ed. Robert S. Levine (Cambridge: Cambridge University Press, 1998), p. 200). Citing these words, in an essay on 'Gender and Sexuality' in Melville, Leland S. Person likewise seeks to propound the notion of a critical 'queer model' in terms of uncertainty: 'Uncertainty is such a common feeling for Melville's readers and contingency such a common experience for Melville's characters, that a "queer model" of approach to just about any issue in Melville's writing makes good sense' (Leland S. Person, 'Gender and Sexuality', in *A Companion to Herman Melville*, ed. Wyn Kelley (Oxford: Blackwell, 2006), pp. 244–5). Uncertainty as a 'queer model' here risks becoming an end in itself, in a sort of repetition of that error by which deconstruction in earlier days became identified with 'indeterminacy' or 'indeterminism'. If queer theory has a special relationship with dubitation, this has to do with *more*, not less, critical and inventive modes of questioning, with trying to affirm and analyse, affirm *by* analysing singularity (whether of signature, event or context), not with referring things back to some generalised logic or model of uncertainty as if for its own sake. The inability to stop reading is still a matter of reading. (*To be continued.*)

43. J. Hillis Miller, *The Disappearance of God: Five Nineteenth-Century Writers* (Cambridge, MA.: Belknap Press, 1963).
44. *The Journals and Papers of Gerard Manley Hopkins*, eds Humphry House and Graham Storey (London: Oxford University Press, 1959), p. 230; cited in 'Justices', p. 239.
45. 'The Wreck of the Deutschland', Part 2, stanza 13, in *The Poems of Gerard Manley Hopkins*, 4th edition, eds W. H. Gardner and N. H. MacKenzie (Oxford: Oxford University Press, 1970), p. 55.

46. *The Letters of Gerard Manley Hopkins to Robert Bridges*, ed. Claude Colleer Abbott (London: Oxford University Press, 1955), p. 66; cited in 'Justices', p. 240.

47. See, for example, Jacques Derrida, *Demeure: Fiction and Testimony* (with Maurice Blanchot's *The Instant of My Death*), trans. Elizabeth Rottenberg (Stanford, CA: Stanford University Press, 2000), p. 41.

48. Jacques Derrida, 'Letter to Francine Loreau', in *The Work of Mourning*, eds Pascale-Anne Brault and Michael Naas (Chicago: Chicago University Press, 2001), p. 95.

Outside the château at Cerisy, July 1997. Jacques Derrida [gesturing toward the sward]: 'Look, there is the mole . . .'. (Reproduced by permission of Marie-Louise Mallet.)

Forgetting Well

Forgetting well. It is necessary to forget well. This phrase occurs, in a manner at once easy and peremptory, in the 'dialogue' with Elisabeth Roudinesco published in English as *For What Tomorrow* . . . . He is on to what is perhaps his most cherished but terrible topic, that is to say mourning. Mourning is his hobby-horse. Of course it is impossible, the impossible hobby-horse. He says to her, as he has said to others, in so many different writings, interviews, speeches and discussions:

> Mourning *must* be impossible. Successful mourning is failed mourning. In successful mourning, I incorporate the one who has died, I assimilate him to myself, I reconcile myself with death, and consequently I deny death and the alterity of the dead other and of death as other. I am therefore unfaithful. Where the introjection of mourning succeeds, mourning annuls the other. I take him upon me, and consequently I negate or delimit his infinite alterity . . . . Faithfulness prescribes to me at once the necessity and the impossibility of mourning. It enjoins me to take the other within me, to make him live in me, to idealise him, to internalise him, but it also enjoins me not to succeed in the work of mourning: the other must remain the other. He is effectively, presently, undeniably dead, but, if I take him into me as a part of me, and if, consequently, I 'narcissise' this death of the other by a successful work of mourning, I annihilate the other, I reduce or deny his death.[1]

In this way he tries to formulate the double-bind of mourning. Mourning is necessary but impossible, necessary *and* impossible. It fails to happen, it fails in happening, it never completely finally happens, except in failing. To the extent that it succeeds in happening, mourning fails, it fails to happen.

His remarks are not limited to what happens or *must* fail to happen in the case of the death of a friend or beloved or beloved friend. (The interlacings and interleavings between love and friendship, as he shows in *Politics of Friendship*, are complex: 'friendship consists in loving', 'it is a way of loving', he says.[2] No love or friendship without *aimance*: 'Beyond all ulterior frontiers between love and friendship, but also between the passive and active voices, between the loving and the being-loved, what is at stake is "*aimance*" [p. 7]. In a footnote [pp. 24–5, n. 5] he says this word was invented by his friend, the 'poet-thinker' Abdelkebir Khatibi. George Collins translates *aimance* as 'lovence'; I prefer David Wills's suggestion of 'lovingness'.) He is talking, in *For What Tomorrow . . .*, about the nature of being, the very constitution of the self, culture and memory. What he says concerning this negation or annulment of the alterity of the other applies also, for example, in the case of immigration, in other words 'the integration of the immigrant, or the assimilation of the foreigner'. And he goes on: 'This "mourning effect" does not wait for death. One does not wait for the death of the other to deaden and absorb his alterity' (FWT, p. 160). As he pithily proposes elsewhere, in an interview with Maurizio Ferraris: 'I mourn therefore I am.'[3]

Now Elisabeth Roudinesco doesn't go along with any of this, it would seem, she won't or can't. She says: 'It seems to me, on the contrary, that a successful work of mourning is not an act of infidelity. It makes it possible to invest in a new object that perpetuates the memory of the old one' (FWT, p. 160). She speaks the language of a more traditional Freudian perspective, the established historian of psychoanalysis. Mourning comes to an end, it is successful in that it allows for a new investment: our capacity for love is freed up and we are able (to borrow Freud's words from the haunting essay, 'On Transience') 'to replace the lost objects by fresh ones equally or still more precious'.[4] In response he says to her:

> Yes, but the loved object is perpetuated in being betrayed, in being forgotten. The one who has died must of course be forgotten, must be forgotten *well*. As I once said – and it is basically the same transubstantiation – 'of course one must eat/one must eat well'. Faithfulness is unfaithful. [*Oui, mais l'on perpétu l'objet aimé en le trahissant, en l'oubliant. Il faut bien, il faut* bien *oublier le mort, comme j'ai dit un jour, et c'est au fond la même transubstantiation, 'il faut bien manger'. La fidélité est infidèle.*] (FWT, pp. 160/258–9)

What sentences!

He is alluding to an interview with Jean-Luc Nancy entitled 'Eating Well'. As with eating, then, it is a matter of 'conception-appropriation-assimilation of the other'.[5] It is a question of 'the "Good" [*Bien*] of every morality', and of 'determining the best, most respectful, most grateful, and also most giving way of relating to the other and of relating the other to the self' (pp. 281–2). As the English translators note, the original French title of this interview is 'Il faut bien manger', which 'can be read in at least two ways: "one must eat well" or "everyone has to eat". In addition, when the adverb "bien" is nominalised as "le Bien", there results the sense of "eating the Good".[6] Do not forget to live, but live to forget. How does one forget well? How is this 'metonymy of introjection to be regulated' (p. 282)? In his conversation with Nancy (and everything here is in conversation, conversing and conversion, passing by way of the mouth, between mouths and ears, minds, hearts), he says:

> The infinitely metonymical question on the subject of 'one must eat well' ['*il faut bien manger*'] must be nourishing not only for me, for a 'self', which would thus eat badly; it must be *shared*, as you might put it, and not only in language. 'One must eat well' does not mean above all taking in and grasping in itself, but *learning* and *giving* to eat, learning-to-give-the-other-to-eat. One never eats entirely on one's own: this constitutes the rule underlying the statement, 'One must eat well'. It is a rule offering infinite hospitality. (p. 282)

You must forget well, you have to forget. Strange double or divided saying, injunction out of joint. And if we pursue further the suggestion concerning what is 'basically the same transubstantiation', we could conclude: forgetting must be nourishing, not only for me; it must be shared, and not only in language; one never forgets entirely on one's own; forgetting well entails an openness to infinite hospitality.

◆

The book with Roudinesco is rich and strange not least for its elisions, crossed wires and missed connections. At times it reads like a sort of dialogue in abyss, at least if we understand by 'dialogue' something like 'an exchange of views in the hope of ultimately reaching agreement'.[7] I am thinking of the cumulative impression, for example, of such interjections or ripostes as 'I don't see it that way' (p. 94), 'I would tend rather to refuse to introduce . . .' (p. 125), 'I didn't say . . .' (p. 160), 'You don't agree with that?' (p. 164), 'I don't know how to respond . . .' (p. 165), 'In my opinion, on the contrary . . .' (p. 174), 'I would tend to think . . .' (p. 195). At some moments more explicitly than at others, Roudinesco seems to want to psychologise his writing, to psychobiographise his philosophy, in particular through identifying him with 'melancholy'.[8] She thinks that all this talk about 'faithful infidelity' and 'successful mourning as impossible mourning' can be seen in psychological terms, boiling down to 'the double character of melancholy: it is the source both of creativity and of destruction' (p. 160).

His distance from this can perhaps be indicated by some remarks he makes in January 1993, in commemoration of the death of his friend

Louis Marin. Mourning is, as always for him, at once singular ('There is no common measure able to persuade me that a personal mourning is less grave than a nuclear war', as we may recall him saying elsewhere)⁹ *and* exposed to the most unbounded generalisation: 'All work in general works *at mourning* . . . The work of mourning is not one kind of work among other possible kinds.'¹⁰ There is, moreover, 'no metalanguage for the language in which a work of mourning is at work'; mourning 'cannot become a theme, only another experience of mourning that comes to work over the one who intends to speak. To speak of mourning or of anything else' (p. 143). He is speaking in 1993, but it is as if he were also, at the same time, dropping words for Elisabeth Roudinesco to hear or read years later: 'In the era of psychoanalysis, we all of course speak, and we can always go on speaking, about the "successful" work of mourning – or, inversely, as if it were precisely the contrary, about a "melancholia" that would signal the failure of such work' (p. 144). Rather, he suggests, it is a question of mourning as a work that works at failing, or more precisely at failing well. And here, above all, his words seem to call out to the figure of forgetting well that appears, as if off the cuff, passed off in passing, in the discussion with Roudinesco. He writes:

> this is the law, the law of mourning, and the law of the law, always in mourning, that it would have to fail in order to succeed. In order to succeed, it would well have to *fail*, to fail *well*. It would well have to fail, for this is what has to be so, in failing *well*. [*Pour réussir, il lui faudra bien* échouer, bien *échouer. Il lui faudra bien échouer, car il le faut, en échouant* bien.] That is what it would have to be. And while it is always promised, it will never be assured. (pp. 144/179)

Affirmation, like the gift, is irreducibly linked to mourning. Mourning is not negative. Neither is melancholy simply a figure of failure. Moreover, as he suggests earlier on in his exchanges with Roudinesco, the 'aporias' of mourning (failing well, the necessary and impossible, and so on) entail working *with* 'the resources' of psychoanalysis but also working *on* 'the limits of psychoanalytic discourse on this subject' (FWT, p. 78).

He speaks of this interminable preoccupation once again in 'Rams', the beautiful text about Hans-Georg Gadamer and Paul Celan that transpired to be one of the last books published in his lifetime.¹¹ Prowling around the extraordinary line in Celan, 'The world is gone, I must carry you [*Die Welt ist fort, ich muß dich tragen*]', he engages with Freud's conception of mourning (in particular, in the essay 'Mourning and Melancholia')¹² in ways that seek, as he puts it, 'to remove the analysis, albeit interminable, from the order of consciousness, from self-presence and from the ego, from all egology'. He goes on:

According to Freud, mourning consists in carrying the other in the self. There is no longer any world, it's the end of the world for the other at his death, and so I welcome this end of the world in me, I must carry the other and his world, the world in me: introjection, interiorisation of remembrance (*Erinnerung*), and idealisation. Melancholy would welcome the failure and the pathology of this mourning. But if *I must* (and this is ethics itself) carry the other in me in order to be faithful to him, in order to respect his singular alterity, a certain melancholy must still protest against normal mourning. This melancholy must never resign itself to idealising introjection. It must rise up against what Freud says of it with such assurance, as if to confirm the norm of normality. The 'norm' is nothing other than the good conscience of amnesia. It allows us to *forget* that to keep the other within oneself, *as oneself*, is already to *forget* the other. Forgetting begins there. Melancholy is therefore necessary [Il faut *donc la mélancolie*].[13]

Such is the beginning of forgetting. Melancholy is necessary. It is not down to his or her or my 'individual pathology' but rather a structure, a situation, how it is.

◆

'The era of psychoanalysis', did I hear myself say, hear him say? Are we still in this era? Or has a kind of somnolence, resistance, indifference and forgetfulness, along with other, arguably more 'active' or 'proactive' forms of educational, cultural and ideological programming, managed to make this topic seem too fuzzy and distant, too vague to talk about? Perhaps his shortest but also most condensed statement on the question of forgetting in the context of psychoanalysis is the mini-text or series of remarks published under the title 'Let Us Not Forget – Psychoanalysis'. Everything is, in a sense, already there in the opening half-dozen sentences:

> Let us not forget psychoanalysis.
> People would like to make us forget psychoanalysis.
> Will we forget psychoanalysis?
> The forgetting of psychoanalysis could not be one forgetting among others and cannot fail to produce symptoms.
> The forgetting of psychoanalysis does not necessarily take place outside psychoanalysis or its institutional space. It can work at the very heart of the psychoanalytical.[14]

This little text of five pages also includes one of my favourite sentences, which also happens to be one of his longest. He is talking about the 'climate of opinion' (the philosophical 'climate of opinion' though clearly not only that), and he is doing this at the Sorbonne in Paris, as part of a forum on 'Thinking at Present', in 1988; but what he has to say is no doubt as topical and urgent now or even more so, and not only in

France or indeed Europe. He is referring to a sort of reaction-formation to what in an Anglophone academic context is sometimes referred to as 'French Freud', the 'return to Freud' or the 'new Freud' that is associated with 'poststructuralist thinking'. Here is the sentence:

> And today, in the climate of opinion, people are starting to behave as though it were nothing at all, as though nothing had happened, as though taking into account the event of psychoanalysis, a logic of the unconscious, of 'unconscious concepts', even, were no longer *de rigueur*, no longer even had a place in something like a history of reason: as if one could calmly continue the good old discourse of the Enlightenment, return to Kant, call us back to the ethical or juridical or political responsibility of the subject by restoring the authority of consciousness, of the ego, of the reflexive cogito, of an 'I think' without pain or paradox; as if, in this moment of philosophical restoration that is in the air – for what is on the agenda, the agenda's moral agenda, is a sort of shameful, botched restoration – as if it were a matter of flattening the supposed demands of reason into a discourse that is purely communicative, informational, smooth; as though, finally, it were again legitimate to accuse of obscurity or irrationalism anyone who complicates things a little by wondering about the reason of reason, about the history of the principle of reason or about the event – perhaps a traumatic one – constituted by something like psychoanalysis in reason's relation to itself. (p. 4)

It is a matter precisely of *analysing* what is going on with this movement whereby 'on pretext of restoring threatened values, and of doing so in the name of reason, responsibility, man, etc.', we are seeing 'a return to a new and very old form of irresponsibility, denial and abdication: obscurantism itself under the mask of humanistic moralism, clear and distinct conscience and consciousness, democratic discussion and consensus' (p. 5).

Let us not forget psychoanalysis, he says, but at the same time, since people evidently are forgetting it, and in a perhaps more blasé and unthinking fashion than ever, let us try to take account of that by focusing on a series of questions: What is forgetting? What does psychoanalysis have to tell us about the nature of reason and forgetting, and the reasons for forgetting? And 'what would one be trying to forget about reason, for what reasons, if, today, one was trying to forget the unconscious?' (p. 7). These are questions that run through everything he writes. As René Major has observed:

> psychoanalysis is what [he] never forgets. He is bound to it, as to his mother tongue, by an originary, which does not mean univocal, bond . . . As with the mother tongue, the relation to the unconscious, which psychoanalysis brings into play, always remains both foreign and familiar . . . [And at the same time] the paths opened up by [his] readings of Freud and Lacan's work have become ones which psychoanalysis cannot forget or foreclose, unless it forget itself.[15]

If there is an era of psychoanalysis he has altered it. He hasn't left it unrecognisable. That's not his way. He has merely displaced and transformed it: at once familiar and foreign to itself.

◆

So, to mourn, to remember and forget well. Without ever being assured, either by him or by myself, by him in myself, or by others. I work hard at this, and therefore doubtless too hard. Work more gently, without force, with the least possible force. How to think on, how to go on? This is one of the places where his writing comes into a profound correspondence with Beckett's, this failing well or failing better.[16] It's weird work, weird words, forgetting well. I do violence to my friend in citing him, consistently, in another language, even no doubt in this translated formulation 'forgetting well' which I cannot help but read in my own way, in a way that *only happens to me*.[17] Working through and over English: that's how it was. I would write to him in English (the only language that I have and that isn't mine) and he would reply in French (his uncanny monolingualism), but when we met (whether in the United States, France or England) he would become host and hostage, turn himself over to 'my' language, speak with me in English because he knew how to, and because he graciously and generously accepted that my French was never going to pass muster.

◆

Forgetting well. It seems as if there is no possibility of a meeting with Roudinesco here, even if he begins by concurring with her. It is there in the simplicity of the 'Yes, but [*Oui, mais*]'. 'Yes, but the loved object is perpetuated in being betrayed, in being forgotten [*Oui, mais l'on perpétue l'objet aimé en la trahissant, en l'oubliant*]': this is both an apparent agreeing and a shifting away, moving on, it happens everywhere, it's one of his signature-effects, a shift of genius-in-asyndeton whereby the loved one is perpetuated not only by being betrayed (a point that is already not Roudinesco's) but by being forgotten, where forgetting the loved one is something new, turning up at the end of the sentence, as if to cover us all (like the snow at the end of Joyce's 'The Dead') in forgetting. He is already onto something else, the next sentence, the extraordinary formulation that seems at once to be a sort of by-product of the preceding sentence (Milton's phrase 'easy numbers' comes to mind[18]), a connective with everything else he has said on the subject of mourning, and an entirely new and strange, indeed impossible saying: '*Il faut bien, il faut* bien *oublier le mort*'. Untranslatable and therefore, as we know from him, the only thing to be translated. The French gives, as Jeff Fort's translation does not, a well [*bien*] up front: how could English respond, transpose, countersign this 'well'? It is well necessary. It is necessary to forget. And at the same time it is necessary to forget *well* the one who has died, the friend or beloved, the beloved friend.

What does it mean to forget well? How would one do it? According to what time frame, starting out from where?

◆

In the essay on Shakespeare's *Hamlet* entitled 'The Time Is Out of Joint', originally presented at a conference at New York University in the autumn of 1993, he argues that the question not just of mourning but of 'the time of mourning' is 'finally the true subject of the play'.[19] *Hamlet* poses, above all, the question of 'what then *is*, in its impossible present, time itself' (p. 19). 'The Time Is Out of Joint' is a provocatively political reading of Shakespeare's play, a sort of mad supplement to *Spectres of Marx*, a supplement on the madness of time and the madness of 'suffering . . . amnesia' (p. 17). It follows *Spectres of Marx* in part by way of what he calls 'a political position-taking . . . *on the subject of* America, and . . . *against* a certain America in the new world order that is attempting to impose itself today' (p. 32).[20] As in *Spectres of Marx*, he explores the relations between deconstruction and justice, starting from the idea of justice as what cannot be deconstructed: 'deconstruction *is* justice' (p. 31), he asserts at one point.[21] And as in *Spectres of Marx* also, this exploration is drawn out of a reading of *Hamlet* as a play about 'absolute disorder, the world out of joint, measurelessness, monstrosity' (TOJ, p. 34).

Taking its bearings from Nietzsche and Celan as well as *Hamlet*, 'The Time Is Out of Joint' focuses on what *one has to know* on the subject of mourning and the time of mourning. In order to put an end to mourning, he says, one has to presume 'that mourning depends on us, in us, and not on the other in us. It presumes above all a knowledge . . . One must indeed know *when* [*Il faut bien savoir* quand]: *at what instant* mourning began. One must indeed know *at what moment* death took place [*Il faut bien savoir* à quel moment *a eu lieu*], really took place, and this is always the moment of a murder' (p. 20). One must know it, one must know it well. Death here would thus come to figure 'the violence of the founding event – which always has something to do with a phantasm' (p. 23). When does death take place? What is a phantasm?

What is life if '[its] affirmation . . . is nothing other than a certain thought of death'?[22] What is mourning if it entails a protestation against 'normal mourning'? What is forgetting well? Uncertainty concerning these questions is at the heart of deconstruction, for deconstruction is what 'begins by questioning, displacing and dislocating' the 'teleological schema' of 'birth, growth, old age, sickness, end or death', and by questioning, displacing and dislocating '[the] opposition between health and sickness, normality and anomaly, life and death' (TOJ, pp. 30–1). Deconstruction would therefore begin from the thought that 'one must stop believing that the dead are just the departed and that the departed do nothing. One must stop pretending to know what is meant by "to die" and especially by "dying". One has, then, to talk about spectrality' (p. 30). The significance of Shakespeare's play is, for him, centred on Hamlet's experience of being 'the heir of a spectre concerning which no one knows any longer *at what moment* and therefore *if* death has happened to him' (p. 30).

He says: Hamlet 'has seen the impossible and he cannot survive what he has survived . . . Because one *should not* survive. And that is what Hamlet *says*, and that is what *Hamlet*, the work, *does*. The work alone, but alone with us, in us, as us. This is what one has to know' (p. 36). And it is from here, he asserts, that 'the call of justice resonates' (p. 37). It is a question of what the work alone does to each one of us alone, in the strange aloneness of bearing witness to the impossible, in particular 'the impossibility of assigning a real date, thus an external, objective reality, to the death of Hamlet's father', in other words 'the impossibility of measuring time and thus of measuring the measure of all things' (p. 33). We are all heirs of spectres and of this deconstructive thinking of the phantasm, with every death, and every experience of mourning, alone.[23]

'The Time Is Out of Joint' might be described as an *occasional piece*, if we allow that phrase to resonate sufficiently with a sense of chance, of what befalls or happens to be the *case*, and with a Shakespearean sense of 'piece' as fragment or remnant.[24] (On the watch, in the night, at the start, Barnardo calls: 'What, is Horatio there?' And Horatio replies: 'A piece of him.'[25]) It is a deceptively casual, disjunctive, out of joint essay, in three parts. Part I ends with a passage from Shakespeare's play concerning the time of mourning and forgetting. Like Hamlet, 'The Time Is Out of Joint' is more than a bit raving, enmeshing us in a certain experience of theatrical repetition. The sense of deranged time is not only Hamlet's but that of reading the essay. As always, his signature is there in the way his writing enacts what he is writing about, as his own sentences rave, race away, like those of the 'last survivor' (p. 33) that he will have been, at work countersigning the 'time out of joint', the phrase from *Hamlet* that he confesses to loving like an obsession (p. 18). It is just before the dumb show and the play-within-the-play. It is perhaps the most acute moment of the madness of suffering memory and amnesia, the delirium of dating, of assigning a time to death, but also the delirium of whether Hamlet is 'truly raving or if he is playing at madness in order to outmanoeuvre his partners, fool everybody, and put the event back on stage, by organising the theatrical repetition in which it already consists, with the sole aim of ensnaring the criminal, trapping him, catching him with his symptom ("The play's the thing / Wherein I'll catch the conscience of the king . . .")' (p. 23). It's just at that point where Hamlet makes a motion to put his head in Ophelia's lap and a joke about her genitals:

HAMLET	Lady, shall I lie in your lap?
OPHELIA	No, my lord.
HAMLET	I mean, my head upon your lap.
OPHELIA	Ay, my lord.
HAMLET	Do you think I meant country matters?
OPHELIA	I think nothing, my lord.
HAMLET	That's a fair thought to lie between maids' legs.
OPHELIA	What is, my lord?
HAMLET	No-thing.
OPHELIA	You are merry, my lord.
HAMLE	Who, I?
OPHELIA	Ay, my lord.
HAMLET	O God, your only jig-maker. What should a man do but be merry? For look you how cheerfully my mother looks, and my father died within's two hours.
OPHELIA	Nay, 'tis twice two months, my lord.

(III, ii, 104–19)

He doesn't cite this passage in full, but writes about how we cannot tell what is going on when Hamlet pretends to put his head between her legs, 'as if to mimic penetration or birth', and he writes about how we cannot tell if Hamlet is speaking figuratively or not when he seems to be 'reducing . . . months into hours' (p. 23). Hamlet is apparently unable to believe or comprehend that it is, as Ophelia informs him, 'twice two months' since his father died:

> So long? Nay then, let the devil wear black, for I'll have a suit of sables. O heavens, die two months ago, and not forgotten yet! Then there's hope a great man's memory may outlive his life half a year. But, by'r Lady, he must build churches then . . .

(III, ii, 120–4)

These lines are cited at the end of Part I of 'The Time Is Out of Joint' (p. 24). The significance of this passage to the essay as a whole is indicated by the fact that Hamlet's incredulous little two-word question

'So long?' (followed by three dots) also forms the essay's solitary epigraph. He says nothing about the citation, cutting it off with three dots mid-sentence and thereby ending Part I of his essay: 'But, by'r Lady, he must build churches then . . .' I can imagine entire books, a proliferation of shelves of books concerned with the study and research of where he quotes without comment, of what he doesn't say, of how to read what is (apparently) not there. Some of his most haunting and memorable effects are built out of these silences, interruptions and ellipses, where he lets himself be read in, through or under the voice of others. It is also, of course, where his work has given rise to fundamental misunderstandings, above all perhaps where commentators think he thinks the same as what he is saying the other is saying. But still, it is a strange place to stop, at the moment of invoking the need to build churches then . . .

◆

Hamlet's language is of course pervasively religious – 'O God', 'the devil', 'O heavens', 'by'r Lady (i.e. Our Lady, the Virgin Mary)', and finally the building of 'churches'. There is no sustained or explicit engagement either in 'The Time Is Out of Joint' or in *Spectres of Marx* with the Christian character of Shakespeare's language. It is a question of reading between words and sentences, between the lines and letters, where (as he says in the early essay on Jabès, first published in January 1964) 'death strolls'.[26] It is a reading in the spirit of what *Spectres of Marx* calls 'a messianism without religion'.[27] It is a matter of exploring 'the time of mourning as messianic time of imminence' (TOJ, p. 23). If a great man is to be remembered even six months after he's dead, he must build churches. Reductively characterising this thought as 'cynicism', the editors of the recent Arden Third Series *Hamlet* compare it with Benedick's comment in *Much Ado About Nothing*: 'If a man do not erect in this age his own tomb ere he dies, he shall live no longer in monument than the bell rings, and the widow weeps'.[28] The proximity with *Hamlet* (written probably a couple of years after *Much Ado*) indeed goes further. Hamlet's supposition that his father has been dead for less than two hours ('within's two hours') picks up, re-sounds and reworks Benedick's reply to Beatrice when asked 'how long is that think you?' Answer: So long as a man makes sure he has his own tomb erected before he dies, he can expect to be remembered for an hour and a quarter, that is to say, as Benedick puts it, 'an hour in clamour [the time of *glas*, the tolling of the funeral bell, but also 'clamour' as vociferation, vehement expression of feeling, outburst, outcry, a mingling of voices] and a quarter in rheum [fifteen minutes of weeping by the widow]' (V, ii, 61–2).

There is something else that links the lines in *Hamlet* with those from *Much Ado*, namely the spectral oddity of Shakespeare's use of the verbs 'live' and 'outlive': the 'memory' of a dead person can 'outlive his life', if only for six months; it is possible to 'live . . . in monument' or memorial. Here, in particular, one might get a glimpse of 'those breaches' described in *Spectres of Marx*, those 'poetic and thinking peepholes [*meurtrières*, slits for watching and firing arrows, literally "murder-holes"] through which Shakespeare will have kept watch over the English language'.[29] Shakespeare's language dislocates and displaces any opposition of life and death, even as it seems to aver death's finality or 'strict arrest'. To outlive one's life, to live in monument: this, in the context of *Much Ado About Nothing*, appears to be a question of living, or living on, not only in the form of the stone of a church-building or other monument (and doubtless the inscription of the name there[30]), but also in the form of sound (the 'clamour') and tears (the 'rheum'). Clamour and tears: let us note these, with a view to coming back to them a little later.

◆

Why does the passage from *Hamlet* get cut off in this manner, mid-sentence, at the end of Part I of 'The Time Is Out of Joint', before he goes on to discuss, in an apparently quite different tone, the question of 'deconstruction in America'? What, if anything, are we to make of this cryptic occlusion of Christianity, this syncopated church-building in memory of? No doubt we are drifting into the region, if we were not already there, of phantom brain-territory.[31] Two possible directions in any case. First, we may recall his consistent concern with the non-theistic, non-theological and non-religious, and we might contrast his account of 'deconstruction in America' (in 'The Time Is Out of Joint' and elsewhere) with the religiously-inflected character of the US academy in which so-called deconstructionist criticism was initially produced in the late 1970s and through the 1980s. (I say *so-called deconstructionist criticism* because 'deconstructionist' is not a word he ever used of himself – indeed it is, as Martin McQuillan has commented, simply 'a word used by idiots';[32] and because the juxtaposition of deconstruction and criticism is a sort of self-cancelling oxymoron: 'deconstruction' is precisely *not* 'criticism' or 'critique'. As we may read, for instance, in *Mémoires for Paul de Man*: 'there cannot be a deconstructive criticism, since deconstruction is more or less, or in any case other than a criticism'.[33]) A quick look at an interview he gave in April 1984 makes it clear that he was from early on sharply aware of the religious character of the 'reception of deconstruction in America': he stresses what he calls 'the protestant, theological ethic which marks the American academic world' and argues that one cannot talk about 'deconstruction in America' without 'mobilising an analysis that . . . focuses on the history of [the US], its religious and moral tradition . . . [the] religious above all'.[34] Then, too, there is the question of what monuments – what institution or institutions, what 'foundations' does he leave us with? As Geoffrey Bennington has suggested, there aren't any, at least in the sense in which Freud, for example, can be said to have left behind a Psychoanalytic Association and a range of institutes across the world. Bennington observes:

> It is probably no accident that [his] death leaves no organised institution of deconstruction whatsoever, no department or school or institute, no institution *of* deconstruction, and at most, at best, but it *is* best, institutions *in* deconstruction . . .[35]

Deconstruction has no institution or monumental centre. One can imagine, perhaps, a centre *for* deconstruction but not a centre *of* deconstruction. Institutions and centres are always *in* deconstruction: that is what his writing and teaching have made clear, all the way from 'Structure, Sign and Play' to 'The University without Condition'.[36]

And as for the second direction – well, it is best and well . . . to try to read the ellipsis, so many ellipses in and of his writings. As I have suggested elsewhere, all of his work can be encapsulated in the elliptical three words: 'To be continued' . . .[37] To be grafted, to be imped. Let us recall, then, how the sentence that he interrupts does indeed go on, and think on how it might inform a reading of 'The Time Is Out of Joint' and the disconcerting, even impossible figure that is our subject here: forgetting well.

It's not two hours, it's four months, Ophelia tells Hamlet. And then the reply:

> So long? Nay then, let the devil wear black, for I'll have a suit of sables. O heavens, die two months ago, and not forgotten yet? Then there's hope a great man's memory may outlive his life half a year. But, by'r Lady, he must build churches then, or else shall he suffer not thinking on, with the hobby-horse, whose epitaph is, 'For O, for O, the hobby-horse is forgot'.
>
> (III, ii, 120–6)

We could dwell on these lines for years – they have been obsessing me already for at least twenty-five (so long?) – dwelling not only on the innumerable scholarly discussions and disputes about the 'suit of sables' and what the devil may wear, or the enigma of this quotation about the hobby-horse, but also and before anything else perhaps on the little words, the seemingly least significant or most forgettable, such as 'so' and 'then' and 'but' and 'for' and 'on' and 'and' and 'O'. 'So long?' 'O heavens, die two months ago, and not forgotten yet?' Hamlet says 'two months', but just a couple of seconds earlier Ophelia said 'twice two months': has he forgotten already? Or is he only pretending to forget? Does he perhaps not even realise that he must seem to have forgotten? (Unless he simply failed to hear? A lengthy digression might be pursued here on the subject of 'psychic deafness', dramaturgic telepathy and the iteraphonic. Deafness is one of the great subjects of Shakespeare's play – 'O, speak to me no more. / These words like daggers enter in mine ears' (III, iv, 87–8), Hamlet's mother tells him. Stop: I am deaf. I want to be deaf. I must be deaf. Of course characters in Shakespeare must be deaf to one another. If they weren't, they would be forever pausing to remark, or at least show signs of having been affected if not completely blown away by the staggering power and beauty of what the last character has said; or correspondingly, to demonstrate aware-ness of the seemingly inadvertent verbal echoes or repetitions – what I would call instances of iteraphonia – whereby one character uses the same word, phrase or image as another. But where does one mark and how would one circumscribe deafness here? Wouldn't 'psychic deaf-ness' in this context also entail a kind of theatrical clairaudience? 'I will speak daggers to her' (III, ii, 179), Hamlet has earlier declared, in the unheard space of a soliloquy. There is psychic *deafness* and there is *psychic* deafness.)

♦

'Where was I?' as he asks, apropos his reading of Hélène Cixous.[38] From her he borrows the faintly delirious portmanteau *oublire,* this is what it is like to read her, he says: 'I read [*lis*] and forget [*oublie*] and forgetread [*oublis*] all the time'.[39] And one of the things it seems he needs to guard against in reading her work is forgetting that it is fiction, or at least a singular kind of writing he names 'hyperrealism': 'let us never forget', he emphasises, that 'we are . . . speaking of literature and fiction'.[40] Forgetreading: isn't that also just the sort of thing Shakespeare draws us into? What is forgetting in literature? What is happening when we read about a character forgetting? Where is this forgetting? What is its time? To what does it attest and how does it signify? These are questions that doubtless connect with, but also veer away from the more familiar sup-position that a character in a play or work of fiction has an unconscious, the supposition that forms the basis for the Oedipus or Hamlet complex.

Literature and forgetting, literature *as* forgetting: let's see what happens if we stop framing things in terms of the 'willing suspension of disbelief', which always sounded at once a bit too volitional and too mechanical, and try instead to think of forgetting well, of how (even or especially in spite of ourselves) we forget, find ourselves lost, forgetting or forgotten in a book. And then how to reckon with the irony that the most memorable, most often quoted, best remembered work of literature in English is arguably the most sustained dramatisation of forgetting in the language? It would be as if the greatest literary works were those bearing some cryptic yet explicit and insistent relation to forgetting, remarking literature itself as a discourse of forgetting, in which you forget, identify with forgetting, share forgetting with the other . . .

Forgetting is the very *mise en scène* of Shakespeare's play. Its 'time out of joint' is a derangement of memory, suffering amnesia and forgetting that afflicts not only Hamlet himself but everyone. It is doubtless most succinctly evoked in the words of the Ghost – 'Remember me' (I, v, 91) and 'Do not forget' (III, iv, 102) – but forgetting wells up everywhere. Bubbling up, oublirious. It begins, perhaps, with forgetting oneself: the *OED* (forget, v. 5) dates the first recorded instance of this formulation of 'forgetting oneself' back to the early thirteenth century. 'Horatio – or I do forget myself' (I, ii, 161): so Hamlet's first words to his beloved friend run. To remember your friend, to recall his name, is the condition of recalling yourself. 'These few precepts in thy memory / See thou character' (I, iii, 58–9), Polonius tells his son. 'Remember well / What I have said to you', the son tells the daughter, who seeks to assure him: ''Tis in my memory locked, / And you yourself shall keep the key of it' (I, iii, 84–6). Then Polonius again, this time to Reynoldo: 'And then, sir, does he this – he does – what was I about to say? By the mass, I was about to say something. Where did I leave?' (II, i, 48–50).

This disjunctiveness and disorder of forgetting also has, let's not forget, a metadramatic dimension, which shows up and enacts, calls on stage and recalls on stage, the very condition of writing and performance, from one instant to the next. It concerns the experience of *learning by heart*, of having to remember one's lines, and above all of remembering lines about trying to remember *other lines*, the lines of a play within a play that was, as Hamlet puts it, 'never acted, or, if it was, not above once; for the play, I remember, pleased not the million' (II, ii, 427–8). Was it acted or not? Remembered or not? Remembered from what? 'One speech in it I chiefly loved', Hamlet tells the Players: 'If it live in your memory, begin at this line – let me see, let me see . . .' And then he misremembers it. The line, apparently, dies: '"The rugged

Pyrrhus, like th'Hyrcanian beast" – / It is not so. It begins with Pyrrhus – / "The rugged Pyrrhus, he whose sable arms . . ."' (II, ii, 437–43). As the Player King declares in The Mousetrap: 'Purpose is but the slave to memory, / Of violent birth, but poor validity . . . / . . . Most necessary 'tis that we forget . . .' (III, ii, 176–80). Hamlet reminds his mother: 'I must to England. You know that?' 'Alack, / I had forgot' (III, iv, 189–90), she replies. The whole thing is a seminar, a teaching or 'document in madness', to recall Laertes's phrase, in other words 'thoughts and remembrance fitted' (IV, v, 180). 'What do you read, my lord?' – 'Words, words, words' (II, ii, 191–2) . . .

Hamlet is in a sense nothing but *forgetreading* – forget-reading and forge-treading (for you cannot get from one end to the other without going, quiet as a mouse, into and if you're lucky out of that forgery known as The Mousetrap, or by way of so many other 'forgeries' (II, i, 20) or fabrications, from the fabricated narrative or 'forgèd process' (I, v, 37) of the King's death, out of which the drama has originally erupted, to the invention or 'forgery' of so many other 'shapes and tricks' (IV, vii, 77), whether in the projected mind of a character, such as Claudius, or in your own).

It is a forgetting well or rather abyss, in which the forgetting of the very line or word carries into that of writing as such, writing itself. Coming very near the end, this is finally perhaps one of the most arresting figures of forgetting in the play. Hamlet is recounting the story of his escape from death en route to England. Apparently as prone to forgetting as anyone else in the play, Horatio needs to be prompted: 'You do remember all the circumstance?' (V, ii, 2), Hamlet asks him. To which his friend replies, in a mirror of indignation: 'Remember it, my lord!' (V, ii, 3). Hamlet explains how, his 'fears forgetting manners' (V, ii, 18), he fingered, unsealed and read the letter or 'grand commission' (V, ii, 19) which Rosencrantz and Guildenstern were carrying to England, requesting his decapitation on arrival. At which point, he tells Horatio:

> Ere I could make a prologue to my brains,
> They had begun the play – I sat me down,
> Devised a new commission, wrote it fair.
> I once did hold it, as our statists do,
> A baseness to write fair, and laboured much
> How to forget that learning; but, sir, now
> It did me yeoman's service. Wilt thou know
> Th'effect of what I wrote?

(V, ii, 31–8)

Wilt thou know? It is almost 'woo't', the word or vocable Hamlet pronounced repeatedly in the preceding scene. He tells Horatio he had worked hard at forgetting how to write in a legible fashion. How is that to be done? It's a madness to think on. Not so much forget-reading, we might suppose, as forget-writing. But at any rate that is no longer the case, not now. For allegedly he has stopped working at this, he has stopped labouring to forget to do something well. It is as if he were writing out of some learned ignorance of the learning and the forgetting, forgotten the forgetting and forgotten himself: his brains have begun the play before he even sits himself down to consider a prologue. And of course it is a forged letter, bearing the seal of his father as a counterfeit to that of the murderous uncle. It is a marvellous case of the *forgetive*, to recall a word Shakespeare uses elsewhere and indeed quite possibly invents: given to forging, in other words, 'creative', 'inventive'.[41]

♦

'Suffer not thinking on': editors gloss this as 'have to put up with being forgotten' or '[suffer] not being thought about'.[42] The word 'suffer' here recalls (everything has to do with this question of recalling, of how Shakespeare's writing recalls while inviting or encouraging us to forget, Shakespeare's *teleanamnesis*, in a word) Hamlet's private words of praise to Horatio a little earlier on in the same scene. Here he says he wears Horatio 'in [his] heart's core': 'For thou hast been / As one, in suff'ring all, that suffers nothing' (III, ii, 60–1, 68). Unless he builds churches a great man must suffer being forgotten – which is, 'in suffering all', in other words to die, no longer 'to suffer / The slings and arrows of outrageous fortune' (III, i, 58–9), in short to suffer nothing, for the dead do not suffer, do they? Except *in memory*, in spirit, in a ghostly fashion. Once again Shakespeare's deployment and derangement of 'suffer' bears spectral force. Like 'thinking on' itself, a phrase elsewhere used specifically in reference to the Ghost, the dead and the impossible time of mourning. As Barnardo says to Horatio, following the first appearance of the Ghost in the opening scene: 'Is not this something more than fantasy? / What think you on't? (I, i, 54–5). 'It' (the 't' of 'What think you on't?') is the something, the ghost, the apparent return of the dead. 'Thinking on' seems to come with this 'it' – Shakespeare's version, perhaps, of the 'es spukt' described in *Spectres of Marx*: 'it spooks', 'it apparitions'.[43]

The murderer did not hear Barnardo use this phrase, but it comes back, an iteraphonic ghost. It is the main verb, the verb we find ourselves waiting for, and are left thinking on, in the first sentence that Claudius pronounces in the play:

> Though yet of Hamlet our dear brother's death
> The memory be green, and that it us befitted
> To bear our hearts in grief, and our whole kingdom
> To be contracted in one brow of woe,
> Yet so far hath discretion fought with nature
> That we with wisest sorrow think on him
> Together with remembrance of ourselves.
>
>   (I, ii, 1–7)

Sorrow should be wise. Think on the dead but don't forget yourself. This is a kind of Freudian formulation. It is a matter of 'mourning duties' (I, ii, 88), as Claudius calls them a little later in the same scene. Mourning has 'some term' (I, ii, 91), Claudius says; it 'comes to a spontaneous end', Freud says.[44] It's one of the most telling and paradoxical enjambments in the play: all focus on the 'him' ends here, cut off without a comma, any supposition that the words following 'think on him' will be *about* 'him' dissolved.[45] It is as though 'think on' *thinks on* by itself, a spectral insister, a piece of strange code, passed from one character to another, with or without their hearing or understanding, part of a ghostly open secret, belonging to no one. In a soliloquy later in the same scene, Hamlet speaks for the first time about his suffering of memory, specifically regarding the transfer of his mother's affections from his father to his uncle: 'Heaven and earth, / Must I remember? Why, she would hang on him / As if increase of appetite had grown / By what it fed on, and yet within a month – / Let me not think on't . . .' (I, ii, 142–6). And it (*'t*) comes back again in the graveyard, gazing at all the human bones scattered about: 'Did these bones cost no more the breeding but to play at loggats with 'em? Mine ache to think on't' (V, i, 87–8). It is as though Shakespeare had invented a new verb, a singular-multiple nonce-phrase, not 'thinking' but *thinking on*: experience out of time, inseparable from the ghost, becoming-ghost, the madness of mourning, suffering memory, the remains of the dead.

◆

'. . . or else shall he suffer not thinking on, with the hobby-horse, whose epitaph is, "For O, for O, the hobby-horse is forgot".' Such would be the fate of the one who doesn't build churches. The reference to the hobby-horse, or to the 'epitaph' or catchphrase of the hobby-horse, is of course meant, on one level, to signify oblivion; and much has been said on the subject of the fact that the popular song or ballad to which Hamlet refers is (as the Oxford editor, G. R. Hibbard, puts it) 'now lost' (I'm in danger of getting lost here, off-track, onto another hobby-horse, the strange 'now' of the Shakespeare editor's 'now lost', the lost now and 'not now'. I tell myself, I hear those words toll once again: *not now*). But this hobby-horse is also being 'perpetuated . . . in being forgotten', to recall the phrase from *For What Tomorrow* . . . Some years earlier, in *Love's Labour's Lost* (1594–5), Shakespeare had already played on this very common image of the forgotten hobby-horse, or its song of forgottenness. Armado, love-sick, sighs: 'But O – but O – ' and Moth supplies: '"The hobby-horse is forgot".'[46] As Harold Jenkins puts it: 'What is certain is that the hobby-horse, while very much remembered, became a byword for being forgotten and as such the occasion for numerous jokes in Elizabethan plays'.[47] Musical knowledge may be lacking, but still we do know that it *was* a song. Jenkins cites *Old Meg of Herefordshire* (1609): 'John Hunt the hobby-horse, wanting but three of an hundred, 'twere time for him to forget himself, and sing but O, nothing but O, the hobby-horse is forgotten.'[48] Likewise, 'epitaph' appears to carry the sense not only of 'a brief composition characterising a deceased person, and expressed as if intended to be inscribed on his tombstone' (*OED*), but also 'a refrain'. There is perhaps a sort of phantom music here, the tracing of a ghostly song. *O, the hobby-horse is forgot.* Sing like cinders, sing-sign the 'der'.[49] As he affirms, so enigmatically, in one of his postcards: 'Only the song remains, it is reborn each time, nothing can be done against it, and it is only it, within it, that I love. Never will any letter *ever* make it heard.'[50]

'Hobby-horse' can be a term of contempt for a 'frivolous fellow' or 'buffoon', as well as a 'loose woman' or 'prostitute'.[51] But originally this compound phrase referred to a small, strong, active horse and, in the song, to a figure in morris dances, associated with May-making, fertility and ghostly sexual power, a man dressed up to look like a horse. A description of the hobby-horse or 'Oss' is given in the *Dictionary of British Folk Customs*:

> He chases the girls, and sometimes corners one of them against a wall and covers her with his huge tarpaulin skirt . . . Every now and then, the Oss dies a magical death . . . The Mayers, and most of the onlookers, sing: 'O, where is St George? O where is he, O?' The Oss sinks to the ground as though he were dying . . . And then, suddenly, the music changes once more, the Oss leaps up high in the air, and off he goes again, as full of life as ever.[52]

Philip Edwards, who cites this passage in the New Cambridge edition of *Hamlet*, goes on to say: 'So the hobby-horse does not die to be forgotten, but comes back with a vengeance, like Hamlet's father.'[53] Forgetting well: as if one could forget that one was dead. 'Now lost', but not forgotten yet. This hobby-horse is like the word 'forget' or 'forgot' itself, for the forging of 'forget' is itself forgotten. 'Forget' is from the Old English *getan* in the sense of 'to hold, grasp'. As the *OED* goes on to observe, apparently without a smile: 'The etymological sense is thus "to miss or lose one's hold"; but the physical application is not recorded in any Teutonic language.' In the 1623 Folio text, immediately following this phrase 'For O, for O, the hobby-horse is forgot', there is a stage direction introducing the dumb-show: 'Hoboys play'. Whoever wrote the words 'Hoboys play' is not so much now lost as never recorded, but in the anagrammatic display of this musical direction the hobby still plays: *O, the hobby*. O the hoboy hobby . . .[54]

♦

How much he doesn't say about *Hamlet*, saying without saying, as if silently acknowledging and welcoming grafts without limit or 'without any limit that *is*'.[55] Inexhaustibly. It is a matter of that strange economy he writes about in 'Biodegradables', of the mixture of ellipsis and loquacity that constitutes the 'singular impropriety' of his signature, gives his work its 'enigmatic kinship [with] nuclear waste' (to adopt his phrase), and means that people will go on reading him, if they are around to read anything at all, for hundreds of years to come.[56] In what was published in English as 'the last interview', entitled *Learning to Live Finally*, originally appearing in *Le Monde* on 19 August 2004, less than two months before his death, he says:

> I have simultaneously . . . the *double-feeling* that, on the one hand, to put it playfully and with a certain immodesty, one has not yet begun to read me, that even though there are, to be sure, many very good readers (a few dozen in the world perhaps, people who are also writer-thinkers, poets), in the end it is later on that all this has a chance of appearing; but also, on the other hand, and thus simultaneously, I have the feeling that two weeks or a month after my death *there will be nothing left*. Nothing except what has been copyrighted and deposited in libraries.[57]

He is divided, possessed of or by a double feeling, 'at war with himself' (to recall the original title of this interview).[58] He suspects that the reading of his work has not or has hardly begun. It is a matter of thinking in terms of years, decades and even centuries to come. And at the same time it is as if he were citing Hamlet or Hamlet were speaking for him. You can't expect a great man's memory to outlive his life more than two weeks or a month. There will be nothing remaining after that, except the books and related material in libraries. That's the way of all flesh, or at least of every philosopher, poet or writer-thinker.

Apropos the death of his friend Sarah Kofman, he suggests that it's a question of place, of wondering what 'a right or just place' is, when everything seems to begin with 'the mourning of this replacement', the replacement of your body by a body of writing.[59] It is a matter of keeping alive the question of the right or just place, of trying to guard it while remaining faithful to the fact that 'the place of a survivor is unlocatable'.[60] As so many of the pieces published in *The Work of Mourning* make clear, you're going to forget, you have to forget, you have to try to forget well, first of all by writing, writing as soon as you can, as fast and close as possible, in all the raw intolerable immediacy of the loved one's death.[61]

♦

Time passes and people forget. *Obstinate rememberers seem to queer themselves.* Queer as day, queer as a survivor.

♦

It is a forgetting well, you keep falling in. Recall that moment of laughter in the film that takes him as its 'star'. They are trying to cross the road and in danger of getting run over. He points to the camerawoman and says in English: 'She sees everything around me but she is totally blind. That's the image of the philosopher who falls in the . . . (how do you say?) well, – while looking at the star. [*pointing to himself*]'.[62]

♦

He himself forgets all the time and this is inevitably bound up with what makes him so interested in keeping or guarding memory. As he says in an interview in 1983: 'I have a huge desire to keep, and yet I am seriously amnesic. I am at the same time astonished by my capacity for forgetting, the facility with which I forget.'[63] 'I love memory' he says, in effect everywhere, in everything he writes. It is the starting point, for example, of his *Mémoires: for Paul de Man*: 'I love nothing better than remembering and Memory itself'.[64] It is one of his most emphatic definitions of the philosopher: 'I write in order to keep . . . The philosopher is above all a guardian of memory.'[65] And it is at the heart of his conception of the university: 'The mission of the university is, in a word, to assure the memory of culture, of thought, of philosophy.'[66] But precisely *on account of* his constant and intense attunement to failure, to not 'know[ing] how to tell a story', to the feebleness of the philosopher as someone who 'ends up with "nothing"', his writings at the same time constitute a sort of letheanalysis.[67] If deconstruction is 'memory work', as he tentatively suggests at one point in *Memoires*, it is also forgetting well.[68]

◆

The word 'suffer': spectral force. It is always coming back. He says nothing about the word, besides citing it, at the end of Part I of 'The Time Is Out of Joint', but so much of what he says can be read in or through it. Suffering is, as he observes earlier on in the essay, at the heart of Shakespeare's play and in particular apropos memory and amnesia:

> [Hamlet's] phrase ('The time is out of joint') does not betray only the symptomatic anxiety of someone whose memory is suffering [*la mémoire souffre*]. His memory is suffering [*Elle souffre*] in fact from a death, and a death is never natural. His memory is suffering [*Sa mémoire souffre*] from the death of a king, a father, and a homonym, but it is suffering [*elle souffre*] first of all and by that very token, *as memory*, from amnesia, from an amnesia that is not natural either. It is suffering [*Elle souffre*] because it cannot remember, thus because it cannot think the event of this so unnatural death, because it is not a memory that is sure of being able to situate, date, determine, objectify the event . . . (TOJ, pp. 17–18)

There is, we might suppose, no death from natural causes: *a death is never natural*. And memory *suffers*. The word 'suffer' or 'suffering' [*souffre*] recurs in this passage, like a refrain or knell. It is another kind of *forgetting well*: like its French counterpart *souffrir*, 'suffer' has to do literally with what carries up from below or underneath.

Let's limit ourselves to drawing up just two buckets from this well: (1) In 'The Time Is Out of Joint' and elsewhere in his writings he foregrounds the ways in which art, and perhaps literature above all, thinks on suffering. Art and literature do not provide us with reprieve or relief from suffering, even or especially when the question of laughter is involved. (We might think here for instance of his work on laughter in Joyce, affirmation and 'yes-laughter' in *Ulysses*; and let's also not forget how funny *Hamlet* is, and how its enduring greatness is bound up, like that of the best jokes, with forgetability.[69]) As he says apropos his friend Sarah Kofman and her writings: she 'interpreted laughter like an artist, she laughed like an artist but also laughed at art, like an artist and in the name of life, not without knowing that neither art nor laughter saves us from pain, anxiety, illness, and death . . . Art and laughter, when they go together, do not run counter to suffering, they do not ransom or redeem it, but live off it.'[70]

(2) However obliquely, his work illuminates the question of animal forgetting or 'bestial oblivion' (IV, iv, 32) in Shakespeare's play, while

opening up new and other pathways for thinking on suffering in the context of animals and animality. This is brought about, first and foremost, through his remarkable analysis in *The Animal That Therefore I Am* of Jeremy Bentham's notorious question, 'Can they suffer?' He questions and disturbs the view (which, he argues, dominates philosophical thinking 'from Aristotle to Heidegger, from Descartes to Kant, Levinas and Lacan') that 'logocentrism is first of all a thesis regarding the animal, the animal deprived of the *logos*, deprived of the *can-have-the-logos*'. Instead, he writes, 'the *first* and *decisive* question [is] whether animals can suffer'.[71] He contends that Jeremy Bentham's simple but profound question 'Can they suffer?' is an index of a crisis that has been going on for some two centuries now, 'a critical phase' in a perhaps ageless war 'waged over the matter of pity' (p. 29). Of course they suffer, he says: 'No one can deny the suffering, fear or panic, the terror or fright that can seize certain animals and that we humans can witness' (p. 28). The suffering of animals is 'indubitable' and even 'precedes the indubitable, it is older than it' (p. 28). He argues that this question about the faculty or power of the 'can', the power of being-able-to ('Can they suffer?'), is 'disturbed by a certain *passivity*'. Thus '"Can they suffer?" amounts to asking "can they *not be able?*"' (pp. 27–8). He concludes:

> Being able to suffer is no longer a power; it is a possibility without power, a possibility of the impossible. Mortality resides there, as the most radical means of thinking the finitude that we share with animals, the mortality that belongs to the very finitude of life, to the experience of compassion, to the possibility of sharing the possibility of this nonpower, the possibility of this nonpower, the possibility of this impossibility, the anguish of this vulnerability and the vulnerability of this anguish. (p. 28)

Hamlet's suffering memory suggests just such a dismantling of the priority of the *logos* or 'discourse of reason'. Suffering – and in particular the suffering called mourning – is *the indubitable* here and even precedes it. To recall his early soliloquy once more: 'Heaven and earth, / Must I remember? / . . . / Let me not think on't / . . . / O God, a beast that wants discourse of reason / Would have mourned longer' (I, ii, 142–51).[72]

♦

Forgetting, then, is not limited to what is called humanity and nowhere is that perhaps more ferociously apparent than in the context of the forgetting *of* animals. *Tout autre est tout autre*, as he says: every other is every other, is every bit other.[73] Every other is also every other animal, for example. We need to be mindful, to be reminded and to become mindful of a more general, even global 'forgetting of violence' towards animals. As he puts it, in *The Animal That Therefore I Am*:

> No one can deny seriously any more, or for very long, that men do all they can in order to dissimulate this cruelty or to hide it from themselves; in order to organise on a global scale the forgetting or misunderstanding of this violence, which some would compare to the worst cases of genocide (there are also animal genocides: the number of species endangered because of man takes one's breath away). One should neither abuse the figure of genocide nor too quickly consider it explained away. It gets more complicated: the annihilation of certain species is indeed in process, but it is occurring through the organisation and exploitation of an artificial, infernal, virtually interminable survival, in conditions that previous generations would have judged monstrous, outside of every supposed norm of a life proper to animals that are thus exterminated by means of their continued existence or even their overpopulation. As if, for example, instead of throwing a people into ovens or gas chambers (let's say Nazi) doctors and geneticists had decided to organise the overproduction and overgeneration of Jews, gypsies and homosexuals by means of artificial insemination, so that, being continually more numerous and better fed, they could be destined in always increasing numbers for the same hell, that of the imposition of genetic experimentation or extermination by gas or by fire. (pp. 25–6)

The world, especially what is still sometimes referred to as the western, industrialised world, is covered with 'bestial oblivion' of the most violent kind, with the forgetting of animals, above all that of industrialised so-called 'meat production' or animal oubliettes.

♦

Shakespeare keeps watch over the English language, I was saying he was saying, through peepholes (such as 'suffer') that can seem so close to his own, so much in anticipation of his countersigning, it appears superfluous to mention. He says it without saying it. Thus for example, as far as I am aware, he never cites or explicitly comments on the passage in which the Ghost of the father leaves the son with the words 'Remember me' (I, v, 91) and Hamlet talks about wiping everything else from 'the table of [his] memory', so that this 'commandment all alone shall live / Within the book and volume of [his] brain' (I, v, 98–103): this passage has 'Freud and the Scene of Writing', with its dazzling exposition of the 'staging of memory', of Freud's development of a notion of breaching as 'a metaphorics of the written trace', written all over it.[74] There is, as we read in *Mémoires*, an 'irreducible link between thought as memory and the technical dimension of memorisation, the art of writing, of "material" inscription'.[75] As well as any philosopher or poet-thinker before or after him, Shakespeare shows that (in the words of the great essay of 1966) 'memory . . . is not a psychical property among others; it is the very essence of the psyche'; and that memory and forgetting are constitutively bound up with inscription, with writing and traces.[76] As Plato's *Phaedrus* says, and as *Of Grammatology* reminds us: 'writing is at once mnemotechnique and the power of forgetting'.[77] Limited inkwell forgetting.

♦

He loves to say 'let us not forget' and even 'let us never forget' or 'what must never be forgotten': a detailed study specifically of this saying or this gesture (rhetorical and otherwise) would require at least a further book or two. I have cited just a few examples, spottily, haphazardly, in these pages.

♦

As a figure that combines the necessity and impossibility of mourning, *forgetting well* is doubtless a strange version of '*il faut bien oublir le mort*'. You can never know if you will have done it, or if you are doing it at this very instant: the form of the present participle ('forgetting') underscores the logic of something at once haunting the present and open, to come. It is a question of justice as the 'experience of the impossible'. How can you forget well, how could you think on 'forgetting well', without some anamnesic logic to watch over the proceedings? It brings to mind what he says about the 'schizopathogenic power of the double bind' of a 'forget me': 'the addressee must keep the command not to keep, without forgetting the request to forget: Grieve for me, therefore keep me enough to lose me as you must'.[78]

Analysis unfinished and interminable: I break off here with two memoranda on forgetting well. Fragments of me and or, more and other, morsels of death and his name, in memoranda.

In its standard current usage a *memorandum* is a note to help remember something or a summary of the state of a question. The first definition of 'memorandum' in the *OED*, however, reads as follows:

> **A.** *int.* In later use only in *Law.* 'It is to be remembered (that)'; placed at the head of a note of something to be remembered or a record (for future reference) of something that has been done. Usu. with *that.* Now *rare.* Perh. *Obs.*

'Memorandum' in this sense is dated back to the late fourteenth or early fifteenth century. It's classified as an *interjection* (what a thought! how he would race away with that, leaping from every jetty imaginable, jetties and interjectiles previously unimagined!). I like the fact that the *OED* says that 'memorandum' in this sense is 'now rare, perhaps obsolete'. The world's greatest authority on the English language thus gives us leave to meddle: no longer 'perhaps obsolete', the sense is hereby revived, fresh as a daisy. As I suggested earlier, one of the effects of his work is to alter our understanding of what is 'obsolete', gone out of use or no longer functional.[79]

◆

Memorandum (1): That he is a great philosopher, the great thinker of deconstruction, inexhaustibly generative and inventive, a hyper-political writer concerned with the pursuit of a new enlightenment, the 'democracy to come'.

◆

Forgetting is characteristic not only of 'subjects' but also of cultures and nation-states, and this is something he meticulously analyses and questions, in terms of producing *resistances to forgetting* and with a view to transformations in the name of justice. As he says in the inter-view entitled 'The Deconstruction of Actuality': 'each country has its own original history, and its own economy of memory, its own way of being economical with it.'[80] We have to deal with what he else-where calls 'the amnesia of which a culture is made'.[81] The notion of forgetting well opens up on to national, international and transnational scenarios. It is there in his reading of Marx: a certain kind of forget-ting is necessary for revolution – one cannot be 'content to forget', for the result of that is simply 'bourgeois platitude'.[82] One has, it would seem, to *forget well*. There is no state, no nation without 'founding violence': this is in turn subject to what he calls, in various contexts, the 'violence of forgetting', that forgetting of violence that is necessary to the formation and survival of a nation – but a forgetting he repeat-edly seeks to recall, in order to question and transform. For example, in *Archive Fever*, he quotes Yosef Hayim Yerushalmi: 'Only in Israel and nowhere else is the injunction to remember felt as a religious imperative to an entire people.'[83] This is a sentence which, he suggests, can make one 'dumbfounded with dread' (p. 77). He wonders, in a gesture of understatement that highlights the 'violence of forgetting' or 'superrepression' that Yerushalmi's assertion calls up, if this sentence is 'just' (pp. 76–7). It is a question of the proper name (here 'Israel') and of exemplarity as 'the place of all violences' (p. 77). He thus seeks to disturb and dislocate that thinking which would assume or assert 'the One, the difference of the One in the form of uniqueness (. . . "Only in Israel and nowhere else") and the One in the figure of totalising assemblage ("to an entire people")'. Taking issue with Yerushalmi he writes: 'If it is just to remember the future and the injunction to remember . . . to guard and to gather the archive, it is no less just to remember the others, the other others and the others in oneself, and that the other peoples could say the same thing – in another way' (p. 77). Every other is absolutely other. *Tout autre est tout autre* (p. 77), he reminds us, knowing we are forever forgetting.

Who else in the past fifty years or more has been as profound a thinker of *place*? Of what a place is, of what takes place, of what gives place to what and how, of displacement, replacement, the unplaceable and the irreplaceable. Of what allows a name, for example, to become 'the place of all violences'. And of what takes place without place, of the crypt and of that 'irreplaceable and unplaceable place' that is called *khora*.[84] If 'the place of a survivor is unlocatable', so too is that of the stranger, the foreigner, the arrivant, absolutely unforeseeable, one must welcome. It is a matter of a 'hospitality without reserve', of a 'messianic opening' that 'renounces any right to property, any right in general', a strange messianism 'without content'. It is a question of being open, in other words, to the coming of this foreigner, and thus of the need to 'leave an empty place, always, in memory of the hope'. This, as he goes on to add, 'is the very place of spectrality'.[85]

'Place is always unbelievable to me, as is orientation', he remarks, while travelling, in *Counterpath*.[86] He tries to think, question and analyse this unbelievability, at once philosophically and politically – from the name and place called 'Jerusalem' and the current 'world war' over its appropriation, to the multiple meanings and implications of globalisation or 'worldwide-isation' (what he calls 'mondialisation').[87] He is the thinker of borders and frontiers and of the deconstruction of all those 'terrestrial places' that are the names or alleged properties of nation-states: deconstruction is/in America, and Israel, *and everywhere else*. He is the thinker of the 'trauma' of the past hundred years or so that he sums up in *Spectres of Marx* as 'the techno-scientific and effective decentring of the earth'.[88] He is the thinker of wells that must not be forgotten. His writing is concerned with registering and criticising every kind of injustice that is at issue in the appropriation and management of those oil-wells on which 'the whole technoindustrial structure of hegemonic countries depends', while also looking ahead to a time when these 'last nonvirtualisable terrestrial places' are themselves gone or have given way to other power-sources.[89] He is the thinker who exposes the madness of that suicidal 'autoimmune' logic which leads governments and states to seek to bring or hasten their own destruction through apparent self-protection, a madness that is as evident in the response of the US and allied forces to 'September 11' or the suicidal 'autoimmunitary' impulses of Israel, as in the kind of 'proliferation' concerning some of those other most terrible military forgetting wells or oubliettes described by Alfred McCoy in *A Question of Torture*: 'Orders from President Bush and Secretary Rumsfeld for the CIA to torture just a few "high-value" Al Qaeda targets quickly proliferated into the abuse of dozens at Bagram, hundreds at Guantánamo, and thousands at Abu Graib and other Iraqi prisons.'[90]

There is, in other words, an injunction to think *forgetting well* and *resistances to forgetting* apropos nation-states and indeed beyond the sovereignty of the nation-state. He is not interested in 'institutions of deconstruction': rather he dreams of 'the untenable promise of a *just international institution*, an institution that is strong in its justice, *sovereign without sovereignty*, and so on'.[91]

Let us not forget, then, the tentative but remarkably general, bracing and embracing definition he offers of the figure of the philosopher, which is also a definition of the role of deconstructive thinking, of thinking on, in the years to come. It appears in the book called *Philosophy in a Time of Terror*, in the context of his questioning of definitions of 'war' and 'terror', 'territory' and 'nation-state', distinctions between '"national" and "international" terrorism', between state and non-state terrorism, and above all perhaps his emphasis on the need for 'radical changes in international law'. He remarks:

> I am incapable of knowing who today deserves the name philosopher (I would not simply accept certain professional or organisational criteria), I would be tempted to call philosophers those who, in the future, reflect in a responsible fashion on these [sorts of] questions and demand accountability from those in charge of public discourse, those responsible for the language and institutions of international law.[92]

The philosopher or, rather perhaps, the philosopher-deconstructor is the thinker of the urgency of the present as the time in which 'justice does not wait'.[93] And that means remembering also his insistence on what is *before memory*, in other words 'the sense of a responsibility without limits, and so necessarily excessive, incalculable, before memory'.[94]

♦

***Memorandum* (2)**: That he is a poet, poematic well of deconstructive genius, a great writer and thinker of poetry and literature, autobiography and fiction.

♦

In memory: where I am, to have been. There is a remarkable book by the American artist Joe Brainard, called *I Remember*, first published in 1970, that takes the form of literally hundreds of sentences or short paragraphs beginning with the words 'I remember'.[95] In evoking here, in a correspondingly zigzag fashion, a few of my memories of the thinker and friend in whose memory I am, I prefer to speak of recalling. No doubt there is something more childlike, more touching and visceral about the anaphora of 'I remember'. 'I recall' may appear more detached, perhaps even a bit more 'English' (cool, embarrassed, embarrassing). But 'I recall' has, perhaps, a certain distinctiveness in turn. It makes, first of all, an apposite if implicit reference to an experience of voice – calling and recalling, evoking and evocating. To recall carries the sense not only of 'to call or bring back (a circumstance, person, etc.) *to* the mind, memory, thoughts, etc.', 'to recollect' or 'to remember', but also 'to bring back, restore, revive, resuscitate (a feeling, quality, or state)' (*OED*, 'recall', v.[1], senses 3 and 4). The example the *OED* gives for the last of these senses is Shakespeare's *Henry VI Part 2*, where it appears specifically in the context of 'recalling' someone to life.[96] There is something spectral about this word, then; and at the same time it is oriented toward the future, by the promise of coming back. It is closely linked to anamnesis, primarily defined in the *OED* as 'the recalling of things past; recollection, reminiscence'. 'Recall' thus calls up and recalls the last words of 'The Deaths of Roland Barthes': 'anamnesis, even if it breaks off always too soon, promises itself each time to begin again: it remains to come'.[97]

I recall reading for the first time 'A Silk Worm of One's Own' and coming to the part where he writes about keeping silkworms when he was a boy, and it made me weep.[98]

I recall standing with him on a sidewalk in Tuscaloosa, Alabama, shortly before he was to deliver his lecture on the 'History of the Lie', and a woman came up and asked him: 'So, what do you think of the natives?' And his shockingly, marvellously spat-out response: 'Natives? Whaddaya mean *natives?*'

I recall sitting with him at lunch or dinner one day in the château at Cerisy-la-Salle and asking him if he would be willing to contribute an essay to a project that was beginning to take shape under the heading *Deconstructions*. I tried to give him the gist of the thing by saying that there would be chapters on deconstruction and this and that, deconstruction and fiction, deconstruction and technology, deconstruction and ethics, deconstruction and drugs, deconstruction and weaving, and so on, and I recall the awesome speed, as-if already laughing flashing in his eyes when he said, with scarcely a second's pause, yes, he would write something about deconstruction and the *and*.

I recall the first time I heard his voice, the trembling and the compelling pauses in his discourse, speaking mostly in French but at certain moments switching into English, at a seminar organised by the *Oxford Literary Review* in the late 1970s. 'When we insist,' he said, and paused: 'we always over-insist.'

I recall once sending him some pipe tobacco (drugs!) and never knowing whether it arrived.

I recall walking with him in Paris past the secondary school where he told me he had taught in the 1950s, the Lycée Charlemagne, and his pointing out the street-name and the pre-Revolution name that was still eerily legible beneath it.

I recall his presentation of *L'animal que donc je suis* (*The Animal That Therefore I Am*), in the library of that 'château of haunted friendship' at Cerisy, when he first came in and you could see the bulk of the typescript of what he was going to read. It took him eight and a quarter hours, delivered over a couple of days, but from near the beginning, already when he was citing *Alice in Wonderland* ('we're all mad here. I'm mad. You're mad'), I developed the bizarre conviction that I could have followed everything he was saying just by the ways in which he moved his hands and gestured, which he did constantly, as he read.

I recall one night in a crowded pub at the end of a conference in England a student at an adjoining table called across to him asking did he ever listen to music. 'Always', he said. Only that word, without further elaboration.

I recall the correspondence, erratic but sustained, over ten years or more, before we ever met, letters, notes and postcards about translations and books. I recall the supposition, so silly in retrospect, that if I was going to be writing a book about his work it would be better not to meet him 'in person'.

I recall the intense excitement and pleasure, mingled with trepidation, of receiving a letter from him, his name signed on the envelope, the most legible of all the words I would then be confronted with.

I recall how, whenever I phoned him, he always recognised my voice immediately. Except once, in the final year.

I recall the occasions, very few, when he phoned me, and the way he pronounced my name, asking if it was me.

I recall being in a minibus at night, returning to the Russell Hotel in Bloomsbury after dinner in the East End, he scribbled what transpired to be the last words he ever wrote to me, an inscription in the little book *Penser à Strasbourg*. The ride was bumpy and his hand jogged, he had to cross out, he had difficulty writing 'as ever' and it turned out looking more like 'a sever'.

♦

Souriez-moi, dit-il, comme je vous aurai souri jusqu'à la fin.
Préférez toujours la vie et affirmez dans elle la survie . . .
   Je vous aime et vous souris d'où que je sois.[99]

These are the words he wrote, shortly before the end, the last words of the brief text that his son Pierre read out at the funeral at Ris Orangis, on 12 October 2004: 'Smile for me, he says, as I will have smiled for you until the end. Always prefer life and affirm survival in it . . . I love you and am smiling from wherever I am.' What simple but devastating words, written in the third person, prosopopeia-in-person. What an unbelievable Cheshire cat, unlocatable, smiling and loving.

♦

You smile and affirm but also weep. It is a matter, finally perhaps, of the eye as forgetting well. As he remarks in *Memoirs of the Blind*: 'Contrary to what one believes one knows, the best point of view (and the *point of view* will have been our theme) is a source-point and a watering hole, a water-point – which comes down to tears'. He contends that

> [d]eep down, deep down inside, the eye would be destined not to see but to weep. For at the very moment they veil sight, tears would unveil what is proper to the eye. And what they cause to surge up out of forgetfulness, there where the gaze or look looks after it, keeps it in reserve, would be nothing less than *aletheia*, the *truth* of the eyes, whose ultimate destination they would thereby reveal: to have imploration rather than sight, to address prayer, love, joy, or sadness rather than a look or gaze.[100]

I say 'he remarks' and 'he contends', but let's not forget that those extraordinary 'memoirs of the blind' are presented in the form of a kind of play, for two or more voices. It ends, you recall, with a reference to Andrew Marvell's image of 'seeing tears' or *tears that see*:

> – Tears that see . . . Do you believe?
> – I don't know, one has to believe . . .[101]

♦

Tears, laughter and song: as always, it's the experience of what cannot be sent, cannot be hurried, the time of tears, song and laughter as incalculable and unreadable.[102]

♦

But in mourning, you should not enjoy the tears or develop a taste for them. Obstinate rememberers must not forget that. The 'well' of 'forgetting well' should not, cannot be a source of pleasure. Let us recall the beautiful sentences on the subject of tears with which he concludes his '*hommage*' to Jean-Marie Benoist:

> One should not develop a taste for mourning, and yet mourn we *must*.
> We *must*, but we must not like it – mourning, that is, mourning *itself*, if such a thing exists: not to like or love through one's own tear but only through the other, and every tear is from the other, the friend, the living, as long as we ourselves are living, reminding us, in holding life, to hold on to it.[103]

◆

What is the word? What would be the right word or words? In a letter to Francine Loreau, written on his own birthday (15 July 1991), about his friend Max Loreau who had died the preceding year, he tries to analyse the sense of being at a loss for the 'right words' [*mots justes*]:

> This being at a loss says something . . . about mourning and its truth, the impossible mourning that nonetheless remains at work, endlessly hollowing out the depths of our memories, beneath their great beaches and beneath each grain of sand [*creusant interminablement au fond de nos mémoires, sous leurs grandes plages et sous chaque grain de sable*], beneath the phenomenal or public scope of our destiny and behind the fleeting, inapparent moments, those without archive and without words (a meeting in a café, a letter eagerly torn open, a burst of laughter revealing the teeth, a tone of the voice, an intonation one day on the telephone, a style of handwriting in a letter, a parting in a train station, and each time we say that we do not know, that we do not know if and when and where we will meet again).[104]

Speech beached. Picture of being at a loss for the right words: the great beaches of our memories, the world of every grain of sand, *undermined* – impossible mourning at work all the time, digging, burrowing, drilling, hollowing out everything. Mourning is at work even, or especially, in and on those moments that are 'without archive and without words'. Being at a loss for words also has to do with a duty, and here again we might recall – in order to think anew – what Claudius refers to as 'mourning duties'. There is 'a duty', he says in the letter to Francine Loreau, 'to let the friend speak, to turn speech over to him, his speech, and especially not to take it from him, not to take it in his place' (p. 95). He recognises the scale of that task and acknowledges his feeling, in writing the letter, that he has already begun to fall short of it: 'no offense seems worse at the death of a friend (and I already feel that I have fallen prey to it)' (p. 95).

He goes on to say: 'I want to let him have the last word here. How to let him have the last word and yet speak of him, of him alone?' (p. 100). He decides to quote some old letters he had received from his friend, remarking: 'I cite them not in order to withdraw or to let him speak alone of himself, but because I like, in transcribing, to under-write [*souscrire*, 'subscribe'] and listen to his voice, and to look at his writing, I mean the way he forms his letters, his manner, his hand' (pp. 100/130).

◆

What is the word? Ouijamiflip. I associate this word, if it is one, with my mother, an attempted transcription of her vocable, her way of saying 'what is the word', 'what-do-you-call-it' or 'thing-a-mi-jig'. At first sight it may suggest the sense of a missing word, of being at a loss for words, or for the right word, with an implication that the word has been forgotten but only temporarily, you are forgetting, yes, but forgetting well, in that it is not really gone, it can come back, it's on the tip of your tongue. But it is never assured, and might just as well be an intimation of insanity, an uncanny figuration of the madness and 'the place of madness' that is the mother.[105] The first little text I ever read in his presence bore that name: *Ouijamiflip*. It attempts to read his work in terms of the double yes (*oui, ja*), chance and telepathy, focusing on his 'Che cos'è la poesia?' and Beckett's 'what is the word'.[106]

◆

I love his handwriting. So finely yet cryptically formed, as if in fall from the start, jetting, constantly at least a little aslant, completely clinamen-tal I'm tempted to say (to recall what he says of the work of art in 'My Chances': it is 'vertical and slightly leaning'[107]), as if always on the verge of falling 'more or less definitively'. How long, so long, I have puzzled over letters he wrote, invariably seeking the help of other friends, trying to decipher the words. What more immediate and powerful way of recalling him (besides a photograph, for example a photo from Blainville-sur-mer, on one of the 'great beaches' of France, not far from Cerisy) than through his handwriting, writing in his own hand? Never forgetting, at the same time of course, that he never stopped questioning the authentic, the inimitable and proper, the opposition of the visible and invisible, the sensible and insensible, stressing (in short) spectrality as the essence of photography and expropriation at the heart of hand-writing. The photograph, for example, requires something 'miraculous', a strange kind of faith 'summoned by technics itself': photographed, we see but don't know, know but don't see, how '[w]e are spectralised by the shot, captured or possessed by spectrality in advance.'[108] Handwriting, on the other hand, will always bear something of the hand of the other, above all the fall of the dead hand: every handwritten letter is a signature tomb. As he writes in *Spurs*, apropos Nietzsche: 'What, after all, is handwriting? Is one obliged, merely because something is written in one's hand, to assume, or thus to sign it? Does one assume even one's "own" ["*propre*"] signature? The formulation of such questions, however, is disqualified by the signature's structure (*la signature/ tombe*) [the signature-tomb, the signature falls].'[109]

◆

What sort of text is 'Che cos'è la poesia?'? It is not like anything else you have read, by him or anyone else. It is a meddling of and with genres, at once poem, dictation, letter, drama for two or more voices, philosophical essay, crypto-telepatho-grammatology, beyond genre, 'beyond languages, even if it sometimes happens that it recalls itself in language' (p. 293). He is responding to the question of the title ('What is poetry?' 'What thing is poetry?'). He proceeds to organise his answer, 'so as not to forget', in the form of 'two words', two axioms or catchphrases, like two memoranda:

> (1) *The economy of memory*. A poem must be brief, elliptical by vocation, whatever may be its objective or apparent expanse. Learned unconscious of *Verdichtung* and of the retreat.
> (2) *The heart* . . . [And above all, that] story of 'heart' poetically enveloped in the idiom . . . 'learn by heart' ['*apprendre par cœur*']. (p. 291)

So, he summarises, 'the poetic . . . would be that which you desire to learn, but from and of the other, thanks to the other and under dictation, by heart'. It is, then 'two in one' (a hendiadys of sorts): the second memorandum 'is rolled up in the first' (p. 291). The poem or, as he comes to call it, the 'poematic' (p. 297) might 'attach itself to any word at all' (p. 299), a beloved phrase or name, the name of who or what is loved for example, or of anything you want to keep and 'learn by heart', but it doesn't return home, it finally never gathers itself together, it is 'beyond the *logos*', 'a-human'. It is a sort of 'converted animal', he suggests, like 'a catachrestic hedgehog' (p. 297) that appears to keep or protect itself by rolling up into a ball but in doing so exposes itself to the unforeseeable, wounding and death. To respond to the question 'what is poetry?' you will have to have known 'how to renounce knowledge':

it entails a 'learned ignorance [*docte ignorance*]', he says, while 'never forget[ting] . . . what you sacrifice' (pp. 289/288).

'Learned unconscious of *Verdichtung* and of the retreat [*Docte inconscient de la* Verdichtung *et du retrait*]' (pp. 291/290). You were trundling on and almost lost sight of that sentence, another of his sentential epics, another invitation to embroil yourself for years. The poem as 'learned unconscious'? What is an unconscious that is 'learned'? ('Learning unconscious': wouldn't that be another way of hearing the strangeness of 'forgetting well'?) And learned unconscious *of* condensation (supposing that '*la* Verdichtung' is indeed principally an allusion, elliptical by vocation, to Freud's concept, elaborated initially in *The Interpretation of Dreams* as a term crucial to an understanding of how dreams work and glossed by Laplanche and Pontalis as also 'one of the essential factors in the technique of joking, in *faux pas*, in the forgetting of words, etc.'[110]) and of the *retrait* (the retreat, the withdrawal or rolling up of the hedgehog, for example, but also everything he has ever written about the re- and the trait, repetition and return, trace and treatment, the retrait of metaphor and deconstruction as work of the retrait or as 'retreatment works')? Everything he says about the importance of not forgetting psychoanalysis, and about listening well to the unconscious, about philosophy, literature and the 'democracy to come', is telegrammed here.

Poetry? It's a madness, it's like 'a photograph [or photography] of the feast in mourning' [*photographie de la fête en deuil*] (pp. 289/288). You love it, you want to 'eat, drink and swallow [its] letter' (p. 293), but it's just a photograph, it's photography in mourning and feast, celebration and name-day in mourning. At the same time it's a condition of the gift, the madness of the gift, 'your benediction before knowledge' (p. 291). It says 'keep me' (pick me up, learn me by heart) but at the same time 'save yourself' (you are in the middle of the road and in danger of getting run over) (p. 295). To learn by heart you have to expose yourself to the deadliness of the mechanical, repetition, by rote. 'No poem that does not open itself like a wound' (p. 297), he says.

◆

It's a dream, it drops. It falls to you. It is 'without subject' (p. 299). There is 'never anything but some poem' (p. 297), it's what 'constitutes you' (p. 293). '*Literally*,' he stresses, 'you would like to retain by heart an absolutely unique form' (p. 293). In order to think on this 'passion of the singular' at the very heart of the now, in order to respond to the question 'che cos'è la poesia?', he declares, you will have had to disable memory, disarm culture, know how to forget knowledge, set fire to the library of poetics. The unicity of the poem depends on this condition. You must celebrate, you have to commemorate amnesia, savagery, even the stupidity of the 'by heart'. (pp. 295–7)

To give it a 'name beyond the name' (p. 297) you might call it 'hedge-hog' [*hérisson*] or, perhaps, 'hobby-horse', a catachrestic hobby-horse. Commemorate amnesia! Forget well, by heart. For let's not forget that when Shakespeare first plays about with this forgotten 'hobby-horse', horsing around in *Love's Labour's Lost*, already in teleanamnesia, it is all about learning by heart, by heart and in heart:

ARMADO	But O – but O –
MOTH	'The hobby-horse is forgot.'
ARMADO	Call'st thou my love 'hobby-horse'?
MOTH	No, master. The hobby-horse is but a colt, and your love perhaps a hackney. But have you forgot your love?
ARMADO	Almost I had.
MOTH	Negligent student! Learn her by heart.
ARMADO	By heart and in heart, boy.

(III, i, 26–33)

♦

There's something perhaps especially demonic about 'Che cos'è la poesia?' It is curiously heterogeneous, in itself and in relation to his other writings. It seems, even in the context of his protean writings, to be a strangely different text every time you read it. It does not appear to present itself as a reading: there are passing references to the Scriptures, Pascal and Heidegger (p. 291), for example, but there is none of the characteristic in-depth commentary or analysis of a specific text or œuvre. Perhaps the only explicit extraneous quotation is the phrase 'demon of the heart' [*démon du coeur*] (pp. 299/298). It appears in quotation marks, but without the attribution of an author, something evidently learnt by heart.

Of the poem or poematic, he remarks:

[i]ts event always interrupts or derails absolute knowledge, autotelic being in proximity to itself. This 'demon of the heart' never gathers itself together, rather it loses itself and gets off the track [*il s'égare*: 'wanders off the point', like his text, we might say, from one moment to the other, in the instant] (delirium and mania), it exposes itself to chance, it would rather let itself be torn to pieces by what bears down on it. (pp. 299/298)

Demonic poematic: to be 'torn to pieces'. What is this 'demon of the heart'? Where does it come from? When I sent him a copy of

'Ouijamiflip', in the autumn of 1995, I asked him. His response (dated 17 January 1996), where decipherable, might be rendered in English as follows:

> I think that 'demon of the heart' is a quotation, but I'm suddenly unsure of whom of what. (Baudelaire, who . . . .. [?] so often demons? Poe's 'Le démon de la perversité' ['The Imp of the Perverse'], translated by Baudelaire, and in which he so often repeats 'I am saved!', a text which is moreover extraordinary? no, I don't remember this 'demon of the heart, [*sic*] forgive me, I confess . . . [*sic*])

Forgetting well: *demon of the heart.* He does not remember, and now it is beyond recall, beyond all recall. He does not remember, even as he appears to mime or parody the crazy narrator of Poe's story ('I confess . . .') and reminds us of his astonishing capacity (which is also a sort of radical passivity) to supplement or graft onto, imp or enter into *everybody*, real or fictional or hyperrealist.

You hear, perhaps, the demon in the demonstration. Poetry has never been named in such an off-the-track way or 'so arbitrarily', says one voice at the end of 'Che cos'è la poesia?', and the other responds: 'You just said it. Which had to be demonstrated [*Ce qu'il fallait démontrer*] . . . "What is . . .?" laments the disappearance of the poem – another catastrophe. By announcing that which is just as it is, a question salutes the birth of prose' (pp. 299/298). We are back, once again, with the 'learned unconscious of condensation' and the imp that he is – his imps, his arts and graces, grafts and traces, his elliptical and singular impropriety, the astonishing ways in which everything he says or writes seems to be grafted or waiting to be grafted to everything else, here for example in the telescoped or tele-lexical engagement with everything he has written elsewhere about 'safe', 'being safe', 'salvation' and 'salut'.[111] To ask 'what is poetry?' is to *salute* the birth of prose.

'I am saved! [*Je suis sauvé!*]', he writes, reciting and recalling Baudelaire's translation of Poe. Or as Poe's original English has it: 'I am safe.'[112] Of course the narrator of 'The Imp of the Perverse' is not safe: the analysis and story he tells us is being recounted on the very eve of his death, having been imprisoned in the wake of enunciating 'the brief but pregnant sentences that consigned me to the hangman' (p. 1226). He has murdered someone and had 'inherited his estate' (p. 1224). Like Claudius, he has apparently got away with the whole thing, at least until the final scene. But the imp of the perverse seals the fate of this anonymous narrator. And like a demented exercise in suicidal autoimmunity, it is the very saying and singsong repetition of the phrase 'I am safe' that will have led him to his death:

– One day, whilst sauntering along the streets, I arrested myself in the act of murmuring, half aloud, these customary syllables ['I am safe']. In a fit of petulance, I re-modelled them thus: – 'I am safe – I am safe – yes – if I be not fool enough to make open confession!'

No sooner had I spoken these words, than I felt an icy chill creep to my heart. (p. 1225)

The phrase 'demon of the heart' does not occur in Poe's text. Nor does '*démon du cœur*' appear in Baudelaire's translation. This is perhaps the nearest we get to an appearance, a sort of apparition of a citation. The French text has '*démon*' in its title, of course, and the demonic effects of the '*je suis sauvé*' are felt to seep or filter into the narrator's heart [*filtrer jusqu'à mon cœur*].[113] But there is no 'demon of the heart': it is like 'the gift of the poem' which, as we read in 'Che cos'è la poesia?', 'cites nothing' (p. 297). It wells. It comes. It's like his definition of 'genius', as 'what happens', as what 'gives without knowing it'.[114]

It would rather let itself be torn to pieces, this imp of the impossible, this *demon of the heart*, because of what links forgetting and the gift. No forgetting well, finally, without that, without that notion of absolute or unconditional forgetting that he talks about in his marvellous book on Baudelaire, *Given Time*. As he puts it:

> For there to be gift, not only must the donor or donee not perceive or receive the gift as such, have no consciousness of it, no memory, no recognition; he or she must also forget it right away [*à l'instant*] and moreover this forget-ting must be so radical that it exceeds even the psychoanalytic categoriality of forgetting. (GT, p. 16)

It is a matter of a forgetting, in other words, beyond any repression that might 'reconstitute debt and exchange by putting in reserve, by keeping or saving up what is forgotten, repressed or censured' (p. 16). This 'absolute forgetting', he says, is in accord with 'a certain experience of the *trace* as *cinder* or *ashes*' (pp. 16–17). It has to do with dissemination, with what 'does not return to the father' or 'does not return in general' (p. 47). He insists on 'forgetting', nonetheless: 'And yet we say "forget-ting" and not nothing' (p. 17). It is a matter of a forgetting that 'forgets itself' (p. 17). He thus concludes:

> What this forgetting and this forgetting of forgetting would therefore give us to think is something other than a philosophical, psychological or psycho-analytic category. Far from giving us to think the possibility of the gift, on the contrary, it is on the basis of what takes shape in the name *gift* that one could *hope* thus to think forgetting. (p. 17)

♦

Unlocatable imp, our survivor: thinker of the poematic *salut*, of mourning and the gift, messianism without religion, 'benediction without any hope of salvation'.[115]

♦

I shall always be in memory of him. Jacques Derrida: *demon of my heart*.

♦

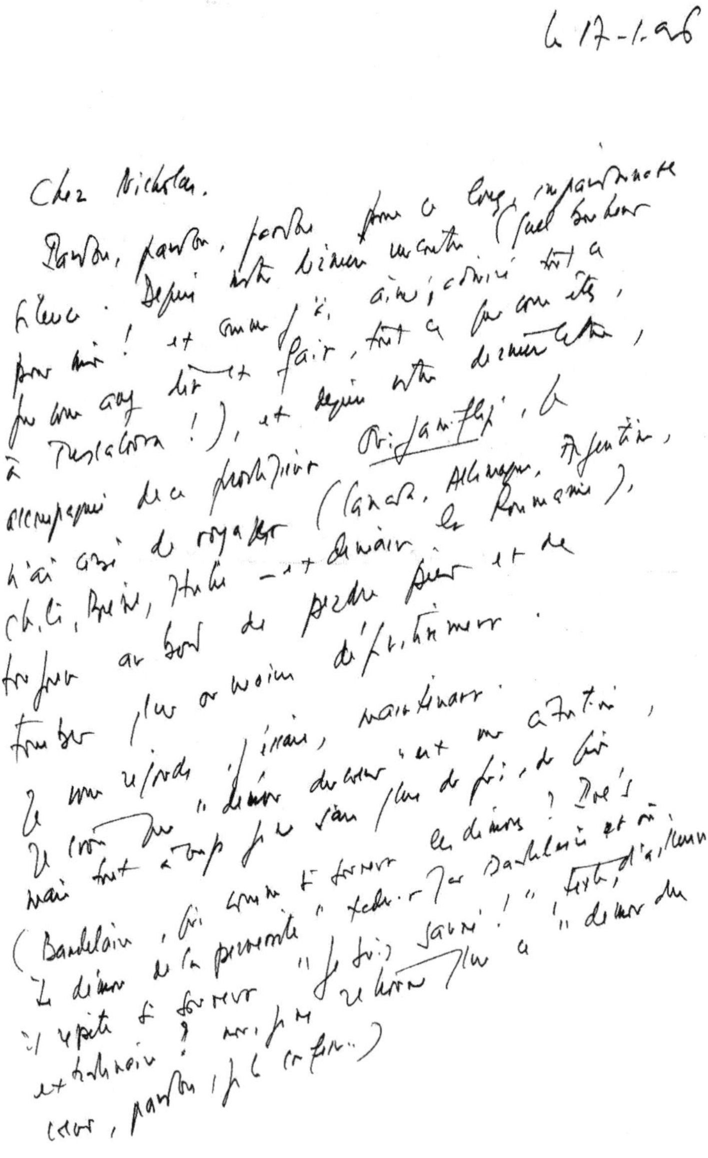

Letter of 17 January 1996[116]

Excuse-moi encore ma participation à la
special issue of OLR, je n'ai rien, sauf, sauf
un long texte INTRADUISIBLE qui
paraîtra dans Les Temps (modernes à suivre ...) pour
un numéro spécial sur Levinas. Je viens
de le finir et, si vous le souhaitez, je pourrai
vous l'envoyer bientôt. Mais s'il a un rapport
certain à la télé et à la télépathie, il est un
rapport indirect et ce texte est écrit sur un
mode si français, si français... Dites-moi.

A bientôt, cher Nick, avec mon admiration
et fidèle affection et la demande répétée
pour ce pardon immédiat, c'est-à-dire
instantanément télépathique.

Yours, as ever,

Jacques.

Notes

1. Jacques Derrida and Elisabeth Roudinesco, *For What Tomorrow . . . A Dialogue*, trans. Jeff Fort (Stanford, CA: Stanford University Press, 2004), pp. 159–60, tr. sl. mod.; *De quoi demain . . . Dialogue* (Paris: Fayard/Galilée, 2001), pp. 257–8. Further page references are given parenthetically in the main body of the text, abbreviated 'FWT', with the page reference to the original French text following a slash, where appropriate.
2. Jacques Derrida, *Politics of Friendship*, trans. George Collins (London: Verso, 1997), p. 8. Further page references are given parenthetically in the main body of the text.
3. See *'Istrice 2: Ick bünn all hier'*, trans. Peggy Kamuf, in Jacques Derrida, *Points . . . Interviews, 1974–1994*, ed. Elisabeth Weber (London: Routledge, 1995), p. 321.
4. Sigmund Freud, 'On Transience', trans. James Strachey, in *Art and Literature*, ed. Albert Dickson, Pelican Freud Library, vol. 14 (Harmondsworth: Penguin 1985), p. 290.
5. See Jacques Derrida and Jean-Luc Nancy, '"Eating Well", or the Calculation of the Subject', trans. Peter Connor and Avital Ronell, in *Points*, pp. 255–87: here, p. 281. Further page references to '"Eating Well"' are given parenthetically in the main body of the text.
6. '"Il faut bien manger" ou le calcul du sujet', in *Points de suspension: Entretiens*, ed. Elisabeth Weber (Paris: Galilée, 1992), pp. 265–301. For the translators' comment here, see *Points*, p. 475, n. 15.
7. See *Chambers Dictionary*, 10th edn (Edinburgh: Chambers Harrap, 2006), p. 413. Of course, this is a strikingly different sense of 'dialogue' from that which emerges elsewhere in Derrida's work, in particular in 'Rams: Uninterrupted Dialogue – Between Two Infinities, the Poem', trans. Thomas Dutoit and Philippe Romanski, in *Sovereignties in Question: The Poetics of Paul Celan* (New York: Fordham University Press, 2005), pp. 135–63. There he remarks that *dialogue* is 'a word [that is] foreign to my lexicon, as if belonging to a foreign language' (p. 136), before going on to elaborate a deconstructive reading, relating dialogue to what is 'interior' and uncanny (*unheimlich*), preceding any monologue: see 'Rams', p. 138 ff. For a more detailed exploration of this topic, specifically in the context of *Antony and Cleopatra*, see 'Woo't' (above).
8. Roudinesco sees Derrida's *Spectres of Marx* as 'a profoundly Freudian book' (p. 175) that is also about the 'the melancholy of the Revolution' (p. 77), haunted by the melancholy of Althusser and of course Shakespeare's Hamlet: 'You choose Hamlet and not Oedipus, that is, the guilty rather than the tragic conscience . . .' (p. 78).
9. See Jacques Derrida, 'No Apocalypse, Not Now (Full Speed Ahead, Seven Missiles, Seven Missives)', trans. Catherine Porter and Philip Lewis, *Psyche: Inventions of the Other*, vol. 1, eds Peggy Kamuf and Elizabeth Rottenberg (Stanford, CA: Stanford University Press, 2007), p. 403.
10. See Jacques Derrida, 'By Force of Mourning', in *The Work of Mourning*, eds Pascale-Anne Brault and Michael Naas (London: Chicago University Press, 2001), pp. 142–64 (here, pp. 142–3); 'À force de deuil', in *Chaque fois unique, la fin du monde* (Paris: Galilée, 2003), pp. 177–204. Further

page references are given parenthetically in the main body of the text, with the page number of the original French text following a slash, where appropriate.

11. 'Rams' was originally published in French as *Béliers: Le dialogue ininter-rompu: entre deux infinis, le poème* (Paris: Galilée, 2003).

12. Sigmund Freud, 'Mourning and Melancholia', trans. James Strachey, in *Pelican Freud Library*, vol. 11, ed. Angela Richards (Harmondsworth: Penguin, 1984), pp. 245–68.

13. 'Rams', *Sovereignties in Question*, p. 160, tr. sl. mod.; *Béliers*, p. 74. He speaks of his text *Béliers* 'prowling' around this line from Celan in the Foreword to *Chaque fois unique, la fin du monde*, p. 11.

14. Jacques Derrida, 'Let Us Not Forget – Psychoanalysis', trans. Geoffrey Bennington and Rachel Bowlby, in *Psychoanalysis and Literature: New Work*, eds Nicholas Royle and Ann Wordsworth, *Oxford Literary Review*, 12 (1990), 3–7; here, p. 3. Further page references are given parenthetically in the main body of the text.

15. René Major, 'Derrida and psychoanalysis: desistantial psychoanalysis', in *Jacques Derrida and the Humanities: A Critical Reader*, ed. Tom Cohen (Cambridge: Cambridge University Press, 2001), pp. 297–8.

16. See Samuel Beckett, *Worstward Ho* (London: John Calder, 1983), p. 7: 'Ever tried. Ever failed. No matter. Try again. Fail again. Fail better.'

17. This phrase ('it only happens to me') is, of course, not mine but borrowed from Derrida: see 'Envois', in *The Post Card: From Socrates to Freud and Beyond*, trans. Alan Bass (Chicago: Chicago University Press, 1987), p. 135, and 'Circumfession', in Bennington and Derrida, *Jacques Derrida*, trans. Geoffrey Bennington (Chicago: Chicago University Press, 1993), p. 305.

18. In his poem 'On Shakespeare' Milton describes how Shakespeare's 'easy numbers flow', perhaps alluding to Heminges and Condell's prefatorial remark in the First Folio: 'His mind and hand went together: And what he thought, he uttered with that easinesse, that wee have scarse received from him a blot in his papers.' See the *Complete Shorter Poems of John Milton*, ed. John Carey (London: Longman, 1971), p. 123, where Carey also cites the celebrated sentence from Heminges and Condell.

19. Jacques Derrida, 'The Time Is Out of Joint', trans. Peggy Kamuf, in *Deconstruction is/in America: A New Sense of the Political*, ed. Anselm Haverkamp (New York: New York University Press, 1995), pp. 14–38: here, p. 18. Further page references are given parenthetically, together with any reference to the French text (unpub. ts.), in the main body of the text, abbreviated 'TOJ' where appropriate.

20. For an excellent reading of Derrida on and against a certain 'America', see Michael Naas, 'Derrida's America', in *Derrida's Legacies: Literature and Philosophy*, eds Simon Glendinning and Robert Eaglestone (London: Routledge, 2008), pp. 118–37.

21. Derrida speaks and writes about the relationship between 'deconstruction' and 'justice' on many occasions. In a discussion at the University of Warwick in 1993, for example, he remarks: 'justice is what deconstruction is about, and what it has to do. Justice is precisely what couldn't be deconstructed because it is or should be the appeal or desire of deconstruction

... Justice is something which exceeds the deconstructable, it is indeconstructable, it is what deconstruction should perform.' See *Responsibilities of Deconstruction*, ed. Jonathon Dronsfield and Nick Midgley, *PLI: Warwick Journal of Philosophy*, vol. 6 (Summer 1997), 27. On justice and the 'undeconstructible' in *Spectres of Marx: The State of the Debt, the Work of Mourning, and the New International*, trans. Peggy Kamuf (London: Routledge, 1994), see in particular p. 59. For a somewhat earlier and more extensive meditation, see Derrida's 'Force of Law: The "Mystical Foundation of Authority"', trans. Mary Quaintance, *Cardozo Law Review*, 11: 5/6 (1990), 921–1045. In this essay (originally delivered as a lecture in New York in 1989), he relates justice to the notion of deconstruction as 'a certain experience of the impossible' (p. 981). He writes: 'Justice in itself, if such a thing exists, outside or beyond law, is not deconstructible. No more than deconstruction itself, if such a thing exists . . . Justice would be the experience that we are not able to experience . . . I think that there is no justice without this experience, however impossible it may be, of aporia. Justice is an experience of the impossible' (pp. 945, 947).

22. See *The Work of Mourning*, p. 175.
23. 'Alone' is, of course, a word effectively rewritten in Derrida's work. As he remarks in *For What Tomorrow . . .*: 'I am not *alone* with myself, no more than anyone else is – I am not *all-one*. An "I" is not an indivisible atom' (p. 112).
24. For more on the 'occasional', see Julian Wolfreys, *Occasional Deconstructions* (Albany, NY: SUNY Press, 2004), especially pp. 303–4, n. 1.
25. William Shakespeare, *Hamlet*, ed. G. R. Hibbard (Oxford: Oxford University Press, 1994), I, i, 19. Further references are to this edition, unless otherwise indicated.
26. Jacques Derrida, 'Edmond Jabès and the Question of the Book', in *Writing and Difference*, trans. Alan Bass (London: Routledge & Kegan Paul, 1978), p. 71.
27. *Spectres of Marx*, p. 59.
28. See *Hamlet*, Arden Shakespeare 3rd Series, eds Ann Thompson and Neil Taylor (London: Thompson Learning, 2006), p. 306; *Much Ado About Nothing*, ed. F. H. Mares, Updated Edition (Cambridge: Cambridge University Press, 2003), V, ii, 58–60. (Further references are to this edition of *Much Ado*, and are given parenthetically in the main body of the text.)
29. *Spectres of Marx*, p. 18.
30. As the opening line of the following scene would suggest, in which Claudio asks: 'Is this the monument of Leonato?' (V, iii, 1).
31. For more on the 'phantom text' and 'brain-territory', permit me to refer to 'This is not a book-review', in *Angelaki*, 2: 1 (1995), ed. Sarah Wood, 31–5; *The Uncanny* (Manchester: Manchester University Press, 2003), esp. pp. 277–88; and 'Hotel Psychoanalysis: Some Remarks on Mark Twain and Sigmund Freud', in *Angelaki*, 9: 1 (2004), ed. Sarah Wood, 3–14.
32. See Martin McQuillan, 'Introduction: Five Strategies for Deconstruction', in *Deconstruction: A Reader*, ed. McQuillan (Edinburgh: Edinburgh University Press, 2000), p. 41.

33. Jacques Derrida, *Mémoires: for Paul de Man*, trans. Cecile Lindsay, Jonathan Culler and Eduardo Cadava (New York: Columbia University Press, 1986), p. 84.

34. See 'Deconstruction in America: An Interview with Jacques Derrida', trans. James Creech, *Critical Exchange*, 17 (1985), 1–33: here, pp. 12, 2. The kind of subterranean reading I am advancing here would perhaps gather additional support from some of the preliminary remarks that Derrida makes in 'The Time Is Out of Joint'. First, in the context of the idea that deconstruction is 'sans merci' (it is 'a practice of implacable ingratitude, without thanks') – '*deconstruction is merciless*', he says (in English in the original) – and he concludes this with a little joke: 'Enough on this thanks and the thanksgiving of deconstruction' (p. 16). Second, apropos the 'is' in his title-phrase and the title of the colloquium at which the text was originally presented (i.e. 'Deconstruction is/in America'), he asks: 'Why should we cross these two quotations . . . at the disjointed juncture, at the crossroads or the crossing of this little "is"? Should we also inscribe it under some erasure in the form of a cross?' (pp. 16–17). This reference to the cross ('en forme de croix') perhaps resonates beyond its more Heideggerian usage (words 'sous rature').

35. Geoffrey Bennington, 'Foundations', in *Textual Practice*, 21: 2 (2007), 243.

36. 'Structure, Sign and Play in the Discourse of the Human Sciences', in *Writing and Difference*, trans. Alan Bass (London: Routledge & Kegan Paul, 1978), pp. 278–93; 'The University Without Condition', in Jacques Derrida, *Without Alibi*, ed. and trans. Peggy Kamuf (Stanford, CA: Stanford University Press, 2002), pp. 202–37.

37. See 'Portmanteau', *New Literary History*, 37: 1 (Winter 2006), 237–47.

38. Jacques Derrida, *H.C. for Life, That is to Say . . .*, trans. Laurent Milesi and Stefan Herbrechter (Stanford, CA: Stanford University Press, 2006), pp. 96, 147.

39. Ibid., p. 23.

40. Ibid., p. 38. Cf. also p. 29, where Derrida speaks of Cixous's 'fictional hyperrealism'.

41. Falstaff notes of good-quality sherry: 'It ascends me into the brain, dries me there all the foolish and dull and crudy vapours which environ it, makes it apprehensive, quick, forgetive, full of nimble, fiery, and delectable shapes': see *Henry IV, Part 2*, ed. René Weis (Oxford: Oxford University Press, 1998), IV, ii, 93–7. The *OED* warily specifies 'forgetive' as 'A Shakespearian word, of uncertain formation and meaning.' The lurking presence of 'forget' in 'forgetive' perhaps at least partly accounts for such wariness.

42. See Hibbard, p. 255, and Thompson and Taylor, p. 306, respectively.

43. See *Spectres of Marx*, p. 172.

44. Freud, 'On Transience', p. 290.

45. There is in fact a comma at the end of the line in the First Folio (1623), but not in the Second Quarto (1604–5): I am here of course following the text of the Hibbard edition which, like Jenkins, and Thompson and Taylor, leaves the line enjambed.

46. William Shakespeare, *Love's Labour's Lost*, ed. G. R. Hibbard (Oxford: Oxford University Press, 1990), III, i, 26–7.

47. See *Hamlet*, ed. Jenkins, p. 501.

48. Ibid., pp. 500–1.

49. I refer here to Derrida's *Cinders*, trans. Ned Lukacher (Lincoln, NE: University of Nebraska Press, 1991); *Feu la cendre* (Paris: Des femmes, 1987). As he puts it in an interview: 'Forgetting itself is forgotten. Everything is annihilated in the cinders. Cinders is the figure of that of which not even cinders remain in a certain way' ('Passages – from Traumatism to Promise', trans. Peggy Kamuf, in *Points*, p. 391).

50. Jacques Derrida, 'Envois', in *The Post Card*, p. 43. I try to explore this and related remarks more fully in 'Jacques Derrida, Also, Enters Into Heaven', *Angelaki*, 3: 2 (1998), 113–16.

51. C. T. Onions, *A Shakespeare Glossary*, rev. ed. R. D. Eagleson (Oxford: Oxford University Press, 1986), p. 132. These are the senses that Moth goes on to play with in *Love's Labour's Lost*: 'The hobby-horse is but a colt ["young horse" but also "lascivious man"], and your love perhaps a hackney ["horse kept for hire", but also "whore"]' (III, i, 29–30, and see Hibbard's notes in *Love's Labour's Lost*, p. 133).

52. Cited in *Hamlet Prince of Denmark*, ed. Philip Edwards, New Cambridge Shakespeare Updated Edition (Cambridge: Cambridge University Press, 2003), p. 170.

53. *Hamlet*, ed. Edwards, p. 170.

54. Who wrote Shakespeare's stage directions? It is generally reckoned that this passage of the text, in the Folio, was set by 'Compositor B', in William Jaggard's printing shop: see Thompson and Taylor *Hamlet*, Table 4, p. 526.

55. I recall here Derrida's concern to 'recast the concept of text by generalising it almost without limit, in any case without present or perceptible limit, without any limit that *is*': see 'But, Beyond . . . (Open Letter to Anne McClintock and Rob Nixon)', trans. Peggy Kamuf, *Critical Inquiry*, 13 (1986), 167.

56. See Jacques Derrida, 'Biodegradables', trans. Peggy Kamuf, *Critical Inquiry*, 15: 4 (1989), 845.

57. Jacques Derrida, *Learning to Live Finally: An Interview with Jean Birnbaum*, trans. Pascale-Anne Brault and Michael Naas (Hoboken, NJ: Melville House, 2007), pp. 33–4.

58. The interview originally appeared in *Le Monde* (19 August 2004) under the title 'Je suis en guerre contre moi-même'.

59. It is *as if*, he goes on, it is 'as if' one's 'dying wish' were: '"this is my body", "keep it in memory of me", and so, "replace it, in memory of me, with a book or discourse to be bound in hide or put into digital memory. Transfigure me into a *corpus*. So that there will no longer be any difference between the place of real presence or of the Eucharist and the great computerised library of knowledge".' See *The Work of Mourning*, p. 169.

60. Ibid., p. 170.

61. It is not a question of supposing that there is some moment or time (even in so-called *grand deuil* or high mourning) in which we do not forget at all, in which there is no forgetting (however well or badly). Cf. David Krell's remarks on the 'do not forget', 'never forget this', in his provoking study *The Purest of Bastards*. He writes: 'Of course we will forget it. Memory is finite. If we keep mourning in mind, we must also mourn memory, and

thus mourn mourning itself . . . We cannot forever remain faithful to the departed one . . . not merely because our attention span is too limited but because, in a sense that is difficult to articulate but hard to deny, these loved others *were never fully there* for us when they were alive, never fully present to us, never palpable in the way our dreams promised – if only because *we* were never fully there *for us* while they were alive.' See David Farrell Krell, *The Purest of Bastards: Works of Mourning, Art, and Affirmation in the Thought of Jacques Derrida* (University Park, PA: Pennsylvania State University Press, 2000), p. 18.

62. See *Derrida: Screenplay and Essays on the Film* (Manchester: Manchester University Press, 2005), p. 57. Derrida is playing out a version of the story about Thales told by Socrates: the philosopher is the figure who is so busy gazing up to study the stars he doesn't see what is at his feet and tumbles into a well. To be a philosopher is to be always 'open to such mockery'. See 'Theaetetus' 174a, in *The Collected Dialogues of Plato*, eds Edith Hamilton and Huntington Cairns (Princeton, NJ: Princeton University Press, 1961), p. 879.
63. '"Dialanguages"', trans. Peggy Kamuf, in *Points*, p. 146.
64. Jacques Derrida, *Mémoires*, p. 3.
65. '"Dialanguages"', p. 145.
66. 'Deconstruction in America', p. 7.
67. The citations here are from *Mémoires*, p. 3, and ' "Dialanguages"', p. 145, respectively. Cf. also his remark in *Mémoires*: 'one must not forget Lethe' (p. 80).
68. *Mémoires*, p. 73.
69. See Jacques Derrida, 'Ulysses Gramophone: Hear Say Yes in Joyce', trans. Tina Kendall and Shari Benstock in *Acts of Literature*, ed. Derek Attridge (London and New York: Routledge, 1992), pp. 256–309.
70. *The Work of Mourning*, p. 173; *Chaque fois unique, la fin du monde*, p. 213. Brault and Naas translate '*souffrance*' here as 'pain' and '*mal*' as 'suffering'.
71. Jacques Derrida, *The Animal That Therefore I Am*, ed. Marie-Louise Mallet, trans. David Wills (New York: Fordham University Press, 2008), p. 27. Further page references are given parenthetically in the main body of the text.
72. We might here recall also what Derrida says in *Aporias*: 'Although the innumerable structural differences that separate one "species" from another should make us vigilant about any discourse on animality or bestiality *in general*, one can say that animals have a very significant relation to death, to murder and to war (hence, to borders), to mourning and to hospitality, and so forth, even if they have neither a relation to death nor to the "name" of death as such, nor, by the same token, to the other as such, to the purity as such of the alterity of the other as such. But neither does man, that is precisely the point!' See Jacques Derrida, *Aporias: Dying – awaiting (one another at) the 'limits of truth'*, trans. Thomas Dutoit (Stanford, CA: Stanford University Press, 1993), pp. 76–7.
73. See Jacques Derrida, *The Gift of Death*, trans. David Wills (Chicago: Chicago University Press, 1995), pp. 82–115, and *passim*.
74. See Jacques Derrida, 'Freud and the Scene of Writing', in *Writing and Difference*, pp. 196–231: here, in particular, p. 200.

75. *Mémoires*, p. 107.
76. 'Freud and the Scene of Writing', p. 201.
77. *Of Grammatology*, p. 24.
78. Jacques Derrida, *Given Time: I. Counterfeit Money*, trans. Peggy Kamuf (London: Chicago University Press, 1992), p. 57. Further page references appear parenthetically in the main body of the text, abbreviated 'GT' where appropriate.
79. See 'Or Again, Meddling', above.
80. 'The Deconstruction of Actuality: An Interview with Jacques Derrida', trans. Jonathan Rée, in *Deconstruction: A Reader*, ed. Martin McQuillan (Edinburgh: Edinburgh University Press, 2000), p. 545.
81. 'Biodegradables', p. 813.
82. See *Spectres of Marx*, pp. 109–10.
83. Yosef Hayim Yerushalmi, *Zakhor: Jewish History and Jewish Memory*, cited in Jacques Derrida, *Archive Fever: A Freudian Impression*, trans. Eric Prenowitz (Chicago: Chicago University Press, 1996), p. 76. Further page references to *Archive Fever* are given parenthetically in the main body of the text.
84. See 'Khora', trans. Ian McLeod, in Jacques Derrida, *On the Name*, ed. Thomas Dutoit (Stanford, CA: Stanford University Press, 1995), pp. 87–127: here, p. 111.
85. *Spectres of Marx*, p. 65.
86. Jacques Derrida, in Catherine Malabou and Jacques Derrida, *Counterpath: Travelling with Jacques Derrida*, trans. David Wills (Stanford, CA: Stanford University Press, 2004), p. 147.
87. For the 'appropriation of Jerusalem', see *Spectres of Marx*, p. 58; on globalisation, see, for example, 'Autoimmunity: Real and Symbolic Suicides. A Dialogue with Jacques Derrida', trans. Pascale-Anne Brault and Michael Naas, in Giovanna Borradori, *Philosophy in a Time of Terror: Dialogues with Jürgen Habermas and Jacques Derrida* (Chicago and London: Chicago University Press, 2003), especially p. 121 ff.
88. See *Spectres of Marx*, p. 98.
89. See 'Autoimmunity: Real and Symbolic Suicides', p. 106.
90. Alfred W. McCoy, *A Question of Torture: CIA Interrogation, from the Cold War to the War on Terror* (New York: Henry Holt, 2006), p. 195.
91. 'Autoimmunity: Real and Symbolic Suicides', p. 191, n. 14.
92. Ibid., p. 106.
93. See 'Force of Law', p. 967.
94. Ibid., p. 953.
95. Joe Brainard, *I Remember*, rev. edn, with an afterword by Ron Padgett (Harmondsworth: Penguin, 1995).
96. It is a matter, in particular perhaps, of the desire or fantasy of tears, groans or sighs that would bring someone back to life. Margaret says of the murdered Duke of Gloucester: 'Might liquid tears or heart-offending groans / Or blood-consuming sighs recall his life, / I would be blind with weeping, sick with groans, / Look pale as primrose with blood-drinking sighs, / And all to have the noble duke alive.' See William Shakespeare, *The Second Part of Henry VI*, ed. Michael Hattaway (Cambridge: Cambridge University Press, 1991), III, ii, 60–4.
97. See 'The Deaths of Roland Barthes', in *The Work of Mourning*, p. 67.

98. He writes about letting himself be 'invaded . . . gently . . . by a child-hood memory, a true childhood memory, the opposite of a dream'. See 'A Silkworm of One's Own (Points of view stitched on the other veil)', trans. Geoffrey Bennington, in *Derridas*, ed. Timothy Clark and Nicholas Royle, *Oxford Literary Review*, 18 (1996), 3–65: here, p. 48.

99. For a photographic reproduction and English translation of this brief handwritten text, see Jacques Derrida, 'Final Words', trans. Gila Walker, in *The Late Derrida*, eds W. J. T. Mitchell and Arnold I. Davidson (Chicago: Chicago University Press, 2007), p. 244.

100. Jacques Derrida, *Memoirs of the Blind: The Self-Portrait and Other Ruins*, trans. Pascale-Anne Brault and Michael Naas (Chicago: Chicago University Press, 1993), p. 126.

101. Ibid., p. 129.

102. See 'Envois' in *The Post Card*, pp. 14–15. The original French runs: '*Ne m'intéresse au fond que ce qui ne s'expédie pas, ne se dépêche en aucun cas.*' See *La carte postale: de Socrate à Freud et au-delà* (Paris: Flammarion, 1980), p. 19. Cf. also his remarks in 'Passages – from Traumatism to Promise', in *Points*, p. 388.

103. 'The Taste of Tears', in *The Work of Mourning*, p. 110.

104. 'Letter to Francine Loreau', in *The Work of Mourning*, pp. 94–5; *Chaque fois unique, la fin du monde*, p. 124. Further page references to this letter are given parenthetically in the main body of the text.

105. On this and related issues, including the terror of the mother becoming mad, as well as, more radically, the mother as 'what makes madness possible' and as the madness of 'the place of language', the madness of 'the mother tongue', see Jacques Derrida, *Monolingualism of the Other; or, The Prosthesis of Origin,* trans. Patrick Mensah (Stanford, CA: Stanford University Press, 1998), pp. 88–9. For 'Ouijamiflip', see *Oxford Literary Review*, 30:2 (2008), 235–55.

106. Jacques Derrida, 'Che cos'è la poesia?', trans. Peggy Kamuf, in *Points*, pp. 288–99. *Points* presents the text of the French original (even pages numbers) facing the English translation (odd page numbers). Further page references here are given parenthetically in the main body of the text.

107. See Jacques Derrida, 'My Chances/*Mes Chances*: A Rendezvous with Some Epicurean Stereophonies', trans. Irene Harvey and Avital Ronell, in *Psyche: Inventions of the Other*, vol. 1, p. 361.

108. See Jacques Derrida and Bernard Stiegler, *Echographies of Television: Filmed Interviews*, trans. Jennifer Bajorek (Cambridge: Polity, 2002), p. 117.

109. See Jacques Derrida, *Spurs: Nietzsche's Styles/Eperons: Les Styles de Nietzsche*, trans. Barbara Harlow (Chicago: University of Chicago Press, 1979), pp. 127/126 (tr. sl. mod.).

110. At the beginning of a section of *The Interpretation of Dreams* entitled 'The Work of Condensation', Freud observes:

> The first thing that becomes clear to anyone who compares the dream-content with the dream-thoughts is that a work of *condensation* on a large scale has been carried out. Dreams are brief, meagre and laconic in comparison with the range and wealth of the dream-thoughts. If a dream is written out it may fill half a page. The analysis setting out the dream-thoughts underlying it may occupy

six, eight or a dozen times as much space . . . [I]t is in fact never possible to be sure that a dream has been completely interpreted. Even if the solution seems satisfactory and without gaps, the possibility always remains that the dream may have yet another meaning. Strictly speaking, then, it is impossible to determine the amount of condensation.

See Sigmund Freud, *The Interpretation of Dreams*, Pelican Freud Library, vol. 4, trans. James Strachey (Harmondsworth: Penguin, 1976), 383–413 (here, p. 383). And see also Jean Laplanche and J.-B. Pontalis, *The Language of Psycho-Analysis*, trans. Donald Nicholson-Smith (London: Hogarth Press and Institute of Psycho-Analysis, 1973), pp. 82–3.

111. See, for example, '*Fors*: The Anglish Words of Nicolas Abraham and Maria Torok', trans. Barbara Johnson, in Abraham and Torok, *The Wolf Man's Magic Word: A Cryptonymy*, trans. Nicholas Rand (Minneapolis, MN: University of Minnesota Press, 1986), pp. xi–xlviii; '*Sauf le nom (Post-Scriptum)*', trans. John P. Leavey, Jr, in *On the Name*, ed. Thomas Dutoit (Stanford, CA: Stanford University Press, 1995), pp. 35–85; 'Faith and Knowledge: the Two Sources of "Religion" at the Limits of Reason Alone', trans. Sam Weber, in *Religion*, eds Jacques Derrida and Gianni Vattimo (Cambridge: Polity Press, 1998), pp. 1–78; and 'Salve: Untimely Postscript, for Want of a Final Retouch', in *On Touching – Jean-Luc Nancy*, trans. Christine Irizarry (Stanford, CA: Stanford University Press, 2005), pp. 300–10. For a fine account and overview of this topic and of the remarkable figure of '*salut*' in particular, see Kas Saghafi, '*Salut*-ations', in *Mosaic* 39: 3 (September 2006), 151–71.

112. See Edgar Allan Poe, 'The Imp of the Perverse', in *Tales and Sketches*, vol. 2: 1843–1849, ed. Thomas Ollive Mabbott (Urbana, IL: University of Illinois Press, 2000), 1219–27: here, p. 1225. Further page references appear parenthetically in the main body of the text.

113. 'Le Démon de la perversité', trans. Charles Baudelaire, in *Nouvelles histoires extraordinaires par Edgar Poe (œuvres complètes de Charles Baudelaire)* (Paris: Louis Conard, 1933), p. 8.

114. See Jacques Derrida, *Geneses, Genealogies, Genres and Genius: The Secrets of the Archive*, trans. Beverley Bie Brahic (Edinburgh: Edinburgh University Press, 2006), pp. 78, 75.

115. *On Touching*, p. 310.

116. A transcription of this letter would run as follows:

17ᵗʰ January 1996

Cher Nicholas,

Pardon, pardon, pardon, pour ce long, impardonnable silence. Depuis notre dernier rencontre (quel bonheur pour moi! et comme j'ai aimé, admiré tout ce que vous avez dit et fait, tout ce que vous êtes, à Tuscaloosa!), et depuis votre dernière lettre, accompagnée de ce prodigieux Ouijamiflip, je n'ai cessé de voyager (Canada, Allemagne, Argentine, Chili, Brésil, Italie – et demain la Roumanie), toujours au bord de perdre pied et de tomber plus ou moins définitivement.

Je vous réponds, j'essaie, maintenant.

Je crois que "démon du coeur" est une citation, mais tout à coup je ne sais plus de qui, de quoi (Baudelaire, qui [. . .?] si souvent les démons? Poe's "Le démon de la perversité" traduit par Baudelaire et où il répète si souvent "Je suis sauvé!", texte d'ailleurs extraordinaire? non, je ne retrouve plus ce "démon du coeur, pardon, je le confesse . . .)

En ce qui concerne ma participation à la special issue of OLR, je n'ai rien, <u>sauf</u>, <u>sauf</u>, un <u>très long</u> texte <u>INTRADUISIBLE</u> qui paraîtra dans <u>Contretemps</u> (Un ver à soie . . .) pour un numéro special sur <u>Le voile</u>. Je viens de le finir et si vous le souhaitez, je pourrai vous l'envoyer bientôt. Mais s'il a un rapport certain à la <u>tekhnè</u> et à la technologie, c'est un rapport indirect et ce texte est écrit sur un mode bizarre, bizarre . . . Dites-moi.

A bientôt, cher Nick, avec mon admiration et grande affection et la demande, urgente pour un pardon, immédiat, c'est à dire instantanément télépathique.

Yours, as ever,

Jacques

Last

I was late with the manuscript, it was promised months earlier, and the publisher had been in touch to ask for details of chapter titles, in order to update their database, they said. Perhaps it was simply a new means of gently nudging me to realise it was time to complete the book. In any case it forced my hand and I responded more or less straightaway. I knew that whatever it was I was writing did not consist of *chapters* and that it would be necessary at some point to try to signal that fact, but at the same time I didn't imagine the publisher's database was going to be particularly interested in such seeming technicalities. I also knew that the *order* of the pieces was not clear to me and indeed was never going to be. But I supplied, as requested, a list of the provisional titles of the pieces I envisaged including. At the end, after 'Forgetting Well', I specified the addition of something called 'Last'. The moment I dispatched the message containing this list I began to feel anxious and troubled about the last title, the 'Last' title. I had, in truth, no idea what induced me to propose it, besides the rather inarticulate desire to try to explore various kinds of duplicity and uncertainty in the English word (last, *the* last, *to* last, *to the* last, a vague sense of tying this up with shoemaking and the figure of the cobbler at the beginning of *Julius Caesar*, footstep and trace) and the conviction that there would be no 'last word' or 'last words'. And of course what was there possibly to be said that hadn't already been said about the *dernier mot* or the *last word* or the afterword or postscript or any number of other equivalent *terms*, in an *interminable* logic of the supplement, by Jacques Derrida himself? And at the same time, how was I to go about trying to leave or give the last word to him? And not least while seeking to acknowledge the force of Hélène Cixous's suggestion that 'no dead person has ever said their last word'.[1] My anxiety on this subject increased throughout the day but was dispelled that night when I woke up – to the moon, beyond the window, as if magically illuminating the great verdant promontory

called Seaford Head – with what I experienced as a perfectly serendipi-
tous solution, an instantaneous lasting response, the most calming and
magnificent of dreams, which I wrote down first thing:

> *Tonight I dreamt he was alive again – and was with me in some far off place,*
> *very green ('Annihilating all that's made / To a green thought in a green*
> *shade': does he cite that in* Memoirs of the Blind*?) – he was being, as ever,*
> *very warm, loving and friendly – but he became anxious, wanting to call*
> *his two sons – there was no telephone we could find – then the agitation he*
> *showed passed and we were talking again – and I asked him what year it*
> *was – he must have seen that I was asking this question as a visitor, or not*
> *in the same world as him, for he laughed (very beautifully) and replied in a*
> *reassuring simple fashion: 'Oh, it's no problem. I can jump around from one*
> *time to the other.'*

Note

1. Hélène Cixous, *OR, les lettres de mon père* (Paris: Des Femmes, 1997), p. 25.
Cited by Jacques Derrida in *H. C. for Life, That is to Say . . .*, trans. Laurent
Milesi and Stefan Herbrechter (Stanford, CA: Stanford University Press,
2006), p. 124.

Index of Works by Derrida

'Afterw.rds', xii, 39
'Afterword: Toward an Ethic of
    Discussion', x
The Animal That Therefore I Am,
    157–8, 164
'Ants', 94
'Aphorism Countertime', 5, 32
Aporias, 181n72
Archive Fever, 60–1, 114, 115,
    160–1
'Autoimmunity: Real and Symbolic
    Suicides', xiv n1, 103–6, 161–2

'Before the Law', 29
'Biodegradables', 154, 160
'But, Beyond . . .', 180n55

'Che cos'é le poesia?', 6–7, 21–2, 45, 83,
    87n34, 167, 168–72
'Choreographies', 115
Cinders, 153
'Circumfession', 1, 87n32, 121–2,
    131n42, 141
Counterpath, 161

'Deconstructions: The Im-possible', xv
    n10
'Deconstruction in America', 146–7,
    155
'The Deconstruction of Actuality', 61–2,
    160
'Deconstruction: A Trialogue in
    Jerusalem', 39
Demeure: Fiction and Testimony, 7,
    23–4, 29, 32, 60, 84n7, 89
'Dialanguages', 8, 78–9, 118, 155
'Différance', 42

Dissemination, 117
'The Double Session' ('La double
    séance'), 58n48

The Ear of the Other, 47
'Eating Well', 136
Echographies of Television, 167–8
'Edmond Jabès and the Question of the
    Book', 145
'Ellipsis', 28
'Envois', 15, 16n12, 22, 23, 25, 28, 34,
    94, 113, 141, 153, 165
'Et Cetera. . .', 39–40, 111n44

'Fichus', xiv
For What Tomorrow . . . A Dialogue, x,
    90–1, 105, 107, 108–9n5, 135–8,
    141–2, 153, 178n23
'Force of Law', 106, 162, 178n21
'Fors', 47–8, 79
'Freud and the Scene of Writing', 100,
    111n40, 114–15, 158–9

*Geneses, Genealogies, Genres and
    Genius*, 115, 172
The Gift of Death, 59, 157
Given Time, 28–9, 159, 172
Glas, 79, 95, 107, 145

H. C. for Life, That is to Say. . .,
    87–8n35, 94, 115
'History of the Lie: Prolegomena',
    112n47, 163

'I Have A Taste for the Secret', x, 3, 5,
    30, 52, 118, 119
'Istrice 2', 136

'Ja, or the faux-bond II', 92, 107, 108n5
Jacques Derrida, 95
'Justices', 125–7

'Khora', 161

'Language is Never Owned: An Interview', 92–3, 97
'Language (*Le Monde* on the Telephone)', 93–4, 95, 97
'The Law of Genre' ('La loi du genre'), 46, 49
Learning to Live Finally, 154
'Let Us Not Forget – Psychoanalysis', 139–40
'Limited Inc', 28, 41, 61, 95–6, 100–1, 117, 118
'Living On/ Border Lines', 38, 41, 43, 44–6, 74, 85n18

'A "Madness" Must Watch Over Thinking', 109–10n21
[Meddling AfterwORd], 53–5
Mémoires: for Paul de Man, x, xi, 60, 85n13, 146–7, 155–6, 158
Memoirs of the Blind, 165, 187
Monolingualism of the Other, 26, 39, 46, 167, 183n105
'My Chances', 63, 167

'Negotiations', 26, 36n22
'No Apocalypse, Not Now', 25–6, 80, 138

'Of an Apocalyptic Tone Newly Adopted in Philosophy', 26
Of Grammatology, ix, xiv n 1, 27–8, 29, 45, 98, 99, 103, 110n23, 118, 119, 159
On Touching – Jean-Luc Nancy, 173
The Other Heading, 1, 97
'Ousia and Grammē', 26–7

'"Le Parjure", Perhaps: Storytelling and Lying', 43, 105
'Passages – from Traumatism to Promise', 180n49
'Passions: "An Oblique Offering"', 22, 32, 119

Politics of Friendship, 4, 6, 78, 11, 13, 17n18, 72, 125, 131n 40, 1356
Positions, 47
'Psyche: Inventions of the Other', 8, 61
'Psychoanalysis Searches the State of Its Soul', 111

'Qual Quelle', 7, 18n30

Rams (Béliers), 68, 82–3, 138–9, 176n7, 177n13
'The Rhetoric of Drugs', 95
Rogues, xiv n1, 93

'Signature Event Context', 28, 96
Signsponge, 66
'A Silk Worm of One's Own', 163, 183n98
Spectres of Marx, x, 3–4, 5, 13, 30, 34, 48, 49, 61, 62, 71, 106, 111n 43, 118, 142, 145, 146, 151, 160, 161, 176n8, 178n21
Speech and Phenomena, 27
Spurs, 168
'Structure, Sign and Play in the Discourse of the Human Sciences', 147

'Telepathy', 94, 101
'"There is No *One* Narcissism"', 44
'This Strange Institution Called Literature', 62, 65
'The Time is Out of Joint', 3, 21, 23, 29, 30–1, 32, 34, 46, 78, 142–7, 156, 179n34
'The Time of a Thesis', 13
'Title (to be specified)', 70, 85n17
The Truth in Painting, 24, 91–2
'Two Words for Joyce', xi–xii
'Typewriter Ribbon: Limited Ink 2', 40, 41–2, 112n53

'Ulysses Gramophone', 65, 94–5, 100
'The University without Condition', 147

'Voice II', 12

The Work of Mourning (Chaque fois unique, la fin du monde), 68–71, 82, 127, 138, 155, 156, 163, 166–7, 180n59

Index of Names

Abbott, E. A., 2–3, 12, 13
Abraham, Nicolas, 47–8
Aeschylus, 16n14
Althusser, Louis, 69, 91, 176n8
Archer, William, 11
Aristotle, 26–7, 157
Austin, J. L., 40–4, 51, 55, 96

Bakhtin, Mikhail, 95, 109n19
Barthes, Roland, 90, 163
Baudelaire, Charles, 171–2
Bawcutt, N. W., 51
Beckett, Samuel, ix, 99, 141, 167
Benjamin, Walter, 91
Bennett, Andrew and Nicholas Royle,
    73, 85n14, 114, 116
Bennington, Geoffrey, 3, 36n30, 95, 147
Benoist, Jean-Marie, 166
Bentham, Jeremy, 157
Berger, Anne, 78
Bersani, Leo, 113, 128n2, 132n42
Bevington, David, 76–7
Bin Laden, Osama, 101, 103, 105–6
Blair, Tony, 97, 101–2, 103, 104
Blanchot, Maurice, ix, 68, 89–90, 92,
    93, 110n23
Blits, Jan H., 19n47
Borradori, Giovanna, 103, 104
Bowen, Elizabeth, 72–6, 155
Boxall, Peter, 35n9
Brainard, Joe, 163
Brault, Pascale-Anne, 68, 69–70
Bush, George W., 101, 103, 162
Butler, Judith, 113, 121

Cahen, Didier, 69
Carey, John, 177n18

Carroll, Lewis, 164
Castricano, Jodey, 47, 48
Celan, Paul, 60, 82, 83, 92, 138, 142
Cheney, Dick, 112n51
Cixous, Hélène, ix, 2, 22, 87n32,
    87–8n35, 115, 148, 186
Clark, Timothy, 27, 109n19
Clery, E. J., 48, 49
Collins, George, 136
Condell, Henry, 177n18
Connor, Peter, 136–7
Conrad, Joseph, 114, 116
Coppola, Francis Ford, 26

de Man, Paul, xi, xii, 40, 43
Descartes, René, 157
Delacampagne, Christian, 93
Deleuze, Gilles, 16n14, 108n3
Dick, Kirby, 59
Dickens, Charles, 112n47
Dobson, Michael, 20n52
Dollimore, Jonathan, 115–17, 119–21,
    122, 124, 127, 129n24, 130–1n36
Dunbar, William, 116
Dutoit, Ulysse, 113

Ebeling, Herman L., 15n11
Edelman, Lee, 124–5, 131n38
Edwards, Philip, 76–7, 153
Ellmann, Maud, 85n14

Farrell, Kirby, 13
Fathy, Safaa, 108
Ferraris, Maurizio, 30, 118, 136
Forster, E. M., 88n35, 116, 117, 119–21,
    122–4
Fort, Jeff, 108–9n5, 142

Foucault, Michel, 91
Freud, Sigmund, 60, 94, 114–15, 119,
    140, 147, 176n8
  The Interpretation of Dreams, 169,
    183–4n110
  'Leonardo da Vinci and a Memory of
    his Childhood', 122
  'Mourning and Melancholia', 73,
    138–9
  'A Note on the Unconscious', 100
  'On Transience', xii, 136, 152
  'The Uncanny' ('Das Unheimliche'),
    111n43

Gadamer, Hans-Georg, 82, 138
Gaston, Sean, 26
Gentleman, Francis, 14
Granel, Gérard, 68
Greene, Thomas M., 5, 17n19
Guattari, Félix, 108n3

Halpern, Richard, 8
Hamacher, Werner, 28
Hari, Johann, 86n29
Hegel, G. W. F., 26
Heidegger, Martin, 26, 111n43, 157, 170
Heminges, John, 177n18
Henry, Thierry, 99
Hibbard, G. R., 32, 76–7, 85n21, 152
Hodge, Joanna, 84n7
Hodsdon, Amelia, 86n29
Hoggart, Richard, 90
Holland, Norman N., 10
Hopkins, Gerard Manley, 116, 125–7
Hueffer, Ford Maddox, 114
Husserl, Edmund, 27, 39

Jabès, Edmond, 145
James, Henry, 73, 116
Jay, Martin, 101, 102, 111n43
Jenkins, Harold, 32, 65, 76–7, 153
Johnson, Samuel, 77, 98
Joudeh, Jinan, 108n1, 126
Joyce, James, ix, xi–xii, 65, 94, 141, 156

Kafka, Franz, 43
Kamuf, Peggy, 3, 36n33, 109n7
Kant, Immanuel, 16n14, 71, 140, 157
Kaula, David, 17n18
Kayser, John R., 17–18n26, 20n55
Kermode, Frank, 10, 18n37

Khatibi, Abdelkebir, 136
Kierkegaard, Søren, 43
Koestenbaum, Wayne, 114
Kofman, Amy Ziering, 59
Kofman, Sarah, 69, 70, 155, 156
Krell, David, 180–1n61

La Fontaine, Jean de, 96, 98
Lacan, Jacques, 91, 140, 157
Laplanche, Jean and J.-B. Pontalis, 169
Lawrence, D. H., 89, 108n3
Lenin, V. I., 118, 129n17
Lettieri, Ronald J., 17–18n26, 20n55
Lévi-Strauss, Claude, 91
Levinas, Emmanuel, 157
Lioliou, Persephone, 34n1
Loreau, Francine, 166
Loreau, Max, 69, 166–7
Lyotard, Jean-François, 69, 70–1, 91

MacAskill, Ewen, 112n51
McCoy, Alfred, 162
MacDonald, George, 78
McKee, David, 22–5
McQuillan, Martin, 146
Major, René, 140
Mallarmé, Stephane, ix, 45, 55
Mallet, Marie-Louise, 44
Margree, Vicky, 34n1
Marin, Louis, 138
Marshall, Cynthia, 12, 19n44
Marshall, William, 48
Martin, Robert K., 122, 132n42
Marvell, Andrew, 165, 187
Marx, Karl, 61
Melville, Herman, 113–14, 121–2,
    125–6, 131–2n42
Miller, J. Hillis, 43, 125–6
Milton, John, 141, 177n18
Monty Python, 105–6

Naas, Michael, 68, 69–70, 177n20
Nancy, Jean-Luc, 136–7
Neill, Michael, 76–7
Nietzsche, Friedrich, ix, 142, 168
Norris, Christopher, 105
North, Sir Thomas, 9–10, 11–12

Paris, Matthew, 23
Parkin-Gounelas, Ruth, 47
Partridge, Eric, 20n50, 38

Pascal, Blaise, 170
Paster, Gail Kern, 12, 17n18, 19–20n50
Person, Leland S., 132n42
Piggford, George, 122
Pires, Robert, 99
Pirovolakis, Eftichis, 34n1
Plato, ix, 23, 159, 181n62
Plutarch, 9–10, 11–12, 19n42
Poe, Edgar Allan, 171–2
Ponge, Francis, 66
Price, Hereward T., 8
Punter, David, 19n40

Rackin, Phyllis, 5–6, 15–16n11
Ridley, M. R., 76
Ronell, Avital, 20n54, 136–7
Roudinesco, Elisabeth, 90–1, 135–8, 141, 176n8
Rumsfeld, Donald, 162

Saghafi, Kas, 184n111
Searle, John, 41, 96, 100
Sedgwick, Eve Kosofsky, 43
Shakespeare, xiii, 49–51, 62, 76–7
   All is True, 1
   Antony and Cleopatra, 62, 76, 77, 79, 80–2, 83
   As You Like It, 62
   Coriolanus, 38
   Hamlet, xiii, 3–4, 25, 29–34, 49, 61, 62, 63–5, 76, 77–80, 81, 82, 83, 98–9, 142–54, 156–9, 166, 176n8
   2 Henry IV, 85–6n21, 151, 179n41
   Henry V, 87n33
   2 Henry VI, 51, 163, 182n96
   3 Henry VI, 62
   Julius Caesar, xiii, 1–20, 38, 186
   King John, 51, 62
   King Lear, 63
   Love's Labour's Lost, 62, 153, 170, 180n51

   Macbeth, 4, 30, 49
   Measure for Measure, 48, 50, 51
   A Midsummer's Night Dream, 51
   Much Ado About Nothing, 145–6, 178n30
   Romeo and Juliet, 9
   The Sonnets, 3
   The Tempest, 62
   Timon of Athens, 38, 62
   Troilus and Cressida, 4, 38
   Venus and Adonis, 81
Sinfield, Alan, 20n52
Socrates, 23
Sophocles, 16n14
Spenser, Edmund, 10
Spevack, Marvin, 2, 18n35, 19n42, 19n43
Suetonius, 10, 14

Taylor, Neil, 80
Thatcher, Margaret, 102
Thomas, Henri, 43
Thompson, Ann, 80
Thomson, Stephen, 34n6
Torok, Maria, 47–8

Valéry, Paul, 7
Vitoux, Pierre, 57n29
von Fritz, Kurt, 17n26

Walpole, Horace, 47, 48–53
Weber, Samuel, 8, 10, 18n31, 96, 97
Whitaker, Brian, 112n51
Wikander, Matthew H., 16n17
Wilders, John, 76–7
Wills, David, 136
Wilson, Richard, 19–20n50
Wolfreys, Julian, 47, 178n24
Wood, Sarah, 105

Yerushalmi, Yosef Hayim, 160–1